The Pulse of Humanitarian Assistance

The Pulse of Humanitarian Assistance

Edited by
KEVIN M. CAHILL, M.D.

A Joint Publication of
FORDHAM UNIVERSITY PRESS
and
THE CENTER FOR INTERNATIONAL
HUMANITARIAN COOPERATION
New York • 2007

International Humanitarian Affairs Series
ISSN 1541-7409

Library of Congress Cataloging-in-Publication Data

The pulse of humanitarian assistance / edited by Kevin M. Cahill.—1st ed.
  p. cm.—(International humanitarian affairs series, ISSN 1541-7409)
  Includes bibliographical references and index.
  ISBN 978-0-8232-2715-0 (cloth : alk. paper)—
  ISBN 978-0-8232-2716-7 (pbk. : alk. paper)
  1. Humanitarian assistance.   2. International relief.   3. Disaster relief.   4. Conflict management.   I. Cahill, Kevin M.
HV553.P85   2007
363.34′526—dc22

                                                          2007010674

Printed in the United States of America
09   08   07   5   4   3   2   1
First edition

For Jan Eliasson

whose extraordinary diplomatic career has been marked by a passionate, and compassionate, identification with the victims of war, armed conflicts, and natural disasters.

CONTENTS

ACKNOWLEDGMENTS

THIS TEXT is the eighth volume in the International Humanitarian Affairs series published by Fordham University Press. I express my gratitude to the contributors for their chapters, and for their patience and goodwill during the editing process. The text was typed, and retyped, by Mrs. Renée Cahill; Sean Cahill proofread the manuscript; the staff of the Institute of International Humanitarian Affairs graciously offered assistance throughout. Father Joseph McShane, S.J., President of Fordham University, and Mr. Robert Oppedisano and his staff at Fordham University Press provided both personal and institutional encouragement and support.

ACRONYMS

ACBAR	Agency Coordinating Body for Afghan Relief
ADO	Australian Defense Organization
AI	Amnesty International
AIDS	Acquired Immune Deficiency Syndrome
AIMS	Afghanistan Information Management Service
ALNAP	Active Learning Network for Accountability and Performance in Humanitarian Action
ALSS	Advanced Logistic Support Site
APOD	Air Ports of Disembarkation
BAPSC	British Association of Private Security Companies
BSG	Brigade Support Group
CA	Civil Affairs officers
CAP	Consolidated Appeals Process (UN)
CCA/UNDAF	Common Country Assessment/UN Development Assistance Framework
CDC	Centers for Disease Control
CERF	Central Emergency Revolving Fund
CHAP	Common Humanitarian Action Plan
CIA	Central Intelligence Agency
CIHC	Center for International Humanitarian Cooperation
CIMIC	Civilian-military cooperation
CINCEUR	Commander-in-Chief, U.S. European Command
CMOC	Civil-military operations centers
CONDO	Contractors Deployed on Operations
CONLOG	Contractor Logistics
CPA	Central Provisional Authority
CRED	Center for Research on the Epidemiology of Disasters
CRS	Catholic Relief Services
CWS	Church World Services
DAC	Development Assistance Committee

DFID	Department for Foreign International Development (UK)
DOB	Deployed Operating Bases
DRC	Democratic Republic of the Congo
ECHO	European Community Humanitarian Office
ECOMOG	Economic Community of West African States Monitoring Group
ECOSOC	Economic and Social Council
ECOWAS	Economic Community of West African States
ERC	Emergency Relief Coordinator
FAO	Food and Agriculture Organization
FMB	Forward Mounting Base(s)
FRSA	Force Rear Support Area
GEMAP	Governance and Economic Management Assistance Program
HDC	Humanitarian Dialogue Center
HEWS	Humanitarian Early-Warning System
HPN	Humanitarian Practice Network
HRR	Humanitarian Response Review
HRW	Human Rights Watch
IAPTC	International Association of Peacekeeping Training Centers
IASC	Inter-Agency Standing Committee
ICC	International Criminal Court
ICRC	International Committee of the Red Cross
IDHA	International Diploma in Humanitarian Assistance
IDP	Internally displaced person
IFRC	International Federation of Red Cross and Red Crescent Societies
IHL	International Humanitarian Law
IIHA	Institute of International Humanitarian Affairs, Fordham University
ILO	International Labor Organization
IMF	International Monetary Fund
IOM	International Organization for Migration
IRC	International Rescue Committee
IRIN	Integrated Regional Information Networks
L of C	Line of Communication

LRRRC	Liberia Refugee Repatriation and Resettlement Commission
MONUC	United Nations Mission in the Democratic Republic of Congo
MSF	*Medicins sans Frontieres*—Doctors Without Borders
NATO	North Atlantic Treaty Organization
NDMA	National Disaster Management Authority
NGO	Nongovernmental organization
OAS	Organization of American States
OCHA	Office for the Coordination of Humanitarian Affairs
OECD	Organization for Economic Cooperation and Development
OFDA	Office of Foreign Disaster Assistance (U.S.)
OSCE	Organization for Security and Cooperation in Europe
OSOCC	Onsite Coordination Center
RSOI	Reception, Staging, Onward Movement, and Integration
SARS	Severe Acute Respiratory Syndrome
SITREP	Situation report
SPLA	Sudan Peoples Liberation Army
SPOD	Sea Ports of Disembarkation
UNAMIR	United Nations Assistance Mission in Rwanda
UNDAC	United Nations Disaster and Coordination
UNDP	United Nations Development Program
UNEP	United Nations Environment Program
UNESCO	United Nations Educational, Scientific, and Cultural Organization
UNHCR	United Nations High Commissioner for Refugees
UNICEF	United Nations International Children's Emergency Fund
UNIENET	International Disaster Management Information Network
UNMIL	United Nations Mission in Liberia
UNOCI	United Nations Operation in Côte d'Ivoire
UNPROFOR	United Nations Protection Force (in Yugoslavia)
UNRWA	United Nations Relief and Works Agency for Palestine Refugees

UNTAG   United Nations Transition Assistance Group
USAID   U.S. Agency for International Development
WFP   World Food Program (UN)
WHO   World Health Organization

The Pulse of Humanitarian Assistance

INTRODUCTION

Kevin M. Cahill, M.D.

EVERYTHING EVOLVES and grows or it stagnates and dies. This is clearly true in nature, where plants and animals need to constantly adapt for their species to survive. It is also obvious that the philosophic, economic, and even religious bases of civilization change in response to unforeseen challenges, sometimes influenced by new technology and knowledge, often in reaction to failures.

In the medical world the humbling process of an autopsy—a detailed postmortem examination—allows pathologists and clinicians to better understand the causes of death. It is, simultaneously, a study intended to stimulate solutions in the endless fight against disease and to improve our methods of treating, and even preventing, fatal complications. Individuals and societies striving to create a more peaceful world must learn from past mistakes as well, constantly analyzing practices and principles once accepted as inevitable. If a better approach to the terrible problems that divide humanity seems feasible, then mankind must have the wisdom, and the courage, to try new paths forward.

This is the essence of diplomacy—the art of searching for a common ground while avoiding the seductive trap of dogmatic posturing. Productive diplomacy promotes cooperative efforts that can replace the ultimately futile cycles of violence and warfare. While laws and treaties, international conventions, and ecclesiastical doctrines have helped codify mankind's most basic beliefs, every generation must reevaluate these tenets. Constant interpretation and alteration to meet new realities is always necessary to advance the human journey toward global peace.

In this sad, almost patently self-destructive era, those of us privileged to work in humanitarian assistance find ourselves struggling to maintain noble traditions when the very foundations of civilization seem to be collapsing. At times it seems we are trying to help the victims of natural disasters or armed conflicts with tools and approaches that may have been better suited to the political structures of earlier generations.

Compassion, sensitivity, respect for the dignity of every person, and, ultimately, love are but some of the timeless virtues that motivate our actions. Yet still more is needed. Competent, professional, and effective programs in complex emergencies demand new techniques and improved skills. Over the centuries the rules, regulations, and usual practices of humanitarian assistance have evolved. We must recognize that change is neither inherently good nor bad. But adhering rigidly to the standard approaches of the past is an almost certain recipe for failure. We should be able to adapt without abandoning fundamental values.

This book considers some of the challenges to humanitarian action posed by emerging external forces. The impact of globalization, the privatization of military forces, the tensions of military-civilian interaction, the plight of internally displaced persons, and the mores of NGOs are some of the factors that will determine how, where, when, and even if humanitarian assistance will be offered in the decades ahead. Increasingly, voluntary agencies and faith-based organizations are reassessing their own modus operandi through thoughtful adaptation coupled with a reaffirmation of the principles behind their very being.

Taking the pulse—a basic diagnostic tool in medicine—is an ancient and trusted clinical exercise. At the bedside the physician uses a gentle, tactile measurement to see if the patient has a strong and steady circulation or one that is weak, irregular, thready, or even terminal. Taking the pulse is often the initial test performed by a medical doctor trying to establish an objective record rather than depending merely on a patient's subjective complaints. The nature of the pulse may lead to more refined studies, gradually building a foundation for rational therapy. Trying to detect a pulse is often the final act for a physician trying to determine if life has passed into death.

So, too, in a series of linked chapters, this book considers the pulse of humanitarian action today. It attempts to diagnose some of the major current problems that afflict the humanitarian profession; it also offers prognoses—predicting a way forward. If one is to address human suffering in the chaos that characterizes complex humanitarian crises, especially those in the developing world, then the etiologic significance of poverty and ignorance, corruption and incompetence, and the all too often evil effects of religion and politics are areas of study as valid as the life cycles of microbes. Professionals in humanitarian assistance must try to measure these factors constantly, just as one carefully records the pulse on the bedside chart of a sick patient.

For example, the semantic specificity that is expected in medicine is equally necessary in disaster management. "Humanitarian crises" are rarely the result of just a failure of the humanitarian system. Solutions, therefore, will not be found by merely addressing unmet humanitarian needs. It is often a dangerous and deceptive exercise to indulge in a "humanitarian intervention," implying that supplying food, water, shelter or medical relief satisfies obligations when, in reality, such activities are often only a convenient way for governments to avoid dealing with difficult underlying political or military problems. The awareness that humanitarian aid can be a "band-aid" approach—satisfying but ultimately futile—is a humbling but essential realization for those who accept leadership positions in the field.

Slowly, but steadily, philosophic interests led me, more and more, deeply into the uncharted seas that influence complex humanitarian crises. Some factors—medical, demographic, epidemiologic, logistical—are easily measured, and an effective response can usually be formulated. Yet it is those less definable, more subjective forces that can so often determine the course of events. As in human relations, it is those subtle but utterly essential influences of natural empathy and understanding—a respect for the diversity of humanity; an appreciation of others' values and customs; a willingness to cooperate, and share; the courage to give, to love—that most often provide the critical defining balance between success and failure. Professionals in humanitarian assistance learn to approach those in pain in a nonjudgmental manner. They learn to leave behind their pride, and their preconceptions, and to sublimate their own interests and agendas in an act of solidarity with refugees and displaced persons who need their help.

Effective humanitarian action requires a comprehensive approach. From both a philosophic and a professional point of view, I have long disagreed with those who believe a physician should be confined solely to the socially accepted parameters of clinical medicine. It was in Somalia, and later directing health services following earthquakes in Nicaragua and Guatemala, and in the war zones of the Middle East, and in the Southern Sudan, that I learned to appreciate the incredible, and beautiful, complexity of humanitarian assistance, and the danger—indeed folly—of believing that merely concern, compassion, or a good heart matter very much.

Those responding to humanitarian crises usually mean well, though sometimes individual organizations, and even nations, become involved for self-serving reasons. Far too often, ill-conceived assistance ends up doing more harm than good. It is difficult to predict which volunteer group will help and which might hurt recovery. Until a decade or so ago, there were no universally accepted training programs for relief workers, and there were few standard criteria to judge the efficacy of humanitarian efforts. The pulse of humanitarian assistance was rarely taken, and the inexperience of those trying to measure results often led to seriously inaccurate readings.

One cannot embark on a career in law, or teaching, or plumbing, or even cosmetics and hair styling without appropriate training and passing a qualifying exam. Yet in humanitarian crises virtually anyone could—and did—go into the most troubled areas of the world, almost arrogantly believing that their mere presence would somehow automatically help alleviate suffering. Even today an inordinate percentage of time in international relief work is spent dealing with problems caused by untrained volunteers searching for their own salvation.

It is also critically important to understand that humanitarian assistance is not merely an altruistic undertaking—it is a big business by anyone's standards. The U.S. government contributed $2.2 billion in 2004 to international humanitarian assistance efforts while America's private sector donated even more. Total worldwide humanitarian assistance is annually more than $10 billion. It is interesting that at a governmental level the U.S. contribution to foreign assistance ranks first, but, if viewed as a percentage of gross national product, the only remaining superpower is in last place.

There are many dilemmas facing international humanitarian assistance today, challenges that probe deeply, conceptually, sometimes painfully, into the very philosophic basis of our work. In the first of four sections of this text a number of these topics are considered by some of the most experienced and respected figures in our field. Bernard Kouchner, who revolutionized modern humanitarian assistance as one of the founders of Doctors Without Borders, now poses a new universal challenge for a new generation: "Patients Without Borders." He considers first the inevitable impact that globalization will have on humanitarian action as we have known it, and then the necessity for innovation and adaptation in our response in the future. Other contributors in this section propose expanding the mandate of the humanitarian field to include basic security issues of beneficiaries, arguing from both an ethical and historical point of view that intervention is sometimes necessary and that military-civilian cooperation is indispensable in such situations.

The role of the military in complex humanitarian crises has been considered in previous volumes in this series. It has been one of the most contentious, as well as the most essential, areas where mutual understanding, respect, and cooperation are necessary if we are to realize maximal efficacy in crises where demand is almost always vastly greater than the supplies or personnel available. While major changes have occurred in the relationship of military and humanitarian workers, new challenges are on the horizon and some are considered in the second section. For example, the problems posed by the emerging presence of private military organizations are carefully considered by, among others, Major General Tim Cross. General Cross has commanded field forces and relief operations in both the Balkans and Iraq, and his authoritative analysis is the product of vast experience. Positive lessons of military-civilian partnership are carefully presented in two linked chapters that focus on the use of the cluster approach in dealing with the 2004–2005 Pakistan earthquake.

There are other fundamental challenges that permeate this field. As an example, consider the easy danger of using *human rights* and *humanitarian assistance* as interchangeable terms. While they derive from similar impulses of an insistence on human dignity, there are ethical and practical reasons to distinguish the two. The simplistic approach, almost inevitably linking them in a judgmental manner, is the one followed in one-minute media sound bites that, unfortunately, so often become the basis for both the political and public understanding of complex events in distant lands.

When human rights violations are involved in a humanitarian crisis, there is a temptation to condemn one party as "wrong" and evil and to offer comfort and aid only to the "right" party, the victims. Unilateral condemnation would, in fact, almost mandate providing help to only one side in such a conflict. But the situation in most conflicts is quite confusing, or has a history that makes individual actions inevitably part of a very old pattern.

It is often—maybe almost always—helpful for humanitarian workers to remain as impartial as possible and be able to assure access to all parties in a conflict. To take such a position is not to condone human rights violations or justify invoking a simplistic neutrality, as was done in Belsen and Auschwitz. Nonetheless, it does pose a dilemma, one that is easily avoided by posturing politicians who do not have to face the very real and immediate tensions and dangers that threaten humanitarian workers in the field.

Another dilemma that will influence the future of humanitarian work is how to find the right balance in mobilizing, funding, and crediting both the large international agency that responds in times of crisis and the local indigenous aid agency. It is an unappreciated reality that international relief and development organizations depend, to a very great degree, on local partners to implement almost all aid programs. One problem is that the major donors—governments and foundations—encouraged by the public relations sections of large humanitarian organizations give support almost solely to the established international entities, forgetting, especially between crises, the need to maintain and build local capacity.

Both local and international organizations are necessary actors in humanitarian dramas—but different standards and support are definitely applied. Understanding where responsibility begins, and particularly where it ends, and how goals mesh, between these two actors remains dangerously unclear. In addition, there are troubled areas of the world where recurrent crises are so predictable that it would be logical for major donors to greatly strengthen local humanitarian groups and not merely wait to fund yet another, utterly expected, expensive, and inefficient "fire brigade" response by the international community.

How professional humanitarian workers can improve this reaction, especially in conflict and post-conflict situations, is considered in the third section. The lessons of West Africa on societies in transition are applicable to other parts of the globe scarred by constant warfare. The unique problems of internally displaced persons in civil wars, and especially in the chaos of rebel conflicts, are presented as unsolved dilemmas with, nonetheless, clearly discernible patterns that can help us devise better approaches for handling future crises.

Inherent in many of these conflict settings for those delivering international humanitarian assistance is the grave question regarding the legitimacy of major actors. The private aid sector is far outstripping the public sector in international aid—significantly influenced by donor nations funneling public grants through nongovernmental organizations. There is a deep-seated temptation to view all official, especially UN, efforts as bloated or worse—and all NGO or private efforts as efficient. There are resultant demands for transparency and accountability for UN programs while there is far less scrutiny on the private or NGO vehicles delivering aid in disasters. This imbalance can produce a self-fulfilling prophecy with inordinate time and energy devoted, for example, to UN reform, while showing little appreciation of the reality on the ground in major humanitarian crises. In such situations the United Nations must handle most of the direction, coordination, and delivery of international assistance with utterly inadequate funding.

While funding for the major international NGOs has steadily increased, many NGOs are undergoing an important soul-searching exercise. Can NGOs accept government grants and still retain their independence? Can they remain faithful to the reasons for which they were founded? Does he who pays the piper always call the tune, so that foreign assistance, even through NGOs, represents the political positions of governments? Three chapters in part 4 discuss the attempts of a major international NGO and two faith-based organizations to maintain their mores and yet adapt sufficiently to fit a new world.

Another growing problem raised throughout the book is preserving "humanitarian space," where the delivery of assistance can be accomplished without unduly endangering relief workers. This "space" is dangerously compromised by a confusion of roles in crises in which intervention is undertaken without international authorization. Even when recognized states are involved in non-sanctioned joint operations, who gives legitimacy to those "coalitions of the willing" that function beyond UN mandates? It is especially in these zones where military and intelligence agencies purposely blur the lines by using humanitarian relief efforts as but one method in psychological warfare. Clearly, oppressed masses in affected nations often perceive such groupings and activities as illegitimate, almost as a new manifestation of imperialism, and they tragically—and increasingly—target humanitarian workers as part of some evil, invading force.

Still another dilemma facing humanitarian workers is determining how the world will deal with the obvious double standards currently employed in responding to crises. Instant communications expose gross preferences and prejudices. One doesn't have to be a genius to understand the links between big-power politics and humanitarian aid. Try to make sense, for example, out of the disparity of funding in the patently created development projects in Kosovo while the vastly more serious needs of the Congo or Sierra Leone are simply denied.

Expanding humanitarian interventions have been used to cover military expediency and, by neglect, exacerbate the "forgotten crises" that scar our globe. These double standards cry out for a response from humanitarian organizations that should be in the forefront of advocacy rather than becoming compliant vehicles for politically acceptable funds. One can also ask how often funds donated for humanitarian purposes in one crisis are diverted to other causes. Do the recipient nations have any role in such decisions? Sooner rather than later, silence will provoke a dangerous response from the disaffected and their supporters to such obvious wrongs in the current international humanitarian system.

Nevertheless, I am still convinced that, despite all our failures, we can—with commitment, perseverance, and confidence—cooperate in efforts to heal the wounds of war and eliminate the causes of widespread violence. We must continue to identify solutions not only to seemingly intractable old problems but also to emerging challenges. By carefully following the pulse of humanitarian action, being flexible and imaginative as we adapt therapy to address changing signs and symptoms, we can construct a new framework to support society's endless search for justice and health, stability and peace.

We must remember that the relief and development system has shown great resiliency throughout its history. The experiences and lessons of recent crises provide, I believe, a reasonably solid foundation for the current transition to how humanitarian assistance will be offered in the future. The evolution of humanitarian assistance, with all its expected rough edges, continues to grow as a tender bud of eternal hope for all who can still dream, a bud determined to become a rose. The pulse of our discipline may seem solid and steady, but the range of safety is narrow. The good physician knows that calamity can strike at any time, and appropriate preparation is an integral part of any therapeutic plan.

Humanitarian assistance is entering a new and complex era. The needs of suffering victims seem to grow ever greater, but so also does the awareness of the global community. It is in this constantly shrinking world, where knowledge and capacity steadily improve, that a new dawn rises, one where we have no choice but to move cautiously forward, believing that mankind will survive and that somehow decency and goodness will prevail. But even if that unreasonable optimism is accurate, we also know that we will reach the promised land only through constant struggle based on academic analyses of field experiences.

That is what this book offers. This volume, the eighth in a series published to explore the multifaceted dimensions of international humanitarian action, brings together renowned experts and unresolved problems. It provides professional perspectives, emphasizing good practices as well as predictable dangers, for a discipline where the strengths and nobility of humanity grapple with extreme frailty and suffering on a vast scale.

There are no easy or final answers. We must constantly monitor the pulse, changing our approaches as new problems and new tools develop. As Samuel Beckett once summarized life's journey: We must "try again, fail again, fail better."

Part 1
Moving Targets

1

Patients Without Borders

Bernard Kouchner, M.D.

THE BIRTH OF A NEW CONCEPT OF HUMANITARIAN ACTION

FOR MANY YEARS I have been involved in fields of work that look
different but which in fact converge: humanitarian action, politics, and public health. In all three areas I have promoted a now
famous medical concept, very easy to state but difficult to set up:
better to prevent than to treat. In many occasions, and in various
capacities as volunteer or as a government minister, I have been
confronted with the same problem: how to take care of poor people's health, how to provide them access to prevention and care?

Biafra

In 1968, I was studying medicine, when the May '68 movement
led by students exploded in France. It was a very restless and cre-
ative year. But it was also a very selfish one. Few really cared about
"remote" people's misery. Most Westerners were focused on domestic or personal matters, surely worthy of interest, but with no
comparison with the difficulties that were assaulting those whose
voice was never heard. France had entered into a new long-lasting
period of abundance and mass consumption.

That year my personal and decisive shock was the war in Biafra.
There, I worked with the International Committees for the Red
Cross (ICRC)[1] and faced reality. The wounded, the starving children . . . all of them were denied respect and care because of the
supposedly protective Geneva agreements. But we were doctors
and we wanted to help different people whose pain and poverty
we discovered. The profession had the advantage of being productive across borders and serving a quasi-universal ethical interest. If the sick called on us, we would come, especially if it was
forbidden, and sometimes when it was impossible.

The Responsibility of Protection

Nationalism was a permanent threat, and indeed often an enemy. In the 1950s and 1960s, the principle that dominated international law was based essentially on the idea of sovereignty of nations. It was therefore out of the question to interfere into the internal politics of states that depended only on existing governments, even if these did not emanate from the sovereignty of the people.

Any interference generated unanimous criticism from international law specialists from both Western and Eastern countries. But in Biafra we discovered the necessity of free speech, and we became illegal in order to change the law. The other people's suffering belonged to no one. It is intolerable for governments to consider themselves as the owners of the suffering that they cause. I respect the power, sovereignty, and the legal power of every state, especially since these are supposed to guarantee the well-being of its people.

We only demand that these powers be exercised in a manner that is more humanitarian and, therefore, more human. I believe that a government that has nothing to hide could not pull a victim away from the stethoscope of a doctor, or deprive an ordinary man from the advice of a lawyer. Our methods were based on a principle of subsidiarity. It was only after all national resources have been exhausted that external assistance should be provided. This is what led me, with some of my friends, to create, in 1971, Doctors Without Borders, today known as the "French doctors." We were taken for fools for a long time before being awarded the Nobel Peace Prize in 1999.

The French doctors are now fifteen thousand worldwide; they operate in forty countries, and, only for France, its yearly budget amounts to 115.2 million.[2] Unfortunately, moving from one humanitarian crisis to the other, we had to face problems of leadership—inside our group, which like any other, soon developed power struggles in its own ranks, but also, of course, within the country, with the political and social system that we were suddenly involved with and which, in turn, had to deal with us. We had to face diversity within our organization—doctors and nurses coming from various religious, philosophical, or political obediences.

Our challenge was primarily to confront and convince various ethnic groups that did not share our own conception of medicine and health care. In 1981 I founded "Doctors of the World," which is now present in forty-six countries.

In 1987, at a Law and Humanitarian Morality symposium, I proposed, with my friend Mario Bettati, that the French government should adopt the notion of the right of interference. In 1988, United Nations Resolution 43–131 recognized the right of access to victims of natural disasters or similar emergency situations. It was welcomed in Western countries, and was not opposed by, though it sometimes worried, developing countries that feared colonialism in disguise. Thanks to this new approach, French organizations were able to enter Soviet Armenia in 1988. Six months later, François Mitterrand affirmed: "the obligation of non-interference stops exactly where the risk of non assistance begins." In his speech of July 14, 1991, he reminded us that: "France took the initiative for this rather extraordinary right in world history, which is a kind of right of interference inside a country when a section of its population is persecuted." The following year, Pope John Paul II rallied to the right of interference in order to block the aggressor's hand in Bosnia.

STATE OF AFFAIRS

Health Inequalities

I have spent almost forty years working in nongovernmental organizations (NGOs), not in administrative headquarters, but in the field, on all continents and in almost all the wars and conflicts the earth has suffered since the 1970s. I still refuse to accept that the sick are dying while treatments exist, and I want to explain why this is not enough, why we, all together, have to develop a new idea, to work on "Patients Without Borders."

The inevitability of suffering and needless death can be eased, perhaps even broken. This is yet to be seen. It will depend on the rich—those of us with wealth and security—on our money and our taste for risk. I tend to be an optimist. It is a race against time. We know what has to be done: a worldwide health insurance system. We can start small but the movement is now taking form for a worldwide tax, a universal income. I am not claiming it will be financially easy, nor would it be simple in terms of infrastructure, but it is a fight we are winning. It is a trend that is catching on.

In poor countries, nearly eight hundred million people do not have enough to eat to stay healthy. Every day, without a guaranteed source of food, they begin their quest; that was their main occupation. Then AIDS arrived, the desert increased, wars multiplied, entire populations were dispersed, and what once was considered worse still is now imaginable. Particularly in Africa, where humanity itself began, the ills of the earth and the sufferance of people are accumulating.

The health of the continent in greatest difficulty requires concrete and urgent action. On top of increasingly lethal infectious diseases, famine or, at the very least, nutritional deficiencies and chronic malnutrition is a problem for many, coupled with the increasing emergence of new and related pathologies. The figures speak for themselves; cases of child mortality, an avoidable problem, can be counted in millions. Diarrhea, pneumonia, measles, tetanus, meningitis, tuberculosis, and malaria subsist when all that is needed is to improve hygiene, to obtain drinking water, and to provide proper vaccinations and some basic medicines.

This is all acquired knowledge, and yet these children continue to die, mainly from indifference. Despite the efforts made by some NGOs, despite the basic treatment and vaccination programs provided by the World Health Organization (WHO) and United Nations Childrens Fund (UNICEF), despite the World Food Program (WFP) and the Food and Agriculture Organization (FAO), children are dying because we provide them with only drops of aid in the desert. We who suffer from plethora and obesity do not know how to share or distribute. We have made the twentieth century one of spectacular growth in inequalities of health, living standards, and knowledge. The relationship of wealth between rich and poor countries has risen from four to eighty in one hundred years (i.e., twenty times greater). But I am not only speaking of statistics.

The WHO reports that:

> While a baby born in Japan today can expect to live about 85 years, a girl born at the same moment in Sierra Leone has a life expectancy of 36 years. This Japanese child will receive education, vaccination services and adequate nutrition. If she becomes a mother

she will benefit from high quality maternity care. Growing older she will have good treatment services and will receive medication worth about 550 dollars a year. The Sierra Leone girl will be under weight throughout childhood and won't have any immunizations. She will marry in adolescence and will give birth to six or more children without any assistance. One or more of her babies will die in infancy. If she falls sick she will have an average medication worth about 3 dollars a year. Surviving middle age, she will develop chronic diseases but without any access to treatment. She will die alone.[3]

Africa is the poorest continent. For example, in rich countries, the total of annual health expenses per inhabitant is $3,100 (11 percent of gross domestic product [GDP]) in 2002,[4] whereas it represents only $81 (6 percent GDP) in developing countries.[5] In Africa, the situation is even worse with an average of $37 per inhabitant (5.5 percent GDP). The number of hospital beds is 7.5 per 1,000 inhabitants in rich countries while it is 1.2 in Africa. The number of doctors is 1 per 500 inhabitants in rich countries and only 1 per 25,000 in the poorest countries.

Fighting Hunger and Malnutrition in the World

Nutrition in Africa is an ongoing tragedy; malnutrition begins in the womb. It worsens at birth by undernourished breastfeeding women. Calorie insufficiency leads to malnutrition, growth and development problems, measles, diarrhea, and bronchitis. But these are not the only diseases, which we describe as "everyday," that are killing children. There are many other diseases that thrive on malnutrition and, in turn, contribute to malnutrition.

AIDS an Example of International Cooperation

This epidemic renews today the awakening of the need for an international solidarity. It reveals essential needs. The virus was announced for the first time in 1981 within the American male homosexual community. In 2005, 40.3 million people are living with HIV, 4.9 million are newly infected, and 3.1 million are dead. These figures are underestimations since millions of patients from China and India need to be recorded.

Several recent initiatives have given a new impulse to the fight against AIDS. In particular was the launching, at the end of April 2001, by UN Secretary-General Kofi Annan of a Global Fund devoted to the fight against AIDS, tuberculosis, and malaria. The goal of this fund is to collect $7–10 billion per year in contributions from rich nations; the United States is to give $200 million, while France has committed €150 million over three years. The fund seeks the assistance of the large, transnational corporations, companies, and private foundations.

Some of the private foundations also implement their own programs, with the AIDS Vaccination Initiative (IAVI) launched in 1994 by the Rockefeller Foundation. This program develops vaccines against AIDS and coordinates research. Virologists, immunologists, and vaccinologists work together to study the scientific barriers with the development of the vaccines against AIDS, and in 1998 IAVI published its "Scientific Blueprint for AIDS Vaccine Development," a strategic plan to coordinate the efforts of world scientists.

At the Abidjan Conference (CISMA) in 1997, France strongly defended equal access to health care for HIV/AIDS treatment. Because of this position and recommendations from the Extraordinary General Meeting of the United Nations on HIV/AIDS of June 25–27, 2001, the French government took the initiative of setting up Esther.[6]

In order to improve the developing countries' capacity to provide treatment for people living with HIV/AIDS, the Esther public interest group supports partnerships that coordinate care through hospitals and social networks in a long-term perspective. Its main objectives are implementing high-quality care for people living with HIV/AIDS, encouraging access to existing services, and helping to improve the social and economic environment of persons affected.

Its program is based on five work axes: focus on hospital twinning and the partnership approach, improving health care conditions by enhancing technical platforms and hospital equipment supply, supporting national health care strategies for people living with HIV/AIDS by encouraging national solidarity systems, promoting and supporting the implementation of a continuous care strategy, and taking part in developing joint actions.

As a result of these initiatives, 1,128 health care professionals from the social sector and associations have been trained, equipment set up, conventions signed with 10 countries: Mali, Senegal, Burkina Faso, Ivory Coast, Benin, Cameroon, Gabon, Cambodia, Vietnam, and Morocco. One million seven hundred thousand euros have already been devoted to financing medicine, reagents and consumables in eight countries where Esther intervenes. This sum makes up 40 percent of Esther's financial commitments on the ground, while waiting for the financing of antiretroviral therapies (ARVs) by the Global Fund, and provides relief in cases where there is a lack of consumables and reagents. There is, however, insufficient antiretroviral therapy in the whole of sub-Saharan Africa despite recent efforts by countries such as Botswana, Cameroon, Nigeria, and Uganda. Another priority for the Esther public interest group is intensifying prevention programs by fighting stigmatization and discrimination.

Finally, let us not forget the third major problem still not under control: malaria. Again, Africa is the worst affected continent, with 90 percent of the world's cases of malaria. The situation worsened when the parasite developed a resistance to most medicines, in particular to chloroquine. How can we ever really be sure how many die from the disease when they live so far from treatment and medication? Does this data, often gathered empirically, provide us with a benchmark below which the situation becomes unacceptable? As we search in the secure environment of our own countries, our own levels of acceptable risk are so miniscule that even our sophisticated devices cannot measure such a small risk. How can we judge levels of acceptability?

Consider, for example, the complications this lethal disease has for pregnant women: severe anemia, hypoxia for the unborn child, development problems. Pregnancy remains the greatest risk for a woman: giving birth often becomes a question of death. In some African countries, the maternal mortality rate can reach more than 1,000 for 100,000 births, or one woman in every hundred dying during or as a result of her pregnancy. Is this not the most shocking of risks? Has AIDS distorted our ability to look at the dysfunctions of the world?

What can be said of those forgotten and abandoned diseases that no one is taking care of, like sleeping sickness, which still kills thousands, and whose sources of transmission are on the increase due to disorganized health systems? It can only be treated with fifty-year-old medicines that are dangerous and toxic; no other treatments are available because no medical research has been undertaken. Pharmaceutical companies simply are not interested in these sick people, who most often remain untreatable. Less than 10 percent of health research funding is devoted to the 90 percent of diseases that make up the burden of diseases in the world.

CONCLUSION

If we believe that the health of people is a universal good, capable of transcending cultures, religions, and beliefs, if we all aspire to this around the world, we need to define a level of health that is compatible with life, and not merely with survival. Let us not take solace in the naïve concepts of the WHO; for example, their definition of health as "the complete state of physical and mental well-being." No one aware of the state of the world we live in could accept such a mechanistic definition, except for rare moments of lovemaking ecstasy.

As a distinguished French philosopher[7] has pointed out, health is not the absence of disease, but an ability to withstand one's environment. Withstanding all these ills is to refuse the factors that create them. What are the choices we have? Refusal. Refusal of fatalism, barbarity, and dictatorship, refusal of the confiscation of goods, technology, knowledge, and power. The struggle against illiteracy, and the promotion of the place of women in schools, and in decisive positions, with concrete actions whose positive effects are largely valued and recognized.

These actions are a primary necessity, but this alone is not enough. The world's organization should be built on respect for the rights of its inhabitants. Then a world in which there is the inevitability of massive and recurrent famine would not exist. Our planet can feed six billion human beings today and ten billion tomorrow. We only need to make a choice: a choice to share and to intervene, a choice to respect the rights of life.

The French health monitoring system analyzes and surveys the various populations of the world and is able to identify the risks and anticipate health and human catastrophes. Warning is, therefore, possible. Must we, and can we, let these hungry people die? The choice of society is a political one, a choice for which we have to accept responsibility. Therein lies the ability to act. All those who share the immense privilege of living in a democracy have the responsibility to become directly involved.

We must fight against our fears, fears that generate useless, disproportionate, harmful withdrawal. Of course every victim has the right to our compassion. And they should be counted one by one. But think how we react to disasters with such a feeling of indifference. The six hundred dead from Severe Acute Respiratory Syndrome (SARS) in Asia in 2005 shook the world with a frightening and unprecedented media frenzy, while several hundreds of thousands of children died in silence and indifference from curable diseases. A cliché, some will say, but this is the forgotten reality of exclusion. Our fears are the instruments that orientate our policies, be they health or otherwise.

We must recognize the urgency and the importance of the policies of health for the development of the poorest countries. We should reaffirm the importance of the bilateral cooperation in the medical field, and promote a method of intervention based on partnership and involving all the actors.

2

Protection of Civilians in Armed Conflict: A Decade of Promises

Sheri Fink, M.D.

THE IDEA THAT civilians merit protection during armed conflict began to arise many centuries ago. The principle is currently enshrined in international humanitarian law under the Geneva Conventions for the Protection of War Victims of 1948 and their two Additional Protocols (1977). These instruments specify that civilians, medical personnel and other categories of noncombatants are not legitimate targets of violence during wartime and are to be afforded protection and other specified rights.

The Conventions also confer rights and responsibilities on humanitarian actors during wartime. Humanitarians aim to relieve civilian suffering and, as such, to protect civilians from many of the harmful or deadly effects of war including deprivations of food, shelter, and medical care. The humanitarian role in physical protection from violence is less clear-cut. Some analysts argue that the mere presence of humanitarian actors provides protection to civilians. However recent experience has suggested that presence may also confer a false sense of protection, and that humanitarian presence may paradoxically present an obstacle to effective military action aimed at neutralizing aggressive forces. Inappropriate interpretation of the humanitarian principle of neutrality may also prevent humanitarians from conceiving of certain populations as endangered and in need of physical protection from aggressive forces.

The genocides of the mid-1990s in Rwanda and Bosnia highlighted the failures of established international systems to protect civilians during armed conflicts, even in cases where the aim of the conflict was clearly the destruction of a civilian population.

These failures have been acknowledged to varying degrees
United Nations, its Member States, and humanitarian or
tions. A number of investigations have been undertaken, proposals issued, and commitments made to improve the security of
civilians and other noncombatants. Over the past decade, several
positive steps have been made. For example, the ability of leaders
to commit grave breaches of humanitarian law within the borders
of their own countries with impunity and without fear of international intervention has been reduced.

However, on the decennial of the Rwandan genocide, at a high-
level conference on genocide prevention, UN Secretary-General
Kofi Annan lamented, "I long for the day when we can say with
confidence that, confronted with a new Rwanda or a new Srebrenica, the world would respond effectively, and in good time. But
let us not delude ourselves. That day has yet to come and we must
all do more to bring that day closer."[1]

That "we" includes humanitarians, who are often among the
few outsiders present in situations of extreme violence and whose
traditional role has been to both assist and protect the vulnerable.
While responsibility for ensuring the physical protection of civilians during wartime rests primarily with governments and militaries, humanitarians must also embrace this goal as central to their
work, including regularly examining their activities as contributing to or detracting from this aim.

BACKGROUND

The right of noncombatants to protection in wartime, and the
duty of others to protect them, currently extends from three bodies of law: international humanitarian, refugee, and human
rights. International humanitarian law, as embodied by the Geneva Conventions and other related instruments, requires that
belligerents respect the four principles of *discrimination* between
military and nonmilitary objects, *proportionality* (the degree of
force used should be proportional to anticipated military advantage and should be weighed against the risk of "collateral" damage to civilians), *precaution* to minimize noncombatant risk, and

protection of noncombatants. Noncombatants include not only civilians having nothing to do with the fighting, but also injured and captured fighters, refugees, and humanitarian, medical, religious, and journalistic personnel carrying out their duties in the conflict area. Refugee law gives nations the duty to grant asylum, thus protecting refugees when their home countries have failed to do so. Finally, human rights law protects certain "non-derogable" rights that are not to be limited during time of war or national emergency. These include the rights to life; juridical personality and legal due process; and freedoms of religion, thought, and conscience. Human rights law also prohibits torture, slavery, and degrading or inhuman treatment or punishment in wartime as well as peacetime.

To summarize, the protection to be afforded noncombatants during wartime is, at base, protection against suffering and death, whether from physical violence, wartime deprivations, or the violation of inalienable human rights. The responsibility for providing this protection rests primarily upon states and members of armed forces. They in turn must allow humanitarian organizations to operate whenever noncombatant needs outstrip the ability of states or militaries to provide for them.

The question, then, becomes how those with a role in providing protection may go about ensuring it. The rest of the chapter will examine this question in the context of various conflicts. Particular attention will be paid to the role of humanitarians and whether and how they may contribute to the physical protection of civilians.

CASE EXAMPLES

Bosnia[2]

The Bosnian war erupted as Yugoslavia dissolved in the early 1990s. Bosnians voted in a referendum to secede from Yugoslavia. Ethnic Serbs opposed the vote and Bosnia and Herzegovina's April 1992 declaration of independence. Backed by Yugoslavia, which was by then dominated politically and militarily by Serbia, Serb forces rapidly came to control roughly two-thirds of Bosnian territory. Human rights researchers, journalists, and international monitors substantiated widespread reports of war crimes, including massacres of civilians.

In response, the United States, France, Britain, Germany, and the Russian Federation formed a "contact group" to work with the region's political and military leaders toward a negotiated end to the war. In addition, the UN Security Council designated several remaining pockets of non-Serbs as "safe areas" under the watch of small contingents of UN forces.

However, the main action taken by outside nations in response to the conflict was the use of UN peacekeeping forces to facilitate the delivery of humanitarian assistance. The war wore on for three years with continuous shelling of civilians, obstruction of humanitarian relief convoys, and officials reneging on cease-fire agreements. The United Nations maintained an arms embargo on not only Slobodan Milosevic's Yugoslavia—which was accused of fueling the atrocities through its support of the Bosnian Serb military—but also on the Bosnian government, whose citizens were bearing the brunt of the atrocities.

The inaptly named UN Protection Forces, known as UNPROFOR, operated under a mandate allowing them to use force to protect only themselves and humanitarian assistance, not the Bosnian civilians being targeted. Thus, UN protection forces on the ground and their North American Treaty Organization (NATO) counterparts providing air support rarely retaliated against military forces responsible for violations of international humanitarian law.

European and American politicians often asserted that international military action aimed at ending the war was untenable as it would require withdrawing the massive international humanitarian operation underway to feed and deliver medical support to the victims. The UN High Commissioner for Refugees (UNHCR), the International Committee of the Red Cross (ICRC), and perhaps hundreds of nongovernmental organizations (NGOs) were providing relief in the conflict zone.

In July 1995, the United Nations and NATO failed to counter a Serb-led attack on the safe area of Srebrenica. The Dutch peacekeepers stationed in Srebrenica allowed the Serb military to take control of the townspeople seeking shelter on the grounds of a UN military compound. Thousands of men and boys were bussed away and massacred, as were men, women, and children who attempted to flee the enclave and were captured by Serb forces.

Humanitarian aid workers from Medecins Sans Frontieres (MSF, Doctors Without Borders) were present in the town before and during its fall. For months before the genocide, certain headquarters staff members believed the situation of the "safe area" was untenable, but the organization refrained from conducting advocacy in light of the tenuous presence the aid workers had in the town. (MSF was the sole NGO with international staff in the enclave, and each staff rotation required difficult negotiations with Serb authorities, who controlled all access points to the "safe area".) In contrast, over the roughly two weeks that the town was falling and its inhabitants were targeted and terrorized, the organization did go to the media with testimony from its two international staff members.

The few words the staff members were able to exchange directly with Serb military chief Ratko Mladic clearly did not deter him from carrying out the genocide. However, the MSF international staff did succeed in protecting eight national staff members and five of their family members by bravely refusing to evacuate without them.

Weeks later, a brief but determined NATO air campaign against Bosnian Serb military targets that coincided with a combined Bosnian and Croatian Army ground offensive against Serb forces at last brought about a cease fire and ultimately the Dayton Peace Agreement that ended the war. In 1999, the successor to Boutros Boutros Ghali as UN Secretary-General, Kofi Annan, who had been Undersecretary for Peacekeeping Affairs at the time of Srebrenica's fall, delivered a critical report on the United Nations' role in the fall of Srebrenica. He wrote:

> Srebrenica crystallized a truth understood only too late by the United Nations and the world at large: that Bosnia was as much a moral cause as a military conflict. The tragedy of Srebrenica will haunt our history forever . . . the provision of humanitarian assistance could never have been a solution to the problem in that country. The problem, which cried out for a political/military solution, was that a Member State of the United Nations, left largely defenseless as a result of an arms embargo imposed upon it *by the United Nations,* was being dismembered by forces committed to its destruction. This was not a problem with a humanitarian solution.[3]

Rwanda

In April 1994 the masterminds of Rwanda's genocide, power-hungry Hutu extremists, gave the signal for Rwandan Hutus to begin killing their Tutsi and moderate Hutu neighbors. Over the course of roughly one hundred days, Hutu militias and other killers slaughtered an estimated eight hundred thousand Rwandans.[4]

The United Nations and some leaders of the world's most powerful countries have issued solemn apologies for failing to act to either prevent or stop the genocide, as the 1948 Convention on the Punishment and Prevention of the Crime of Genocide requires. The genocide did not come without notice to the international community. UN and NGO staff had been on the ground in Rwanda for several years prior to the genocide, responding to humanitarian needs resulting from fighting between forces of the Hutu-led government and Rwandan Patriotic Front (RPF) rebels, the latter composed mainly of Tutsi exiles.

The Arusha accords of August 1993 brought about a cease fire, a power-sharing agreement to end the civil war, commitment to refugee returns, and an election. The UN Security Council established the UN Assistance Mission for Rwanda (UNAMIR) in October 1993 to promote security and help coordinate humanitarian assistance and monitor the ceasefire. In January 1994, it is often forgotten, Rwanda took up a rotating seat on the UN Security Council.

During the year prior to the genocide, UN military and humanitarian personnel as well as NGO staff and academic researchers were warned by Rwandans that an organized genocidal attack on Tutsi and an assassination of moderate Hutu was being prepared. In the UN case, these warnings included information on death-squad target lists, distribution of weapons, and plans for civil unrest and killings of UN soldiers. By late 1993, hate speech and exhortations to decapitate Tutsis were being regularly broadcast on radio and television.

A few days after the violence commenced, in the context of widespread killings of civilians and fighting between RPF and government forces, six hundred French troops entered the country. They did not come to protect Rwandan civilians, but rather to evacuate expatriates and some Rwandan politicians. At this time,

nearly all international humanitarian personnel departed the
country, leaving behind their terrified national staff.

Less than two weeks later, spurred in part by Belgian political
pressure following the brutal killings of several Belgian peacekeepers, the Security Council drew down UNAMIR from 2,539 to
270 troops on the ground in Rwanda. As the killings continued,
the few remaining humanitarians and lightly armed UNAMIR
troops struggled to provide physical protection and assistance to
a small proportion of the Rwandans at risk.

On the one hand, provision of traditional humanitarian assistance did not always prevent the killings of beneficiaries. For example, the UN Advanced Humanitarian Team, which arrived in
Kigali in late April, delivered modest amounts of aid to threatened populations. These groups were subsequently targeted by
militias.

However, brave efforts to protect civilians sometimes paid off.
Philippe Gaillard, then head of delegation of the International
Committee of the Red Cross mission in Rwanda, has estimated
that the organization saved sixty to seventy thousand lives during
the genocide.[5] For example, in Kabgayi thirty-five thousand
mainly Tutsis survived in a hospital and nearby buildings. In Cyan-
gugu the ICRC convinced authorities not to kill the area's remaining nine thousand Tutsis. They were brought to a camp in
Nyarushishi and watched over until the French "Operation Turquoise"—a controversial UN-approved intervention to secure the
southwest of the country—took control of the region in late June
1994.

Gaillard points to several factors that he believes allowed the
ICRC to protect civilians. First, early in the genocide, the organization broke its traditional silence of neutrality and went to the
media about two instances where the organization's ambulances
were attacked and injured patients taken off and killed before the
eyes of the ICRC staff. "The effect in Rwanda was immediate,"
Gaillard said in an October 1994 address at the International Museum of the Red Cross and Red Crescent in Geneva.[6] "The Rwandan government and media changed tack and set out to polish
their badly tarnished image by mounting an awareness campaign
on the right of the wounded to care and on the role of the Red

Cross. Within a few days, our ambulances no longer had any difficulty in moving about freely in Kigali."

Gaillard also attributed the ICRC's ability to function in the midst of genocide to its continued dialogue with military actors, including the genocidaires. According to Gaillard, "Dialogue is the expression of a calm strength which sometimes recharges the batteries of the person you are talking to."

These factors were undoubtedly important, but to focus on them exclusively would miss the fundamental point. The ICRC was able to protect people because it set out to protect them. The organization visited and sometimes remained with groups of threatened people, working to prevent the militias from killing them. Protecting people against violence and genocide, rather than merely providing medical treatment to those lucky enough to survive, was a central goal of the ICRC workers during the Rwandan genocide.

The military success of the Rwandan Patriotic Front in July 1994 brought an end to the genocide. In the aftermath, great numbers of Hutus, including militia members and their families, fled the country, leading to a massive humanitarian crisis outside Rwanda's borders. For example in Goma, Zaire, 850,000 refugees appeared in the span of five days.

This visually compelling situation drew significant media attention. A host of United Nations and nongovernmental aid organizations responded, perhaps two hundred in all. Yet over the following months, tens of thousands in the camps died of diseases such as cholera. Thousands died violently. Many of those violent deaths were attributed to genocidaires—armed killers who took refuge in the camps, benefited from humanitarian aid they diverted from legitimate refugees, and used the camps as bases to rebuild their armed forces and launch attacks into Rwanda and within Zaire.

Western military contingents assisting with relief efforts, as well as the UNHCR, failed to take on the mandate of improving security in the camps. Several aid groups, including Doctors Without Borders and CARE, withdrew from the camps in protest. In November 1994, eight agencies jointly requested the UN Secretary-General to deploy a UN security force in the camps. None was authorized, although Zairian soldiers were deployed to provide security in several camps in January 1995.

The result: the genocidaires were never separated from the refugees, and ultimately the Rwandan army attacked the militant-controlled camps in late 1996. Both refugees and militia members disbanded the camps and fled. The situation of the camps played a role in catalyzing civil war in Congo.

The Steering Committee for Humanitarian Response drew the following lessons in its March 1996 review: "Both inside Rwanda and in the camps of Goma, the humanitarian community was left to steer its own course, attempting to substitute for the lack of political and military action. . . . A key lesson, then, is that humanitarian action cannot serve as a substitute for political, diplomatic and, where necessary, military action."[7]

INTERNATIONAL SOUL-SEARCHING, CREATION OF NEW INSTITUTIONS, AND PROMISES

The failures of the international community to prevent and stop genocide, even as its representatives were on the ground prior to and during the commission of this world's greatest crime in Bosnia and Rwanda, led to some soul-searching in the years that followed. In 1999, the United Nations initiated an independent inquiry into its role in the Rwanda genocide.[8] The same year, UN Secretary-General Kofi Annan delivered a report on the UN role in the Srebrenica genocide.[9]

Both reports drew similar conclusions. The inquiry into the UN's role in Rwanda emphasized that the presence of the United Nations in a conflict area raises among civilians the expectation of protection, whether or not protection is a specific mandate of the operation. "The onslaught of the genocide should have led the United Nations . . . to realize that the original mandate, and indeed the neutral mediating role of the United Nations, was no longer adequate and required a different, more assertive response, combined with the means necessary to take that action."

Both reports faulted the gulf between "mandate and means"—and an institutional adherence to neutrality and impartiality even when confronted with genocide-in-progress—as factors that contributed to the United Nations and its Member States' failures in both genocides. The Rwanda report stated: "There can be no neutrality in the face of genocide, no impartiality in the face of a campaign to exterminate part of a population."

The Rwanda report included a requested list of recommendations. Chief among these, it called on the Secretary-General to initiate a comprehensive UN action plan to prevent genocide. The report also demanded that Member States muster the political will to act to prevent genocide and gross violations of human rights, regardless of where they take place. It highlighted the need to improve the UN's early warning capacity, information flow, and its protection of civilians in armed conflict. The report's authors also called for a change in UN rules to enable the evacuation of local staff from crisis areas.

The Steering Committee for Humanitarian Response report on Rwanda[10] shared many of these recommendations and added several important ideas for promoting future protection of civilians. Among these was the need for UN peacekeeping operations to have a clear mandate to protect civilians when large numbers are threatened by violence. It also called for the expanded use of specially trained police forces in complex emergencies and a strengthened role for regional organizations in conflict prevention and peacekeeping.

The report's authors also made several recommendations pertaining to humanitarian actors: "Urgently develop a UN-sponsored programme through governments, NGOs, and other organizations to sensitize leadership of the international community to genocidal conspiracy and incitement anywhere and to obligations of all governments to prevent and suppress it." It called for better NGO staff training on conducting dialogue with beneficiaries and avoiding themselves creating security incidents.

In the Aftermath of the Recommendations

The Canadian government took the lead in following up on the UN recommendations. During its rotating membership on the

UN Security Council (1998–2000), Canada introduced human security into the Council's agenda, most notably through Security Council Resolution 1265 on the Protection of Civilians in Armed Conflict. At the time that this resolution passed, UN Secretary-General Kofi Annan called for a "culture of protection" in the United Nations. A subsequent resolution in 2000 (SRes 1296) extended the UN's commitments to protecting civilians in wartime.

However, the results of these efforts have yet to alter the bottom line, even by measure of the Secretary-General himself. Five years after the agenda was announced, and ten years following the Rwandan genocide, the Secretary-General's fourth report on the progress of the "Protection of Civilians in Armed Conflict" initiative in May 2004 emphasized that "civilians continue to bear the brunt of armed conflicts."[11] The report highlighted protection problems in countries ranging from Cote d'Ivoire to Nepal, and it pointed to the widespread use of extreme violence, deprivation of aid, and sexual violence as means of warfare around the globe. The Secretary-General condemned the "disproportionate and avoidable civilian deaths and injuries" and violations of international humanitarian law and human rights law against detainees in Iraq.

The report rightly highlighted several areas of progress, including the establishment of ad hoc tribunals for crimes committed in the former Yugoslavia and Rwanda, and of a permanent International Criminal Court with jurisdiction over genocide, war crimes, and crimes against humanity, aimed at ending impunity for those who would organize or commit these crimes. The Secretary-General also pointed to an increased focus on protection issues in Security Council Resolutions and in Security Council missions to areas of conflict in Africa, and the development of a UN aide-memoire on civilian protection.

Other positive developments include the bringing into force, in 1997, of an international convention banning antipersonnel landmines. The United Nations has also made efforts to promote regional stability and prevent conflict, including the Secretary-General's appointment of a Special Advisor on the Prevention of Genocide. In Macedonia, preventive deployment of UN forces succeeded in staving off what would likely have been another terrible Balkan war, showing great promise for the idea of preventive intervention.

The Secretary-General's 2004 report commended the "swifter deployment of peacekeeping troops," often contributed by regional organizations, and a "stronger protection focus in peacekeeping mandates." UN peacekeeping mandates allowed troops to physically protect civilians under imminent threat of violence in countries including Sierra Leone, the Democratic Republic of the Congo (DRC), Liberia, Cote d'Ivoire, and Burundi.

However, both of these last accomplishments have been undercut during the ongoing protection crisis in Darfur, Sudan. Experts estimated that 70,000 to 170,000 civilians died as a result of direct violence in the early months of the crisis, which began in earnest in 2003.[12] The United Nations belatedly backed the establishment of an African Union–led peacekeeping force. However the force's mandate, inexplicably, did not extend to the protection of civilians. Deployment of the needed peacekeepers was also tragically slow.

As in the case of Bosnia, for more than a year the prime international intervention in Darfur was humanitarian relief. However, humanitarian presence alone was not able to guarantee civilian protection. In several cases, attacks on civilians in Darfur came in the direct presence of international humanitarian personnel, and humanitarians themselves have been killed. On the other hand, advocacy from humanitarian agencies such as MSF—although it at times came at the cost of temporary loss of access—arguably helped raise international public awareness of the crisis and contributed to the international community's belated steps to improve security for civilians.

The United Nations, while it cannot bring every rogue militia immediately to heel, at minimum should have the power to control its own operations, and in particular its long-scrutinized and overhauled peacekeeping operations. Thus, it was disheartening that UN Undersecretary General for Humanitarian Affairs Jan Egeland, in his June, 2005 report to the Security Council on the protection of civilians in armed conflict, had to repeat a well worn refrain: "It is essential to define the protection responsibilities of peace-keeping operations and develop appropriate guidance and doctrine to support this role."[13]

The other completely preventable protection shortfall Egeland raised is underfunding. A shortage of funding extends not only

to general UN operations in conflicts, but even more so to UN's specific protection activities. As of June 2005, Member States had funded protection activities at 5 percent of requested levels in Sudan, 1 percent in the Democratic Republic of Congo, and 0 percent in Cote d'Ivoire where, in the words of Egeland, "civilians are abused, killed and raped every day."

PROMOTING A SHIFT IN INTERNAL RELATIONS

Canada made another important contribution to international dialogue on civilian protection. In 2000, it established the International Commission on Intervention and State Sovereignty. The commission addressed the tension between two fundamental concepts in the UN charter: individual human rights and state sovereignty. It also studied the difficulty the United Nations has had in defining intra-state conflict as a threat to international peace and security, a necessary step in authorizing the use of force to intervene in a conflict under Chapter VII of the UN Charter.

The Commission's final report took the concept of humanitarian intervention to its next logical step in a trajectory it had followed since the late 1960s.[14] Prior to that time, humanitarian organizations, chiefly the ICRC, operated in conflict-affected territories only upon the permission of the governments that controlled such territories. Beginning in the late 1960s and early 1970s, humanitarians associated with the "sans frontierism" movement led by Dr. Bernard Kouchner and others asserted the right to intervene for humanitarian purposes whether or not governmental permission was granted. This principle has been widely adopted by humanitarians.

Subsequently, Kouchner, as France's Secretary of State for Humanitarian Action, led France to introduce for debate at the UN General Assembly the concept that nations, too, have the right to intervene to promote protection and assistance for civilians in internal conflicts. This "right to intervene" was asserted by the UN Security Council in 1991 when it authorized "Operation Provide Comfort," a military operation in northern Iraq to secure a safe zone and provide humanitarian assistance for Iraq's Kurds. It

was the same principle that allowed France to send troops into Rwanda during the genocide.

NATO asserted the right to interfere when it launched air strikes on Serb military targets operating against Albanians in Kosovo in 1999. Some optimistic analysts have referred to this as the first example of a "human security war."

The Canadian-led Commission subsequently shifted the terms of the debate over humanitarian intervention versus state sovereignty further in the direction of intervention. Based on the "obligations inherent in the concept of sovereignty" provisions of the UN Charter, international law, and "the developing practice of states," the commission unanimously established the following:"-Sovereign states have a responsibility to protect their own citizens from avoidable catastrophe . . . but . . . when they are unwilling or unable to do so, that responsibility must be borne by the broader community of states."

In such cases, the Commission stated, "the principle of nonintervention yields to the international responsibility to protect." Thus, state intervention to protect civilians may now be spoken of not merely as a foreign policy right, but as a responsibility. UN Secretary-General Kofi Annan, addressing the Stockholm International Forum on Genocide Prevention in 2004, approvingly termed this a "nascent doctrine."[15] The commission entitled its 2001 final report "The Responsibility to Protect" and emphasized the importance of the tri-fold responsibilities to prevent, react, and rebuild, with prevention the chief among them.

UN Member States have now formally embraced this responsibility to intervene across borders to protect civilians under threat of extreme collective violence. In September 2005, the United Nations adopted the 2005 World Summit Outcome Document, stating: "We are prepared to take collective action, in a timely and decisive manner . . . should peaceful means be inadequate and national authorities are manifestly failing to protect their populations from genocide, war crimes, ethnic cleansing and crimes against humanity." After months of negotiations, the UN Security Council endorsed these provisions in a new resolution on protection, Resolution 267 (2006), which also reaffirmed previous commitments to the protection of civilians in armed conflict. What remains to be seen is the extent to which Member States will back up their passionate words with action.

NEXT STEPS FOR HUMANITARIANS

The chief lesson humanitarians appear to have taken from Rwanda, and in particular from the large-scale cholera deaths in the Goma refugee camps, was the need to increase the quality of the relief they provide. Through the SPHERE Project and other initiatives, humanitarians are working to improve professionalism and adhere to minimum standards in core areas such as health services, nutrition, and water supply and sanitation.[16] This is appropriate, because during conflict, preventable diseases sometimes, but not always, cause as many or even more civilian deaths than those due to direct violence.

However, in a major omission, the SPHERE Project's widely distributed manual does not explicitly cover the humanitarian's role in the physical protection of vulnerable populations. Likewise, many key aid agencies fail to include protection in their mission statements, although the U.S. aid consortium InterAction does mention protection in its statement of commitment.

The examples cited earlier in this chapter reveal that humanitarians have the power to play an important role in promoting the physical security of civilians in wartime. For example the ICRC in Rwanda protected threatened groups of people, albeit painfully few, through prioritizing protection, maintaining communication with armed groups, and judicious use of public denunciation.

However there is a tendency of humanitarians to dismiss the promotion of physical protection as a goal beyond their abilities and mandate. Physical security "can only be guaranteed through public order mechanisms," said MSF's Francoise Bouchet-Saulnier when interviewed by the Integrated Regional Information Networks (IRIN) for a March 2003 special report, "Civilian Protection in Armed Conflict." While the examples cited in this chapter show her statement to be true, it is also true that humanitarians, with focused effort, may succeed in physically protecting groups of endangered people. Also, as Bouchet-Saulnier rightly points out, humanitarians have the opportunity to enhance civilian protection by speaking out when others are failing on this account: "Humanitarian actors have to trigger other mechanisms involving states responsibility to respect and make International Humanitarian Law respected." The fact that humanitarians are likely to be on the ground as some of the few outside witnesses to protection crises makes this an important part of their job.

Hugo Slim and Luis Enrique Egurin, in their 2004 pilot guidance booklet for Active Learning Network for Accountability and Performance in Humanitarian Action (ALNAP) entitled "Humanitarian Action," assert that protection from the point of view of a humanitarian agency is "the challenge of making states and individuals meet their humanitarian responsibilities to protect people in war and filling-in for them as much as possible when they do not. . . . This involves engaging those responsible and involving those at risk in an effort to prevent violations and civilian suffering."[17] In this pilot document, and in the final ALNAP protection guide,[18] the authors suggest five modes of action that humanitarian agencies may use to promote protection, including: denunciation, persuasion, mobilization (discreet information sharing), substitution (providing aid), and capacity building (support to other structures providing protection). Engaging in advocacy or sharing of information with those who may more freely advocate for human rights is a critically important protection tool.

In the wake of attacks on humanitarians operating in conflict situations, there is an understandable reticence on behalf of headquarters staff to engage in advocacy of the sort described in the ALNAP guides. However humanitarians who emphasize neutral relief provision over protection and call this a "back to basics" approach are forgetting that protection has been a humanitarian mandate since the establishment of the ICRC in 1863. What prevents these agencies from engaging in advocacy on behalf of civilians threatened by violence may be thoughts of Red Cross founder Henri Dunant's bargain with Napoleon III: a promise of neutrality in exchange for access to aid the wounded on the battlefields of Solferino, Italy. However, at times it is appropriate for humanitarians to risk access to those in need by speaking out about the human rights violations they witness, in particular when no others are able to do so. Hopefully these times will be rare.

In addition, humanitarians have a duty to speak out when the very terms of their work are misused, as they so often are—for example when political leaders use the word "humanitarian" to describe crises that in fact are, at base, crises of human security. Never again should humanitarian presence be used, as it was in

Bosnia, as an excuse by political leaders for not intervening politically and militarily to protect civilians for fear of harming the humanitarian response. Feeding and clothing human beings is a paradoxically harmful activity when it interferes with efforts to stop others from outright killing them.

As obvious as that sounds, humanitarians focused on carrying out their important and difficult assistance mandates do not always step back to review the full contours of their operating environments and the potential negative as well as positive effects of providing humanitarian relief. As onerous as it may be to conduct such assessments, it is incumbent upon humanitarians to do so.

Why? For one thing, the mere presence of humanitarians is often interpreted by civilians as an implicit promise of protection—the UN Rwanda review came to a similar conclusion about UN presence. In fact MSF took this lesson from Srebrenica and has since withdrawn from situations where it felt its presence lent civilians a false sense of security. For example, in August 2000 MSF pulled its medical teams out of parts of Kosovo. The statement announcing the pullout reads as if it could have been written about Srebrenica seven years earlier: "MSF questions the appropriateness of humanitarian medical and psychological assistance when, in the presence of internationally mandated protection forces, the fundamental rights of people are being denied." Not surprisingly, one of MSF's expatriate staff members who had worked in Srebrenica helped draft the statement.

These types of decisions—whether to risk access to populations in need of assistance in order to advocate for their physical security—are wrenching. A much easier protection step for humanitarian agencies to take is to better safeguard the security of their national staff through, among other measures, including them in organizational evacuation plans. However, the United Nations and most humanitarian agencies have not yet taken up the recommendation in the UN Rwanda report that they do so.

John Fawcett and Victor Tanner conducted a survey on national staff security for InterAction.[19] They received forty-six responses from humanitarian agencies operating in various country locations. The authors found serious deficiencies in security provisions for national staff and concluded, "Agencies rarely, if ever, evacuate national staff alongside their foreign colleagues."

Conversely, humanitarian agencies nearly always compose detailed security plans for international staff evacuation. It is shameful that this double standard has not been resolved, particularly as it is often national staff who assume a higher risk than internationals when working for humanitarian agencies. Providing for their protection, including pledging to evacuate them in case of unrest, would not only save lives, but also help mend the unseemly "us-them" and often "north-south" social stratification that international humanitarian agency heads say they wish to overcome.

While some might argue that providing for the evacuation of a proportionately larger "local" staff contingent is impractical and dangerous, experience has proven this wrong. In addition to the example of Srebrenica, another effort worth noting was that of Mercy Corps International in Kosovo. In the spring of 1999, Mercy Corps was forced to evacuate along with most other humanitarian groups when unrest intensified in the province and NATO air strikes commenced. As the largest international humanitarian agency operating in Kosovo, Mercy Corps did not have enough room in its vehicles to carry its entire local staff. Therefore, the senior expatriate repeatedly drove back and forth between Pristina and the Macedonian border, an eighty-kilometer journey, until all staff who desired evacuation had successfully been brought to safety.

A final area in need of improvement is research. Humanitarian agencies are increasingly bringing science to bear on their activities, studying and evaluating the effects of various interventions on the health status of their beneficiaries. It is time to include physical protection and security as endpoints in humanitarian research.

In conclusion, the means, laws, and an international consensus exist for protecting civilians in wartime. However, the number of civilians suffering violence across the globe reveals that the will to put this principle into practice is still lacking.

Humanitarians, who regularly operate in conflict areas promoting the welfare of noncombatants, have an inherent interest in the improved physical security of their beneficiaries. There is a need to pay more attention to this aspect of protection at both agency and interagency levels, including setting priorities and policies, training field personnel, and evaluating agency interventions and public and private advocacy efforts through the lens of protection.

This chapter puts forward some ideas for action. At base, what is needed is a commitment among humanitarians to adopt protection, along with assistance, as an organizational mission in humanitarian operations. Once the commitment is made, and humanitarians begin assessing their interventions from the protection standpoint, their proven creativity and ingenuity will undoubtedly allow them to come up with even better ways to promote the protection of those they serve.

3

No Justice Without Power: The Case for Humanitarian Intervention

Alexander Van Tulleken, M.D.

Blind Justice

Blind Justice is usually portrayed as an iconographic blend of Themis and Justitia, the respective Greek and Roman goddesses of justice. Her figure oversees courthouses throughout the world: a blindfolded lady holding scales and a sword. Her blindfold renders her impartial; the sword she holds gives her power. This power can take many forms: diplomatic negotiation, sanctions and trade embargoes, and, finally, the threat and use of military force.

It is the use of military force with which this chapter is concerned; specifically the use of force for the purposes of human protection (as distinct from purposes of belligerence, self-defense, or democracy promotion). The "Justice" sought by exertion of this power is understood as the enforcement of international human rights laws and norms. For the sake of clarity the term "humanitarian intervention" is used here to describe "the threat or use of force across state borders by a state (or group of states) aimed at preventing or ending widespread and grave violations of the fundamental human rights of individuals other than its own citizens, without the permission of the state within whose territory force is applied."[1]

There are ethical, legal, and practical problems in justifying the use of force in this way. There are very few cases where human rights abuses are so gross as to justify the use of force across international borders, and perhaps an even smaller number where an intervention could be expected to halt, or even ameliorate, suffering. Nonetheless there are situations in which humanitarian intervention is justified.

It can still be said that there are no words for these situations; it is not possible to create succinct definitions when describing such events. Atrocities from the death camps of World War II, to Pol Pot's Cambodian killing fields and Idi Amin's Uganda, to Rwanda and Darfur, do not all fit neatly into one category. Yet however hard it is to define what might constitute unacceptable abuse, or to set a threshold for intervention, it is still possible to appeal to the international community's intuitive sense that, in certain cases, it is simply not acceptable to stand by observing the worst abuses of populations by their states. UN Secretary-General Kofi Annan captured the dilemma eloquently when he asked: "If humanitarian intervention is indeed an unacceptable assault on sovereignty, how should we respond to a Rwanda, to a Srebrenica—to gross and systematic violations of human rights that affect every precept of our common humanity?"[2]

The international community's conventional response to atrocities such as the Rwandan genocide has mainly consisted of humanitarian assistance in the form of, amongst other things, medical and food aid. This has proved woefully inadequate to ameliorate crises or end suffering. In many cases it has prolonged the suffering and dissuaded governments that might have intervened from taking more forceful measures. At best it is only a stopgap, a way for governments and donor populations to be seen to be doing something without becoming involved politically or militarily. During the genocide in Rwanda, the French NGO Medecins Sans Frontieres took out advertisements in *Le Monde* to publicize the crisis which read "On n'arrête pas un génocide avec des médecins,"[3] translating as "You can't stop genocide with doctors." There are circumstances in which humanitarian assistance alone is unable to prevent deaths that are being deliberately inflicted. It can only help as part of a wider response to halt those states that would deliberately abuse their populations.

This suggests a leaning toward military force when confronted with genocide and other crimes against humanity. When the use of force is available as an option it becomes far easier for states to pursue other less controversial and less costly methods of halting atrocities. If the international community, either as a collective body in the United Nations or as individual states, does not lean toward humanitarian intervention there is a risk, seen clearly in Rwanda and other neglected atrocities, that we will lean so far away as to do nothing at all when confronted with gross human rights abuses that might be prevented. The principles of justice, embodied in the Charter of the United Nations and in the legal systems of civilized nations, can achieve nothing when confronted with genocide, with mass slaughter, with crimes against humanity, unless there is a sword to accompany the scales of justice.

THE LANGUAGE OF DEBATE

It is important to recognize that there are widespread and strong objections from the NGO community, among others, to the use of the term "humanitarian" in connection with military force. This debate has great importance; there is something extremely distasteful about former U.S. Secretary of State Colin Powell's comment that NGOs were a "force multiplier" in the 2003 war in Iraq. Professor Hugo Slim in "Humanitarianism with Borders"[4] explains that NGOs do not have a monopoly on humanitarianism. The term "humanitarian" in any context prejudges issues, and perhaps it would be better simply to refer to "civil affairs" and "military affairs" in any work done to ameliorate a crisis caused by human-rights abuses. Nonetheless the term is used as it is still popular in the language of both political and academic debate.

It is important not to equate the terms "humanitarian crisis" and "abuses of human rights." They may coexist but they are not identical. Humanitarian crisis suggests that the suffering is caused by a failure of the humanitarian aid system, and implies that a humanitarian solution should be sought. The crises considered are the result of deliberate actions of states and rulers that choose to abuse their populations and require a wider response.

OVERVIEW

There is a current range of debates and dilemmas surrounding humanitarian intervention focusing on ethical, legal, and practical

problems. Most important is failure of the international community to respond effectively to well-publicized atrocities, creating a
vicious circle, removing disincentives for the perpetrators to stop,
and removing incentives for countries to intervene. Does the international community have the ability to intervene effectively?
The answer lies in the precedents set by the history of humanitarian intervention. How might we best respond to another Rwanda?
What possible ways can the response of the international community be improved?

BREAKING A VICIOUS CIRCLE

There are atrocities in which it would be, or would have been,
possible to effect change for good through the use of international military force, but there are few examples where this has
been done. History shows short-term and long-term consequences of this lack of intervention. Firstly, in a crisis where there
is no potential for effective internal resolution (e.g., through civil
war), there is the potential for it to continue unabated, growing
in scale and severity. Secondly, and perhaps more importantly, a
lack of intervention or a failed intervention in one crisis sets a
precedent of impunity for other perpetrators of crimes against
humanity, who currently can be fairly sure that unless they are
harboring terrorists they are unlikely to provoke a significant response no matter what outrages they commit against their populations. It also sets a precedent for governments in nations that do
not intervene. They discover repeatedly that it is politically acceptable to do nothing to halt abusive governments other than support NGOs and send food and doctors.

    The events that occurred in Srebrenica in July 1995 demon-
strate both the scale of atrocity that can occur and the extent to
which a crisis can be ignored. It would seem that to intervene,
governments need not just evidence that genocide can happen,
but immediate, regional evidence that it has already taken place.
President Bill Clinton's remarks regarding Srebrenica are notable
for their candidness: "Srebrenica was the beginning of the end of
genocide in Europe. It enabled me to secure NATO support for
the bombing that led to peace."[5] It seems remarkable to claim

that the slaughter in Srebrenica was necessary to twist the world's arm; given that the Holocaust had occurred in Europe less than sixty years previously, was this not enough evidence to support early intervention? Using President Clinton's reasoning, the lack of intervention in the Rwandan genocide would serve a similarly useful purpose.

There has been a steady stream of political commitments on the theme of "never again." Samantha Power gives a comprehensive list of the U.S. Presidents' commitments since 1979: Jimmy Carter, ". . . never again will the world fail to act in time to prevent this terrible crime of genocide"; Ronald Reagan, "Like you, I say in a forthright voice, 'never again!'"; George H. W. Bush (after his visit to Auschwitz), "the determination not just to remember, but to act"; Bill Clinton, ". . . the high cost of remaining silent and paralyzed in the face of genocide."[6]

The events that have given rise to this "repulsive marriage of noble rhetoric and heroic constraint"[7] have not provided sufficient incentive to act in time to prevent any of the worst excesses of the twentieth or twenty-first century's barbarism. Despite extensive media coverage, at least in the countries with the resources to act, in the case of Rwanda, Bosnia, and most recently Darfur, no political leader has ever demonstrably suffered as a result of failing to intervene in a genocide or situation of gross and widespread abuses of human rights. Indeed the opposite has often been the case. More damaging than simply gross hypocrisy, the failure of states to live up to their commitments has exposed a series of empty threats. The definition of humanitarian intervention includes the *threat* of force; potentially its most useful tool. This threat now carries little weight.

The combination of failed interventions, perhaps most prominently in Somalia, and stark failures to intervene at all, perhaps most notable in Rwanda, creates a vicious circle. The demonstrable lack of political incentive combined with the financial and political costs have led to fewer interventions. The culture of impunity thus created leads to an almost total lack of deterrent, in the form of the threat of an international response, to perpetrate such crimes, and thus an increasing number of atrocities.

It is however extremely difficult to extrapolate from this that an effective, well-targeted, rapid response to an emerging crisis would turn a vicious circle into a virtuous one. It is not possible to confidently assert that successful interventions would not only demonstrate to would-be perpetrators of crimes against humanity that they would have to consider an emphatic international response. Nor would a successful intervention necessarily demonstrate to governments that effective intervention is an achievable and politically desirable goal. In theory perhaps more interventions will mean fewer atrocities. The problems with this logic in constructing a policy for intervention are legion. The literature is filled with retrospective analysis of events demanding action. In reality no truly successful intervention would be able to measure number of lives saved.

The enormous legal and political obstacles in mounting a military response to crimes against humanity are discussed below. In certain circumstances (for example in Rwanda) humanitarian intervention could likely be part of an effective solution to gross abuses of human rights. The additional value of precedent set might also discourage future atrocities. Any interventionist stance must, however, be tempered by the numerous instances of the failure of use of military force. The conflict in Iraq, albeit not a humanitarian intervention, demonstrated clearly how much harm can be done when military force destabilizes a country without an adequate plan for post-conflict recovery. The U.S. invasion of Iraq does nothing to set a useful precedent to deter governments that would abuse their populations. On the contrary, it is a stark example of how, though the Americans and other governments turned a blind eye to well-publicized reports of the slaughter of close to one hundred thousand Iraqi Kurds in 1987–88 (deemed to be an internal affair) in an effort to maintain warm relations with Saddam Hussein's regime, once terrorism and oil became more pressing issues, human rights was used as one justification for the invasion. There is no value in demonstrating that Western governments are content to ignore human rights abuses as long as there are no economic or political costs at home. The reasons for use of force have to be clear and legitimate. The intervention has to be planned carefully. Nevertheless there are circumstances in which humanitarian intervention can be beneficial.

THE ETHICS OF HUMANITARIAN INTERVENTION

Ignorance, Indifference, and Imagination:
The Compassionate Case for Intervention

There has been a gradual shift through the twentieth and twenty-first centuries from a belief that state sovereignty is sacrosanct towards the idea that individual human rights may trump state sovereignty.[8] Certain people have stood out as protesting more vocally, more passionately, and more effectively in favor of this shift. Raphael Lemkin, the author of the Genocide Convention; General Romeo Dallaire, head of the UN Mission for Rwanda during the genocide; Senator William Proxmire, the man largely credited with getting the Genocide Convention ratified by the United States; these men battled against great resistance to try to improve the response of their nations, and the world, to crimes against humanity.

All of them had witnessed at first hand the impact of abusive governments, and the horrors of mass slaughter, and all of them, perhaps naively, believed that if they could persuade people of the horrors of what they themselves had seen, then the case for a change in policy with regard to humanitarian intervention would be made. Likewise many of the NGO workers in Rwanda were shocked that the international community could respond so little to such well-publicized and shocking events. Witnesses to such crimes rarely need persuading that intervention can be a moral necessity, and yet they are not necessarily better informed than politicians or the lay public at home who have read accounts in the press or seen reports on the news. Very few details are missing from modern media reports of contemporary crises such as that in Darfur; there are almost daily accounts of people's homes being destroyed, rape being used as a weapon of war, and stories of mass murder, mass graves, and families being driven off their lands into refugee or internally displaced persons (IDP) camps by the hundreds of thousands.

Senator Proxmire said that the greatest foes of human rights are ignorance and indifference.[9] To these it is possible to add lack of imagination. It is increasingly hard to argue that Western

48   ALEXANDER VAN TULLEKEN, M.D.

populations are ignorant of human rights abuses going on around the world. It is also clear from the generous responses to appeals for funds from NGOs that people are not indifferent to the suffering of humans in other countries. But a belief that there is a moral responsibility to intervene to stop human rights abuses, combined with a vague desire to do so, does not translate into intervention even when intervention appears to be imperative to firsthand witnesses. The individuals who have done most to further the idea that states should accept some responsibility for protecting other populations have done so with tireless energy and passion, in many cases to the detriment of every other aspect of their lives. This passion must come from imagination. It is only when one imagines leaving everything one owns, witnessing executions and rapes, and having to live in refugee camps for years without a job or a home, that the moral imperative to intervene on behalf of populations not fortunate enough to live in security becomes clear.

People who see such events firsthand do not automatically become more compassionate or better informed. The reason that individuals who have borne witness to these crimes are so much more affected is perhaps that the personal encounters force them to put themselves in the victim's place. Stories in the media, reported from thousands of miles away, require much more effort to do this. European and American citizens do not fear persecution as a group. Certainly through terrorist attacks they have experienced, and do experience, fear from the risk to individuals. But they believe that genocide and mass slaughter happen elsewhere, in less civilized parts of the world. They believe, with some justification, that a free press, trial by jury, democratic elections, and powerful police and armed forces will prevent or stop human right abuses against them and, perhaps more importantly, that there will be no impunity for the perpetrators. They are never forced to *imagine* how they would feel if they themselves became the victims of conflict.

There are many ways in which this process of imagination might be inspired. Films such as *Schindler's List, Hotel Rwanda,* or *Shooting Dogs* force themselves on our imagination in a way that newspaper accounts cannot. *Hotel Rwanda* was successfully linked to an appeal for the victims of atrocities in Darfur. Public sympathy does not justify intervention in itself, but it should go some way toward removing the political apathy so often seen in the face of atrocities, so that use of force may be considered and debated, as part of the spectrum of measures to deter tyrannical regimes.

This is the challenge that should precede a more formal analysis of the ethical arguments; that those of us that live in security must never forget what we would want someone to do if we were that person on the road or in the forest or in the desert, begging soldiers for the lives of our family.

The Ethical Case for Humanitarian Intervention

There is an ethical case for humanitarian intervention that is intuitive; there seems to be no need for a lengthy philosophical justification for the use of force when confronted with the details of the Holocaust of World War II or the Rwandan genocide or the massacre at Srebrenica. The case for intervention is based on a simple set of beliefs: that all human lives are equally valuable, that the instrumental value of the sovereign state is less than the fundamental value of a human life, and that, if a person can do something to help another person, they should. These ideas need little further elucidation; they are fundamental moral norms and their acceptance is widespread. That there is a moral consensus on the importance of human rights and human protection is demonstrated in the Genocide Convention, in human rights legislation, and in the widespread public support for NGOs and governments that champion human rights. These beliefs translate into a case for humanitarian intervention only in certain specific circumstances when atrocities are so horrific as to demand some form of action, and when the only course of action that might be expected to halt the atrocities is the use of military force. The criteria that need to be satisfied in order to justify humanitarian intervention are discussed later in detail.

The use of the intuitive arguments outlined above to justify the use of force in protecting citizens of other nations is not new. Hugo Grotius, the Dutch jurist, argued in 1625 that nations have a right of humanitarian intervention, that "those who possess rights equal to . . . kings, have the right of demanding punishments not only on account of injuries committed against themselves or their subjects but also on account of injuries . . . [that] excessively violate the law of nature . . . in any person whatsoever."[10]

In some cases these are duties, not merely rights. By virtue of our common humanity, human beings have certain moral duties towards one another, and these duties are not limited to people to whom we are closely linked; we cannot be freed from these obligations "by senate or people."[11] It is a morally tenuous position to uphold human rights simply by not violating them: by attaching an intrinsic moral value to human rights, individuals and states have a duty to take action to ensure that they are not violated at all.

As well as the intuitive argument that humanitarian intervention is a moral imperative in certain circumstances, there are specific philosophical arguments to demonstrate the existence of a moral norm. The philosopher John Rawls, in "A Theory of Justice,"[12] examines morally binding norms by asking what contracts rational individuals would create between each other given enough information to make a rational choice, but not sufficient to allow individual entities to take advantage of differences in their situations. If individual human beings are making the contract behind "a veil of ignorance," that is, knowing that some governments were likely to commit atrocities, but not knowing which governments these would be, then they would be likely to create a contract allowing limited humanitarian intervention, while maintaining the benefits of a system of sovereign states. Put simply: if you did not know which country you were going to end up living in, you might well favor a world that leaned toward humanitarian intervention.

A consensus that certain atrocities oblige the use of force alone is not sufficient to build a case for humanitarian intervention. Nonetheless, any fundamental objections to the use of humanitarian intervention must address these basic ethical concepts.

A more comprehensive case to justify a specific intervention must meet certain ethical criteria. A possible version of these is outlined in the International Commission on Intervention and State Sovereignty's document "The Responsibility to Protect":

The Just Cause Threshold:

... To be warranted, there must be serious and irreparable harm occurring to human beings, or imminently likely to occur, of the following kind:

A. large scale loss of life, actual or apprehended, with genocidal intent or not, which is the product either of deliberate state action, or state neglect or inability to act, or a failed state situation; or

B. large scale "ethnic cleansing," actual or apprehended, whether carried out by killing, forced expulsion, acts of terror or rape.

The Precautionary Principles:

A. Right intention: The primary purpose of the intervention, whatever other motives intervening states may have, must be to halt or avert human suffering. Right intention is better assured with multilateral operations, clearly supported by regional opinion and the victims concerned.

B. Last resort: Military intervention can only be justified when every non-military option for the prevention or peaceful resolution of the crisis has been explored, with reasonable grounds for believing lesser measures would not have succeeded.

C. Proportional means: The scale, duration and intensity of the planned military intervention should be the minimum necessary to secure the defined human protection objective.

D. Reasonable prospects: There must be a reasonable chance of success in halting or averting the suffering which has justified the intervention, with the consequences of action not likely to be worse than the consequences of inaction.[13]

The debate surrounding humanitarian intervention does not solely focus on what circumstances might satisfy these criteria. The ethical objections to humanitarian intervention usually center around three main arguments: the sovereign state, the effects on global stability, and the problems of internal legitimacy. This chapter will address each of these in turn.

ETHICAL CHALLENGES FOR HUMANITARIAN INTERVENTION

The Sovereign State

The intuitive case for humanitarian intervention is based on the idea that if individuals have a duty or responsibility to protect other individuals, then states composed of individuals have the same duty. However, one of the ordering principles of international relations has been the rule of nonintervention. The benefits of this principle should not preclude humanitarian intervention but they do raise the threshold for acceptable intervention. Hedley Bull in *Intervention in World Politics* defended the principle nonintervention thus: "Ultimately, we have a rule of non-intervention because unilateral intervention threatens the harmony and concord of the society of sovereign states. If, however, an intervention itself expresses the collective will of the society of states, it may be carried out without bringing that harmony and concord into jeopardy."[14]

When examining the importance of sovereignty it is necessary to distinguish between authorized and unauthorized intervention. Humanitarian intervention when authorized by the UN Security Council does "express the collective will of the society of states" and as such is both legal and far less controversial. It is when intervention occurs against the wishes of the Security Council that great attention must be paid to its impact on sovereignty.

Objections to intervention on the basis of state sovereignty usually emphasize either the fact that the state is a social contract or the practical benefits of the existence of states that serve to maximize efficiency and thus utility. Objections on these bases have either to demonstrate that the state has an intrinsic value or, if the instrumental value of the state is recognized, that the benefits of the state outweigh the harms of the atrocities.

The social contract argument states that if autonomous individuals have created a state as a result of free consent, then violating the borders established by these people violates their human rights. This view, that borders have an intrinsic moral significance, would allow civil wars as permissible acts of humanitarian rescue, but regard humanitarian interventions as unprovoked acts of war. Yet most noninterventionists that take this view would not oppose war as a means of self-defense, which has its moral justification in protection of human rights rather than simply territory per se. It is hard to complete a consistent philosophical argument that acknowledges the human rights abuses as atrocities but denies foreigners a right to intervene on behalf of the victims even if that intervention crosses international borders.

If it is acknowledged that international borders do not have an intrinsic moral significance, and that states have a purely instrumental value, then objections to intervention must argue that the greatest utility is created by an absolute policy of nonintervention, and that this utility will derive either from maintaining state autonomy or from avoiding the destabilizing effect of interventions on the global community.

The benefits of sovereignty derive from the fact that borders secure the stability of social interaction, much in the way that property rights and boundaries allow individuals to maximize their efficiency. This is one reason to respect national borders; giving states exclusive jurisdiction over their territories maximizes global gains. To continue the property rights analogy, however, landowners are not allowed complete freedom within the boundaries of their lands. There is great benefit to the state having jurisdiction over, for example, criminal matters in everyone's land just in the way that, in some well-defined instances, an international body should intervene in the internal processes of a state.

Objections rooted in sovereignty have to prove first that humanitarian intervention damages sovereignty to the point where it is no longer a useful tool, and second that the pragmatic points about the value of sovereignty in the long term are sufficient to allow genocide or other crimes to continue. When considering atrocities such as those seen in World War II, Rwanda, or Srebrenica, these are extremely difficult positions to uphold. However, there are numerous examples of abuses of human rights occurring all over the world that do not merit humanitarian intervention. It is in considering these lesser crimes that the importance of respecting sovereignty in the cause of global stability becomes apparent.

Global Stability

Another objection to humanitarian intervention is that intervention will undermine global stability, both by the intervention itself and by the creation of a precedent open to abuse. This has not, in fact, been the case in previous interventions such as East Timor, Sierra Leone, or Kosovo. These interventions, it could be argued, have improved matters in their respective regions, and their effect on the world as a whole has not been a decrease in order. The objection to humanitarian intervention is based on the idea that global stability, that is, a preservation of the status quo, is a good end in itself. This is not necessarily the case: large numbers of (possibly destabilizing) humanitarian interventions driven by frequent abuses of human rights are not, in themselves, bad things. The surrender of sovereignty by a victimized people to a liberal state may well improve their lot. There is also little evidence that precedents for intervention would open the way for abuse. The conflicts in Chechnya or Iraq are often cited as wars where humanitarianism is used as a smokescreen for an unjust conflict to advance the intervening parties' interests. As the "Downing Street Memo"[15] and other emerging evidence is beginning to suggest, reasons were sought to go to war in Iraq, and the reasons used were not humanitarianism but rather the threat of weapons of mass destruction. War would not have been averted in either Chechnya or Iraq had there been no precedent for humanitarian intervention. Unjust wars may well be fought under a pretext of humanitarianism should a stronger precedent or legal justification emerge to allow governments to do so. It is, however, likely that these wars would be fought anyway under another justification. Objectors who fear "too many interventions" or "an obligation to intervene everywhere" have little credibility in a world that did nothing when it had extensive knowledge of the Rwandan genocide.

It is hard to believe there could be too light a trigger for intervention based on human rights abuses. Intervention is deemed to be more expensive (financially or politically) than nonintervention and governments are therefore reticent to act without great public pressure or ulterior political motives. It is not necessarily the case that the financial or political costs are minimized with a policy of nonintervention, but this is usually perceived to be true at the time when interventions are being considered. This issue is discussed more fully below, using the case of Rwanda.

Internal Legitimacy

The most challenging ethical argument against intervention is the lack of internal legitimacy; it will not be right for a state to coerce its members to fight, against their will, for the freedom of others who are not part of the cooperative agreement formed by the members of that society. In defense of intervention it can be argued that, in a liberal society that believes that in cases of genocide "something must be done," one can invoke a public-good argument similar to that which justifies coercion to ensure that people fight for the nation's defense. It is simpler to argue that coercion of voluntary soldiers is just—they have signed an enlistment contract that devolves the responsibility for choosing the fight to the government. A consistent libertarian argument would say that revealed consent must be upheld, and the alternative in any case would be to allow soldiers to choose the conflicts they fight in—a system that has obvious and abundant flaws.

The problem is more challenging when a government wishes to use conscription to compel people to fight, the best example being the draft in the United States during the Vietnam conflict. The intervention has to have wide support in order to make a compelling public-good argument, and this will not always be the case. This objection to humanitarian intervention, however, does not preclude intervention; it only limits the amount of coercion a government can exercise by recognizing the autonomy of the individual. In the case of multilateral interventions there is less debate.

The United Nations is a part of the social contract of the individuals in states ("We the peoples of the United Nations . . .") and its primary aim is the preservation of international peace and security.[16] While it may be argued forcefully that states are obliged not to compel their populations to fight under their flag to protect foreign populations, it may be argued equally forcefully that they have a duty to assist any intervention deemed just by the Security Council as part of a larger, international social contract.

THE LEGALITY OF HUMANITARIAN INTERVENTION

The legal debate surrounding humanitarian intervention is distinct from the ethical debate. There is, in certain extreme circumstances, a clear and widely accepted moral imperative for humanitarian intervention. That such situations exist and justify intervention is acknowledged in the Charter of the United Nations, and in international agreements such as the Genocide Conventions. Moreover, in interventions such as those that have occurred in Somalia or Haiti, there is a clear legal precedent for authorized intervention. It is the justification of unauthorized intervention (humanitarian intervention without the authorization of the Security Council of the United Nations) that is controversial.

There is currently no unequivocal legal justification for unauthorized intervention, no matter what the precipitating circumstances are. What is becoming increasingly clear, however, is that there is a wide gap between the purposes of the law and the legal system's ability to enforce it. This gap has been highlighted on numerous occasions: in 1999 UN Secretary-General Kofi Annan addressed the failure of the Security Council to "find common ground upholding the principles of the charter, and acting in defense of our common humanity," and has on numerous occasions referred to a developing "international norm" in favor of intervention to protect civilians from wholesale slaughter.

The admission from the Secretary-General that the Security Council is not functioning the way it was intended to allows us to make an argument in favor of unauthorized intervention that would fill the gap between the intention of the law and the legal system's ability to fulfill this. Professor Michael Reisman at Yale Law School proposes a view of the constitutive process of the legal system that attempts to reconcile the apparent conflict between the intuitive idea that human rights abuses should be prevented and the enforcement of international law. He distinguishes between substantive lawfulness and procedural unlawfulness, suggesting that an act can be lawful if "despite procedural irregularities, [it] has purportedly complied with the relevant substantive requirements of lawfulness."[17]

Regarding such acts as legal depends on how well the constitutive process of the relevant legal system functions to enforce the law. If the international constitutive process is a highly effective system then unilateral action will be taking the law into one's own hands. The United Nations, however, the only indisputable enforcement agency for international law, was founded with an expectation of a high degree of cooperation between Security

Council members, which, with the advent of the Cold War, collapsed. By the admission of the current Secretary-General, it is a system that is ineffective for the application of particular norms, in this case due to a lack of consensus on human rights. If governments revert to unilateral action to enforce human rights law because the enforcement through the Security Council cannot be achieved, it can be argued that they do not take the law into their own hands but are simply preempting a decision that a legally designated agency was supposed to take.

The academic idea that an intervention could be regarded as legal in certain contexts even when it occurs without the specific authorization of the Security Council is a long way from a concrete justification of unauthorized intervention. Nonetheless it illustrates the fact that the law evolves and alters through time and circumstances, and is shaped by events as well as documents.

There are four sources that are widely accepted as the bases of all international law, and which are binding on the International Court of Justice: "a. international conventions . . . b. international custom . . . c. the general principles of law recognized by civilized nations; d. . . . judicial decisions and teachings of the most highly qualified publicists of the various nations."[18]

It is useful to examine the different views that can be taken on unauthorized interventions depending on the emphasis placed on each of these sources. Professor Jane Stromseth has described four approaches to unauthorized intervention.[19]

The status quo approach places emphasis on the UN Charter in categorically affirming that unauthorized intervention is illegal as a clear violation of the literal text of the UN Charter. Article 2(4) is commonly cited: "All Members shall refrain in their international relations from the threat or use of force against the territorial integrity or political independence of any state, or in any other manner inconsistent with the purposes of the United Nations."

It can be argued that this does not forbid the use of force per se and that if a humanitarian intervention does not cause territorial conquest or political subjugation then it is allowed. The phrase "inconsistent with the purposes of the United Nations" can be interpreted in the light of Articles 24 and 39–41, which elaborate on at least some of these purposes, and the methods deemed legitimate to achieve them. Nonetheless in Articles 1, 24, 39–41, and others, the UN Charter is explicit regarding the need for authorization of humanitarian intervention.

Article 1(1) outlines the purposes of the United Nations as

> to maintain international peace and security, and to that end: to take effective collective measures for the prevention and removal of threats to the peace, and for the suppression of acts of aggression or other breaches of the peace, and to bring about by peaceful means, and in conformity with the principles of justice and international law, adjustment or settlement of international disputes or situations which might lead to a breach of the peace.
>
> Article 24 explicitly states that "the specific powers granted to the Security Council for the discharge of these duties are laid down in Chapters VI, VII, VIII, and XII."

Articles 39–41 of Chapter VII together state that the use of force is legitimate in response to "any threat to the peace, breach of the peace, or act of aggression" and "may include demonstrations, blockade, and other operations by air, sea, or land forces of Members of the United Nations." It is important to note the precedent for interpretation of these articles: the Security Council does regard massive human rights abuses as threats to the peace, as evidenced by the Chapter VII intervention in, for example, Somalia, where the purpose of the intervention was not to ameliorate the effects of conflict and displaced populations on neighboring countries, but rather to secure food supplies to the population of Somalia.

There exists in Article 2(7) a caveat even to authorized intervention that states "nothing contained in the present Charter shall authorize the United Nations to intervene in matters which are essentially within the domestic jurisdiction of any state." The usefulness of this as a legal objection to humanitarian intervention was addressed by Secretary-General Kofi Annan in a speech to the UN Commission on Human Rights on April 7, 1999, when he said that "ethnic cleansers" and those "guilty of gross and shocking violations of human rights" will find no justification or refuge in the UN Charter.

The status quo approach, regarding unauthorized intervention as illegal, has the advantage of minimizing the use of force internationally, which may promote global stability, and of protecting sovereignty. Yet in its insistence on the authorization of the Security Council it forces a policy of nonintervention in circumstances where this is morally unacceptable. The subsequent approaches described by Professor Stromseth seek to explore the possibility of unauthorized humanitarian intervention in situations where there is no Security Council consensus.

The "excusable breach" approach follows the status quo approach in acknowledging the illegality of unauthorized intervention, but allows for it as a moral and political necessity in certain exceptional circumstances. It relies on the principle that "necessity knows no law," thus avoiding the development of specific criteria for unauthorized intervention. Its proponents contend that unauthorized interventions in exceptional circumstances are illegal actions that are unlikely to be punished or condemned. While this approach is beneficial as it highlights the extreme circumstances that might lead to unauthorized intervention, and reasonable in not condemning such interventions, it seems to fall short of an ideal system where the law would concur with the moral and political views of the majority of the Security Council in cases such as the NATO intervention in Kosovo.

The third approach develops from this shortfall and looks to customary international law to justify unauthorized intervention. Its proponents seek an emerging norm of international customary law by examining interventions that have taken place and the international responses to them. This approach is beneficial as it balances the need for continuing observance of the Charter's principle of nonintervention, and the importance of the Security Council's authorization, while allowing for the legality of certain exceptional unauthorized interventions. It relies heavily on the Security Council as the arbiter of the legitimacy of interventions and also places emphasis on the idea that interventions should have a legal justification at their core. It allows some reconciliation of the literal text of the UN Charter with emerging international consensus on the importance of human rights.

The fourth approach seeks to remove the ambiguity of the second and third approaches and to formally identify a "right of intervention." There are significant drawbacks to the exactness inherent in developing a clearly defined "doctrine of intervention" rather than allowing a more open-ended evolution of international law. Its proponents would argue, however, that the severity of some of the atrocities, which are currently ignored by the international community, merit a specific set of laws to encourage intervention.

The third approach may be the most likely to yield progress in allowing unauthorized interventions without undermining the Security Council or the UN Charter. Analysis of Operation Provide Comfort, which aimed to protect the Iraqi Kurds in the first Gulf War, and of the NATO interventions in Kosovo suggests that there may be some normative consensus in favor of unauthorized humanitarian intervention in exceptional circumstances. The Security Council refused to label the NATO intervention in Kosovo as unlawful and subsequently authorized a follow-up mission in Kosovo. However, neither case could yet be said to have changed international law. Following the Kosovo intervention, the "Group of 77" twice adopted declarations affirming the illegality of unilateral humanitarian intervention.

The legality of unauthorized intervention may be gradually changing to permit the use of force in atrocities where the moral justification is clear. Even should a norm of international customary law emerge, breaches of state sovereignty will be the subject of controversy. It is beneficial and right that this should be so. There are very few circumstances which merit humanitarian intervention with or without authorization, but it is to be desired that a system will develop to close the gap between the purposes of the international law, which have respect for human rights as a central tenant, and the ability of Security Council to enact these purposes.

The Practical Problems of Humanitarian Intervention: Does the International Community Have the Ability to Intervene Effectively?

Lessons from the Past

Even if one can demonstrate a clear ethical and legal case in support of humanitarian intervention, the most compelling case against intervention, and perhaps the most difficult to respond to, is that intervention rarely works. Examples such as post-intervention Kosovo and ongoing high mortality in Iraq suggest that, ethical and legal arguments aside, the use of military force does not effectively ameliorate abuses of human rights, and it often worsens them, adding to the death toll both immediately and in the long term.

The invasion in Iraq was not in large part motivated by humanitarian concerns but, nonetheless, there was a compelling humanitarian case for the removal of Saddam Hussein and his regime. But even with the full might of the most powerful military in the world it has proven, so far, impossible to use force to improve the lot of the citizens of Iraq.

Rwanda

Any case for intervention must rest not simply on abstract moral and legal grounds for intervening; it is essential that both of these arguments have at their core the idea that military intervention can work in at least some circumstances. In examining the Rwandan genocide and the events surrounding it, it is possible to explore whether there were courses of action that would have averted the genocide and whether these included the use of military force. It is also possible to investigate why these courses of action were not pursued and by what mechanisms such neglect can be avoided in the future.

Rwanda is a situation in which there could be said to be "a common humanitarian position on [military] intervention."[20] There is now an almost universal consensus among governments, NGOs, and the general public that the Rwandan genocide demanded fast and forceful international military intervention, which it did not receive. Former White House spokesman Ari Fleischer recently said, in a public statement to justify unilateral and unauthorized action in Iraq, "from the moral point of view, as the world witnessed in Rwanda . . . the UN Security Council will have failed to act once again."

Rwanda was not only the most rapid genocide in the history of the twentieth century, killing eight hundred thousand people in three months, it was also clearly predicted by people in authority in the United Nations as well as rapidly and effectively publicized. The genocide occurred after the United States had ratified the Genocide Convention. It occurred in a small country using simple propaganda methods and even simpler weapons. Rwanda had neither sufficient power, nor sufficiently powerful allies, to deter any intervening force from attempting to stop the killing.

The first lesson, and perhaps one of the most valuable, to be learned from Rwanda, is the effect of precedent in crimes against humanity. To see the effects of precedent on the Rwandan government, on the United Nations, and on the individual governments that might have intervened, we can examine briefly the rise of humanitarian intervention.

The Rise of Humanitarian Intervention

In the forty years during which the Cold War took place, between 1948 and 1988, only thirteen UN peacekeeping missions were deployed. Between 1988 and August 2005 forty-seven missions have been deployed. In 1992 some twelve thousand military and police personnel were operating as UN peacekeepers; as of March 31, 2005, there were over sixty-seven thousand serving.[21]

This increase has been the result of a deliberate policy laid out in "An Agenda for Peace,"[22] analyses and recommendations commissioned by the UN Secretary-General in 1992, which not only emphasized the UN's lead role in international peacemaking, peacekeeping, and peace building, but also the use of UN military force to achieve this. Secretary-General Boutros Boutros Ghali declared, "The time of absolute and exclusive sovereignty has passed." Such a dramatic policy was born of the hope that the end of the Cold War would bring a veto-free era of international consensus. Since the end of World War II the international community, through the United Nations, had been developing the legal tools that outlined the way in which states were to treat other states as well as their own populations. It was hoped, and believed, that the way was now paved to enforce these laws and allow populations to claim their rights.

The initial burst of enthusiasm for military humanitarianism began in Somalia in the aims and the mission title of Operation Restore Hope. This was the first opportunity to demonstrate the effectiveness of the U.S. military as a force for humanitarian intervention, acting through the United Nations, demonstrating to tyrannical governments that they would abuse human rights at the expense of their sovereignty.

ilateral action or at least some level of involvement in the ﬂict would have enabled governments to accurately gauge the ength of feeling of the general public for intervention, military otherwise. Failing these things, any of the powerful members f the Security Council could have urged that the United Nations einforce rather than downsize UNAMIR. If not prepared to support even these measures, then governments could have responded more actively by asking the United Nations for logistical support. The United States was asked to supply armored personnel carriers. When they were eventually delivered to UNAMIR after considerable delay and at a high cost, they arrived without radios or other essential fittings needed for useful operation. Other actions that would have had an impact on the conflict and were well within the abilities of even the most anti-intervention administration were requesting that Rwanda be removed from the Security Council and jamming the hate radio broadcasts that were thought to be driving much of the killing. None of these things amount to anything like the commitment required for unilateral, unauthorized humanitarian intervention. Yet the United States and many other powerful governments did far more to hinder UNAMIR than to help it.

Only once all these options had been explored would governments have needed to consider unilateral or unauthorized intervention. The fear of being drawn into such interventions completely paralyzed political administrations from taking any steps to ameliorate the crisis. The most common argument against humanitarian intervention is that it doesn't work, that use of force makes things worse. But the fear of eventual use of force in Rwanda meant that almost nothing was attempted: no political, diplomatic, or even "soft" intervention (such as jamming the radio).

Having force as a genuine last resort allows a state to explore numerous other options, perhaps the most powerful of which is the threat of use of force. This is currently an empty threat.

The response to the Rwandan genocide demonstrates two things that strongly favor a review of the processes by which nations and coalitions decide to intervene. Firstly, that it is possible for nations not to act in the face of the worst atrocities. Secondly, that intervention would have been very likely to stop or slow the

The operation stumbled on the political cost of American casualties. On October 3, 1993, a seventeen-hour battle in Somalia's capital, Mogadishu, culminated in the deaths of eighteen U.S. soldiers, with eighty-four casualties. Bodies of dead American soldiers being dragged through the streets were shown on international news reports. On October 7 President Clinton responded by withdrawing U.S. troops from Somalia and, by the spring of 1994, all UN troops had been withdrawn. The operation was a complete failure and left a nation still struggling under warlords. But many UN workers at the time felt that had the political will existed to stay, the operation could have been successful.

The failed intervention in Somalia demonstrated to the Clinton administration, and to the world, that the political cost of American casualties was too high to favor humanitarian intervention. In 1993 the massacre of fifty thousand Tutsis in Burundi in response to the assassination of the country's first Hutu president attracted no attention. This lack of reaction did not go unnoticed by hardline Hutus in Rwanda, a neighboring country, with a predominantly Hutu government. Hutu extremists began an extensive propaganda campaign against the country's other major ethnic group, the Tutsis. There was already a small UN force in the country trying to maintain the Aretha Peace Accord between the ethnic groups. The radio and print media proclaimed that once the genocide began, the United Nations would "run away if bluehelmet soldiers began to get killed." This propaganda was a key element in preparing the genocide against the Tutsis. The Hutu government orchestrating the genocide were well aware, after Somalia, that there was a precedent for Western nations not tolerating casualties.

On January 11, 1994, General Romeo Dallaire sent a now-famous fax to UN headquarters stating the Hutu extremists' plans as indicated by an informant: "Belgian troops were to be provoked [at a demonstration] and if Belgian soldiers resorted to force, a number of them would be killed and thus guarantee Belgian withdrawal from Rwanda."

Hutu extremists began targeted killings in Rwanda on April 6, 1994, after a plane, carrying President Habyarimana, was shot down. Colonel Theoneste Bagosora, a hard-line Hutu, took control of the country with the army. Hutu killing squads known as the Interhamwe began a round of political assassinations that would rob the Rwandan government of virtually every powerful moderate within days. On April 7 the prime minister, Agathe Uwilingiymana, was met at home by fifteen peacekeepers. Ten were Belgian and five Ghanaian. They were to accompany her to Radio Rwanda to deliver an emergency appeal for calm. The group was attacked and the prime minister killed along with her family on the spot. The peacekeepers were then separated out: the Ghanaians were led to safety, the Belgian were taken to a military base, tortured, executed, and mutilated.

The killing of the Belgian soldiers produced exactly the result intended: the Belgians had completely withdrawn their troops by April 19. Equally significantly, the Belgian foreign minister, Willie Claes, asked the Americans to support a full UN withdrawal so that the Belgians were not perceived to be leaving on their own. By April 25 General Dallaire, who had originally proposed that a force of several thousand would be needed just to uphold the Aretha Peace Accords, was left with only 503 peacekeepers from an original force of over 2,000. The United Nations mission for Rwanda (UNAMIR) was crippled by this loss of troops.

Throughout the Rwandan genocide there was not merely a lack of support, but active opposition in Western governments to initiatives that would stop the genocide. It can be established from examining documents in the U.S. National Security Archives that there was a clear understanding of the situation in Rwanda as it evolved, and that "any failure to fully appreciate the genocide stemmed from political, moral, and imaginative weaknesses, not informational ones."[23] By April 11 Pentagon Africa analysts had accurately predicted the likely course of events and briefed the undersecretary of defense: "if the peace process fails . . . a massive bloodbath (hundreds of thousands of deaths) will ensue"; the "UN will likely withdraw all forces"; and the United States will not get involved "until peace is restored."[24]

In a statement to the French press, President Clinton addressed some of the reasons for the United States not to intervene: "I think that is about all we can do at this time when we have troops in Korea, troops in Europe, the possibility of new commitments in Bosnia . . . and . . . in Haiti."[25] The United States was wary of even a UN response because it saw two potential outcomes: the

authorization of a new UN force and a new means to implement either; and worse, th United States having to bail out a failed UN mi administration was concerned that the public rea failed intervention would be politically damaging cided very early on that that no circumstances could to get involved.

As well as concerns about cost and public perception another factor leading to the decision not to intervene. memo the Pentagon discusses the feasibility of counterin hate radio that many thought was maintaining the momen of the slaughter. The National Security Adviser was advised th "jamming" the radio would be "ineffective and expensive" an that a "wiser" activity would be to assist the "relief effort."[26] In considering the failure of military intervention it is disturbing to note that the presence of relief efforts may have been a factor militating against use of force.

What Could Have Been Done?

There was no shortage of information for any government or the Security Council to act on. Major NGOs and newspapers publicized reports of hundreds of thousands dead by the end of April. There were a number of courses of action suggested both by government officials and NGOs that were not pursued by the American or any other government. If it appears that there is disproportionate emphasis on the responsibility the U.S. government bears in failing to act, this may be because they have made more prominent statements admitting their mistakes, and also because they were the nation most able to rapidly project power. There were many other governments, especially that of the United Kingdom, whose policies were not merely passive but in fact actively obstructive to individuals advocating intervention of some form.

Not all of the interventions would have required the use of force or committed any intervening state to further action. Diplomatic and political pressure could have been applied, including public condemnation of the Rwandan government, and declaring the conflict a genocide. Attempts to garner public support for genocide. An analysis of the Rwandan genocide supports the ethical, legal, and practical arguments in favor of humanitarian intervention. From this I do not extrapolate that we should intervene in every crisis, only that there are some crises where use of force could be effective. I would contend that use of military force has been done on so few occasions as to make it a poor deterrent for perpetrators and to provide little more than theoretical evidence as to its efficacy. Nevertheless it is hard to believe that even a relatively small UN mission, with a Chapter VII mandate, supplied not even with soldiers but at least with logistical support from nations such as the United Kingdom and the United States, could not have made a difference. Early in the genocide General Dallaire cabled New York saying "give me the means and I can do more." I have found no compelling arguments to suggest that it would have cost any of the Western powers significantly (either politically or financially) to provide more assistance.

In fact, Rwanda provides far less appealing justifications for humanitarian intervention. It would have been far more cost-effective for the United States to intervene early in the crisis. The projected cost of the UN mission was around $30 million. The cost of providing relief to the refugee camps in Goma and other sites as the genocidaires fled the advancing Tutsi army eventually came to $237 million for the U.S. government alone.

Examining Rwanda also demonstrates the potential for the use of military intervention to fail because of questionable motivation and poor execution. In an address to the Security Council on July 11, 1994, French Prime Minister Edouard Balladur said that France had had a "moral duty" to act without delay to stop the genocide and provide immediate assistance to the threatened populations.[27] The UN Security Council authorized the French initiative on June 22, 1994, through Resolution 929.

The French deployed Operation Turquoise with two thousand five hundred French and Senegalese troops with a mandate to "contribute to the security and the protection of displaced persons, refugees and civilians at risk, including through the establishment and maintenance of secure humanitarian areas."[28] The French were not, however, impartial forces, despite their UN mandate. They had long been Rwanda's strongest ally and had been supplying the Rwandan government ever since the Rwandan

Patriotic Front (RPF) attacked the government forces in 1990. French troops had been stationed in Rwanda for many years and Lt. Col. Chollet, the commander of these forces, was appointed adviser to President Habyarimana. French military officers posted with the Rwandan army in their headquarters "necessarily knew what was going on in the Rwanda military structures, they were fully informed that massacres were in preparation," according to Romeo Dallaire, the Canadian general who headed the UN mission sent to Rwanda in 1993.[29]

It has been argued that it was the French government's intention to help the Hutu government and prevent the total victory of the RPF. French bias toward the Hutu government is commonly cited as the reason that Operation Turquoise did not disarm the Hutus, or demilitarize the safe havens they had created. Whether through bias or mismanagement, the camps in these areas, containing 1.2 million people, provided food and shelter but did not protect people. The camps consequently became the focus for ongoing extremist Hutu killings of Tutsis and moderate Hutus.

As well as the problems inside the camps and the lack of neutrality, the safe havens also infringed the Rwandans' right to flee under articles 13 and 14 of the Universal Declaration of Human Rights. The French blocked asylum applications from Rwandans, claiming that they were being protected in their own country.

Operation Turquoise did have some humanitarian benefits. First, it managed to stop the refugee flow to neighboring Zaire, which could have been highly destabilizing, and it is generally estimated that it protected thirteen to fourteen thousand people within the zones. Furthermore the presence of French troops made feasible the delivery of humanitarian assistance. However, as France withdrew from Rwanda in late August 1994 and UNAMIR forces replaced Operation Turquoise, the Rwandan government became increasingly fearful that the safe havens were used as a conduit for arms and the protective regime greatly deteriorated.

It is an interesting rejoinder to those that warn against a precedent for humanitarian intervention, lest it be abused for ulterior motives, to note that this already occurs. The French intervention was legal and performed under a UN mandate. Weaker nations in turmoil and vulnerable populations are always going to be susceptible to exploitation. As it stands the law allows, depending on its interpretation, both too little and too much.

The failure of humanitarian intervention to stop the Rwandan genocide, both in terms of the failure of most nations to intervene at all, and in terms of the poor results of a French intervention with dubious motives, was due to political constraints rather than lack of available resources.

THE FUTURE OF INTERVENTION

It now seems less likely than ever that any nation would commit itself to any charter or resolution more specific than the existing, vague resolutions that currently oblige everyone, and no one, to act to prevent or halt abuses of human rights; and there is little reason to expect that the continuing expressions of regret, and further commitments to preventing and halting genocide, seen at the World Summit at the General Assembly of the United Nations in August 2005 would be of any real value were another situation like Rwanda or Srebrenica to emerge rapidly.

The wording of the draft outcome document from this summit was sufficiently vague to allow almost all Member States to commit to it, but it expresses almost nothing that has not been said on numerous previous occasions and in numerous previous documents. It emphasizes that need to use the UN Charter as the basis for interventions and to act through the Security Council. This second point gives the least cause for optimism that future interventions could be rapid and effective. The Security Council is regularly hamstrung by consistent, overarching conflicts of interest between its members, such that a rapid decision concerning the need for a breach of sovereignty is all but impossible. Even interventions by nations or coalitions, which are not carried out under a UN mandate, are driven by a delicate balancing act. On the one hand, liberal Western governments do not want to be seen as doing nothing in the face of atrocities that are increasingly widely publicized. On the other hand the political cost of seeing soldiers coming home in body bags is perceived to be so enormous that interventions are only begun when there is overwhelming pressure to do so.

It is interesting to consider various ways in which the balance might be tipped in favor of intervention in cases where there appears to be an overwhelming need for intervention. There is a case to develop a quantitative ranking for atrocities much like the system used by Freedom House to measure freedom in different countries. This might be used as a basis for a less politicized, more algorithmic style of decision making with regard to intervention. Apart from the colossal problems of quantifying atrocities and human-rights abuses, there still remains an intrinsic problem that nations, citizens, and governments are reluctant to commit resources to military interventions; fear of the political cost of losing soldiers, mission creep leading to long-term commitments, and a reluctance to set a precedent for breeches of sovereignty that may one day be used against them means that interventions are most likely to be carried out by a third party, a neutral body, such as the United Nations. UN interventions are subject to bureaucracy and starved of funding, and there are few precedents to demonstrate their efficacy.

Another possibility for tipping the balance is multilateral interventions performed by organizations such as NATO or a European Joint Task Force that would be able to circumvent the Security Council. This demonstrated some success in Kosovo, but though less susceptible to veto in the Security Council, such forces as these would still be restrained by political appetite.

Overcoming the severe political constraints imposed on the United Nations by its members has been at the heart of the debate surrounding intervention. An emerging strategy to facilitate rapid intervention without obliging countries to commit their own soldiers is the use of private military companies. Peter Singer of the Brookings Institute puts the case concisely in his article "Peacekeepers, Inc.": "If the public sector is unwilling to get its own house in order, the private sector offers a new way to protect those who would otherwise be defenseless."[30]

Private military companies (PMCs) currently play a variety of roles in conflict from logistics, training, and maintenance to implementation and command work at the forefront of the battle space.

Questions surrounding the use of private military companies (PMCs) for intervention in states are no longer hypothetical. The forces in the Economic Community of West African States (ECOWAS)that intervened in the Liberian civil war in the 1990s had air support, including assault helicopters, staffed by former U.S. and Soviet special forces troops, provided by International Charters, Inc. (ICI), of Oregon. Executive Outcomes was hired by the Sierra Leone government in 1995. Funded in part by multinational mining interests, it was able to defeat the RUF in only a few weeks, allowing elections to be held. Peter Singer contrasts this with the UN's far more prolonged struggle in 1999 to achieve the same result with a bigger budget and more personnel.

There has been ongoing examination of the potential for use of PMCs for peacekeeping and peace building. In 2003, International Peace Operations Association, a consortium of military firms, proposed to work on behalf of the United Nations Mission in the Democratic Republic of Congo (MONUC) in Eastern Congo, offering to create a fifty-kilometer demilitarized zone. The asking price for this was $100–200 million.

There has been considerable support voiced for exploring the potential of privatizing at least some aspects of peacekeeping. One of the prominent PMCs, Sandline, published an extensive list quoting politicians such as British Foreign Secretary Jack Straw speculating that there may be considerable advantages to using PMCs to halt atrocities.

The appeal of PMCs for use by the United Nations is that, potentially, they offer a cost-effective, ready-equipped force that can be rapidly deployed and circumvent the need to go begging for soldiers from Member States. Former UN Undersecretary General and Head of Peacekeeping Sir Brian Urquhart said "there are all sorts of special tasks which possibly these companies are better-trained to perform than a UN force put together at the last minute for the particular purpose. It does seem to me that it will be very foolish to close the door to that."

The increasing availability of PMCs may be one feasible way in which intervention becomes palatable for governments whose political constraints are greater than their financial ones, and may well allow the United Nations to deliver more cost-effective peacekeeping at the same time as overcoming the problems of supplying troops and everything else a mission needs to succeed.

Unsurprisingly, however, the potential and actual problems with private military companies are enormous. The lack of monitoring of private troops in the field, combined with minimal accountability, were demonstrated when employees of Dyncorp working in the Balkans were implicated in a child prostitution ring and the Bosnia site supervisor was found to have filmed himself raping two women. The recruits in PMCs may be from military backgrounds unsuited to the culture of peacekeeping. In addition to these concerns, there are problems with the legal status of contracted peacekeepers.

There is a lack of military law within private organizations to maintain discipline amongst their recruits who would be bound by nothing more than standard employment contracts. More concerning is the lack of clarity regarding contracted peacekeepers under international humanitarian law. Employees of PMCs could potentially be deemed to be mercenaries under Article 47 of the Geneva Convention and thus denied the right to be either a combatant or a prisoner of war. Even if regulated by the United Nations, the difficulties of integrating a well-paid private force into UN forces could be considerable, and the long-term commitment of companies may be hard to guarantee.

The use of PMCs requires monitoring systems, contractual standards, independent observers, and, most importantly, the control of law. Clear provisos regarding military tribunals in the international court of justice would be needed to regulate the actions of troops in combat. A further disadvantage of using PMCs is encouraging growth in a sector that is open to abuse. The defeat of the RUF in Sierra Leone in 1995 was deemed to have benefited the country's citizens, but there is no guarantee that international mining consortiums will always act in the interest of human rights. The same market from which the United Nations can purchase the means to project power also allows other organizations and individuals, such as drug cartels and terrorists, to rapidly take on technology that was previously available only to governments. The same industry that may be used to intervene to protect may be used to create further crises.

Despite all these problems, the existence of PMCs, and their potential for use in emerging conflicts where there are issues of human protection, currently presents the international community with the dilemma of watching people be killed or using privatized peacekeepers. Is there a responsibility to hire protection if there are no governments prepared to commit soldiers to a UN operation?

The amounts of money involved in these interventions do not limit the possibility of hiring PMCs to governments. Executive Outcomes performed a retrospective analysis of whether it would have had the capacity to intervene in Rwanda in 1994. They estimated the cost to provide protected safe havens from the genocide to be $600,000 a day, a total of $150 million. The UN operation cost over $300 million and was deemed to be a complete failure.

It is interesting to speculate on who else may be interested in projecting power in this way. The sums involved are certainly large, but not so large as to be outside the budget of many individuals and organizations that are greatly concerned with human rights, humanitarian aid, and development. The 2001–2002 international budget for operating expenses for Amnesty International was over $35 million. The total expenses for Human Rights Watch in 2005 were nearly $26 million. Peter Takirambudde, Executive Director for Africa, Human Rights Watch, was quoted in *Newsweek International* in 2003 saying "[the use of PMCs in combat] is no longer necessarily a bad thing . . . it is not a crazy idea. . . . Times have changed."

With spending power like this, can we imagine a day when it might be a consortium of NGOs that would consider spending the $150 million asked by a company like Executive Outcomes? And what would the world's response be? At the moment governmental donors such as the European community, as well as individual donors, are quite happy to outsource a great deal of humanitarian work to NGOs. Is it conceivable that the mandate of such NGOs could creep from hired protection for their employees to hired protection of their benefactors to enforced protection of their benefactors and finally perhaps preemptive attacks on groups that threaten security or human rights?

A step further in this speculation is to wonder what wealthy individuals might do with the ability to purchase power and an altruistic streak. Microsoft cofounder Bill Gates has made individual donations worth more than $5 billion. Should he decide to employ a PMC and become more active in the sphere of humanitarian intervention, he would wield considerable power, particularly in areas of the world where governments are content to look the other way or the wheels of the Security Council's bureaucracy turn too slowly.

The dilemmas outlined earlier in the ethics section of this chapter tried to separate the actions of individuals and states. In the last ten years the proliferation of PMCs has meant that, for the first time, military power is available to individuals or is at least within the budgets of individuals. Is it now reasonable to consider the dilemma of a passerby watching an attack and considering intervening, but with the difference that, although the passerby remains an individual, the victim is a minority group within another state, and the only intervention would be a phone call and a money transfer?

The scenarios may be considered far-fetched. Nonetheless, competition among NGOs for donor money leads increasing numbers of NGOs to work in areas of conflict where there may be great need for protection. In the 1990s more workers from the American Red Cross were killed than army personnel. PMCs are increasingly available to provide protection to workers, and there is some precedent for even the organizations most committed to neutrality using armed guards, notably in the form of the "technicals" in Somalia. The benefits of PMCs undertaking activity such as convoy protection may be twofold, not only directly protecting the workers on the ground but also preventing exploitation and control by local aggressors of donor money and resources. This could potentially be a significant step towards the ideal of "do no harm"; there have been many conflicts that have been fuelled by inflow of food and money creating an economy vulnerable to corruption, and a means of manipulating a desperate and hungry population. But the use of the military under a mandate given to them by NGOs may also be the thin end of the wedge, and once there is the capacity to provide convoy protection it is not a huge extension of the role of a PMC to try to create a more consensual environment for their employers. Unrestrained by a UN mandate or political bias, perhaps there would be powerful incentives for

NGOs, previously limited to advocacy and diplomatic pressure, to begin to intervene with force wherever they perceived human rights abuses to be occurring.

Whatever the advantages of PMCs these may well be out-weighed by possible harmful consequences of their use. Where one individual may purchase power for the noble ends of stop-ping atrocities, it is far more likely that another would purchase power to further their own ends, causing more suffering. Iraq is the first example of this, with partially privatized armies being used to further companies closely linked with members of the Bush administration.

The selling points of PMCs in considering their use for humani-tarian intervention is their cost effectiveness and their political independence. Their use may combine a level of public and polit-ical acceptance along with an effective and rapid response to the next Rwanda. It is essential, however, that the industry is tightly regulated and used to support rather than replace existing legal structures, most importantly the United Nations.

CONCLUSION

There will continue to be events that demand humanitarian inter-vention. It is readily apparent from the atrocities that continue in Darfur, Sudan, that governments who abuse their populations are confident that they can do so with impunity, and it is unlikely that there will ever be a completely satisfactory mechanism to cope with such atrocities. The balancing of the tragic consequences of inaction with the need for unity on the part of the international community is a complex problem that will continue to challenge governments regardless of legal norms or new legislation that might emerge, and however much public and political will to pre-vent crimes against humanity might increase. It is right that this should be a focus of controversy and that humanitarian interven-tion should not be undertaken lightly.

Nonetheless the direst atrocities crystallize the arguments sur-rounding humanitarian intervention to allow one firm conclu-sion: it becomes clear when examining crimes such as those that occurred in Rwanda that it is not acceptable to allow such things to occur.

This simple conclusion may seem to be cold comfort in the face of ongoing killing, but that it should have been stated so emphatically by the Secretary-General of the United Nations in his "Action Plan to Prevent Genocide"[31] outlined at the tenth anniversary of the genocide in Rwanda does offer some hope. The first step on the road to improved human protection in all nations has to be acceptance of the idea that it is a moral imperative and that sometimes force as part of many other strategies will be required to achieve it.

Interventions such as that in Kosovo demonstrate that humanitarianism can be a motive for the effective use of force by coalitions of governments. It is also interesting to note the influence of religious groups in America who have lobbied President George W. Bush both to support negotiations in South Sudan and to consider the use of force in both this region and more recently in Darfur. The cease-fire in South Sudan in January 2005 depended in part on this, showing the increasing levels of public interest in conflicts overseas and the power of public opinion in motivating politicians.[32]

History shows that the journey from acknowledgement of the existence of a moral imperative to the time when there is a tangible benefit to an oppressed population is a long and arduous one. William Wilberforce spoke in the British House of Commons on the abolition of slavery in 1789. It was forty-four years before his Abolition of Slavery Act was passed. It took an additional twenty-six years to ratify the Thirteenth Amendment to the U.S. Constitution to abolish slavery in the United States. Mary Wollstonecraft's "A Vindication of the Rights of Women" was published in 1792; voting rights for men and women in Britain were finally equalized over a century later in 1928. Even today there are parts of the world where slavery continues and universal suffrage does not exist. The goal of preventing genocide and crimes against humanity presents challenges just as complex as abolition or suffrage, but it is to be hoped that it will be fought for with the same passion and intelligence as these issues. There is every reason to believe, however frustrating the failures of the recent past, that, in time, this goal can and will be achieved.

Part 2
Military-Civilian Cooperation

4

The Humanitarian Community and the Private Sector

Major General Tim Cross

THE INEXORABLE RISE in the number of private-sector companies engaged in an increasingly wide range of activities in support of military deployments has been quite extraordinary over the last ten to fifteen years. Although their combined impact has significantly influenced the conduct of military operations across the spectrum of complex emergencies right around the globe, their direct impact on the numerous humanitarian and other nonmilitary players has been relatively benign until more recently. The U.S.-led intervention in Iraq in particular has brought the issue to the fore, primarily because of the number of private military/security companies (PMCs/PSCs) that have been hired—often at apparent enormous cost[1]—to help stabilize the country. And many within the humanitarian community are worried about the impact of these companies on "their" space, and perhaps rightly so. But the harsh reality is that this private-sector engagement is not new and it is not going to go away; indeed it could even increase in the years ahead.

This chapter will analyze the backdrop to this engagement and offer some thoughts on where we go from here. It is very much a personal view; no attempt has been made to produce a detailed audit of recent events, but rather to summarize my own experiences and observations. I begin with an overview of how the private sector has "invaded" the military space, setting out a little of the history but with a fairly detailed look at more recent developments to show how we have got to where we are; I then outline my perceptions of the future impact of all this on the humanitarian players, and offer some thoughts on how they should respond.

My operational experience goes back over thirty-five years, with deployments ranging from Northern Ireland in the 1970s and Cyprus with the United Nations in 1980, through to the Balkans in 1995, 1997, and 1999 and the Gulf in 1991, 2002, and 2003. As in the previous chapters within this book series,[2] I stress that I write as a senior British military officer, with all the baggage that this reality implies. But I write too as someone who has had extensive experience in dealing with the nonmilitary players: both the humanitarian agencies and the private-sector contractors. As a young officer thirty years ago I had deep suspicions about the usefulness of anyone other than the military, certainly in terms of efficiency or effectiveness or both. In the fast-moving, high-intensity battlefields of Western Europe, I could see no place for "civilians"; only people in uniform would be welcome. How wonderfully naïve I was!

When forced to reflect back over those thirty-five years (which being asked to write this chapter has forced me to do!) I quickly realized that this private-sector engagement with the military is nothing new; indeed it goes back a long way—certainly long before my time. And an historical perspective is always useful when attempting to assess the present and look out into the future.

THE HISTORICAL MILITARY CONTEXT

Even a cursory glance at the history of the British military reveals that the origins of just about all of our great regiments and corps were built on the foundation of private individuals and companies, and much of our enabling capability around the world came from contracted support. Indeed a large chunk of the British Empire, including its jewel—India—owed its roots to companies such as the East India Trading Company, who operated well outside the control of the British government and employed its own security forces. A couple of hundred years ago officers in the Royal Navy were often only employed on a part-time basis, spending time ashore on half pay waiting to be summoned to go and defeat the Queen's enemies—which of course they did on a regular basis, particularly the French and other European navies in the collective scramble and rivalries to secure our respective empires. And while the size and shape of the British Army itself has waxed and waned over the years, the numbers actually in uniform have, up until 1915–16, never been large. As opportunities arose we have always reduced in size and turned to contractors or locally recruited labor of one form or another to support us on our various deployments.

Eighteen years after the Battle of Waterloo, in 1833, the "state-owned" Royal Wagon Train was disbanded. Europe was in a state of relative peace with itself after the defeat of Napoleon, and the British government was not slow in cutting back on nonessentials like the army as there was no obvious enemy to fight. One of the consequences of those cutbacks was that when the next conflict emerged in the Crimea, Commissioner General William Filder, an aged veteran from Wellington's Spanish peninsular campaign against the French in 1808, was given the unenviable task of collecting transport, forage, and fuel in a country that, in 1853, had even fewer such resources than impoverished Spain forty-five years earlier. He initially had to operate with eighty horses and mules, a few Maltese carts, and eighty native carts captured from the Russians. Local labor—four hundred Turks—unsuccessfully attempted to do the equivalent work of today's military pioneers. Until the construction of the railways, using civilian workers ("navvies") brought out from England, it was simply impossible to get enough stores up into the hills, so horses starved on the plateau while hay and corn lay rotting in the port. Security was poor; there was no coordination, no command grip—no leadership. Ships arrived badly loaded with no manifests, and some were turned around still loaded; a situation not helped when, in November 1854, a storm damaged twenty-one vessels, eight within Balaclava Harbour, and sunk several outside it. In the spring of 1855 military control began to be exerted. Turkish labor was finally organized for construction work, and the railway was completed; Spanish mules arrived from Barcelona, fresh meat and vegetables from Malta. Cheating contractors were purged and warm greatcoats and boots began to arrive. Until the arrival of Florence Nightingale, with 38 nurses, the hospital death rate in the Crimea was 44 percent—6 months later it was down to 2.2%.

The end result was the formation of an all-military Land Transport Corps, the Hospital Conveyance Corps,[3] and, prior to the Boer War, the Army Service Corps in 1891.

In operations in South Africa at the turn of the twentieth century, the resulting supply system of regimental transport, supply columns and parks, railheads and technical transport for artillery ammunition, engineer equipment, and medical supplies—all under state (i.e., military) command and control—proved reasonably effective. But the army was still supported by local labor and contractors—five thousand civilian personnel with Lord Roberts's columns during the long haul from Bloemfontein in February to March 1900, and seven thousand in General French's march in the Transvaal later that year. Contracted functions included the carrying of dispatches, fortification construction, intelligence gathering and scouts, the supervising of horses in the remount and veterinary departments, and sanitary and other labor duties in military camps. But there were shortfalls and concerns. The treatment of contracted labor at Mafeking from October 1899 for seven months gave rise to strikes over pay and conditions; the fair supply and distribution of food broke down and many were irritated by what they saw as the unnecessarily close supervision of their lives by the military—nothing much changes!

The first of the humanitarian organizations, the International Committee of the Red Cross (ICRC), was by now well established. The ICRC was born in 1863 from the Battle of Solferino, and out of the two world wars emerged Save the Children in 1919, OXFAM in 1942, and Care and Relief Everywhere (CARE) in 1945. These, and others, generally operated apart from the actual warfighting—in both time and space—dealing with the fallout of conflict in relative safety; this was to change.

For the British Army the two world wars were a break from our historical past. The conscription that followed the formation of Kitchener's Volunteer Army in 1915, and the return of National Service for World War II, resulted in an army—and indeed a navy and air force—of such large numbers that everything that was needed could be done by men and women in uniform. The size of the forces overall meant that industry "simply" had to churn out the weapons and paraphernalia of war, and the military—government-owned, funded, and controlled—did everything else;

most aspects of logistics, transportation and movement, communications, engineering, and administration were handled by soldiers, sailors, and airmen, and certainly just about every aspect of security, protection, and close engagement with the "enemy" was in military hands. Nonetheless, once again not everything was easy or perfect; in 1916 an industrial dispute in the United Kingdom resulted in serious supply shortages—including the real danger of the army running out of artillery ammunition on the Western Front—and the various dock and mining strikes over the period of both world wars make for sobering reading.

Although it continued elsewhere for longer, British National Service ended in the early 1960s, and we gradually returned to our historical roots of only holding relatively small professional armed forces.[4] Even though much of the fabric of our ability to fight remained in military hands, we had to increasingly rely on commercial support. As we slowly withdrew from empire, fighting a number of "colonial wars" along the way, we constantly turned to contractors for support of one kind or another. But it was all relatively easy. The 1970s–1980s army that I served in was focused on deterring the might of the Soviet Union; our plans were built around pre-positioned stocks of materiel[5] that, during the short-warning times expected, were to be moved out of the military depots to deployed locations around West Germany. Our main Line of Communication (L of C) into Germany, which was NATO's (and therefore our) principal deployment region, went from the United Kingdom through the English Channel ports and on across the Low Countries. Our forces were expected to initially fall back before the onslaught of the Warsaw Pact, shortening the L of C and making it easier to provide support. Contractors had little or no role to play in the high-tempo, intensive warfighting that was expected to last barely thirty to ninety days before one side or the other was forced to "go nuclear" to avoid defeat. Mutually assured destruction was assumed to follow.

Things began to seriously change, however, in the late 1980s and early 1990s. As the Cold War came to an end, governments, initially in the West but increasingly elsewhere, took the opportunity to reduce the size and shape of their militaries even further. Defense budgets were reduced, often dramatically, and the support services—often referred to as the "tail"—suffered most.

Numbers of both people and equipment were cut, and the military found itself facing up to the stark reality that it no longer had limitless resources to call on. Ironically, the demise of the Soviet Union/Warsaw Pact, and the relative safety and stability of the Cold War superpower balance,[6] was replaced by a whole range of conflicts around the world. We moved into a world of relatively small wars and weak states, many of whom needed outside help to maintain security and to develop—or in some cases were at the receiving end of an intervention by the international community. Ethnic cleansing reemerged in Europe and elsewhere, and traditional military engagements abounded. Classic UN peacekeeping deployments, of which there had been relatively few before the 1990s, were largely replaced by peace support or even peace enforcement missions; there were many of them, and they required the deployment of a robust military capability.

THE SITUATION TODAY—THE BUSINESS IMPERATIVE

Unlike the static, "shop window" armies on either side of the inner-German border in the 1960s through the 1980s, which were mostly poorly supported by a largely hollowed-out logistic capability, the expeditionary military forces of the 1990s needed comprehensive support; military capability now had to be deployed and sustained, not just on defensive operations falling back on their L of C within an advanced Western European country, but on offensive/pursuit operations, often advancing hundreds of miles in harsh conditions across unprepared terrain in the process. To get a sense of this, figure 1 shows a schematic of a military deployment from the UK base to a theater of operations somewhere across the world.

The Concept of Operations begins with the outloading of materiel and people from the UK-based depots and bases to the air and seaports of embarkation. Our military forces deploy through what we call the "Coupling Bridge," the pipeline down which our people and all of the supporting materiel—our combat power—flows. This Coupling Bridge may or may not pass through one or more Forward Mounting Base(s), known colloquially as FMBs; somewhere like Gibraltar or the Ascension Islands, used in 1982

Figure 1.   Expeditionary Operations—the Concept

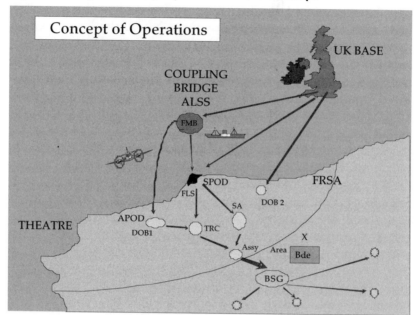

in the move to recover the Falkland Islands, Cyprus for operations in the Middle East over the last fifteen years, or the territory of a friendly ally nation. An FMB is a place where forces can be acclimatized, reconfigured, trained, or held pending political/diplomatic developments; an Advanced Logistic Support Site (ALSS) can also be established where materiel can be modified or held in preparation for follow-on forces. From the FMB the Coupling Bridge moves on out into the theater of operations.

Within the theater itself the Sea and Air Ports of Disembarkation (SPOD/APODs) are established, along with Deployed Operating Bases (DOBs) for aircraft and helicopters; Theater Reception Centers (TRCs) and Staging Areas (SAs) are also set up. Troops and equipment are received into theater through this matrix, and they then move on up into Assembly Areas (Assy Area), where they are married up, equipment is armed/fuelled/up-armored, et cetera, before being passed into, as shown in this example, a Brigade (Bde) Level operations area. The area around the SPODs, APODs, DOBs, TRCs, and SAs is known as the Force

Rear Support Area (FRSA), and the size of it can vary dramatically. For the initial UK moves to the Balkans—both in support of
the United Nations and the subsequent NATO deployments—we
used the Croatian coastal sea and airports at Split, moving our
materiel up by road into Bosnia; so the FRSA was Croatia itself.
For the Kosovo deployment we used the Greek air and sea ports at
Thessalonica for initial entry, and moved on up into Macedonia,
establishing SA/Assy Areas around and to the south of the capital
Skopje; so the FRSA was Greece and Macedonia.

The Brigade Support Group (BSG), shown as being deployed
within the forward operating area, acts as a hub-and-spoke focus
for the support of individual company or regimental locations. It
too can cover a significant area—Bosnia, Kosovo, or large tracts
of desert in Saudi Arabia, Iraq, or Kuwait.

It is through this "architecture" that all of our people and
equipment must flow, both forward and backward. And within
that overall architecture is a whole range of communications, engineering, logistic, and medical capabilities, all of which must be
overseen, commanded, and protected. This is a complex and
hugely demanding business and an expensive one in terms of
manpower, and the reality is that in deployments around the
world over the last fifteen to twenty years an increasing amount
of this capability has had to be undertaken by contractors from
the private sector. This has led to the introduction of a new lexicon. The use of contracted logistic support is known as "CON-
LOG" (Contractor Logistics), while the wider use of Contractors
Deployed on Operations is known as "CONDO." Both of these
have seen enormous growth over the last few years.

There are therefore now two principal pressures, which I sum
up as the business imperative and the operational imperative. In
simple terms, the principal driver must always be the latter, the
operational imperative, because the implications of coming second on the battlefield are in a significantly different league to
doing so in corporate business. However, and not far behind, we
now recognize the realities of resource constraints and ensure
that we conduct operations efficiently as well as effectively. We
need to be—and generally now are—comfortable with the idea
that business imperatives, based around cost and linked to best
business practice, can be, indeed often should be, a major driver

in the way we organize and operate. This applies to a very large extent within the UK base and the Coupling Bridge, but also to a significant, if lesser extent, within theaters of operation. Capabilities like logistics, engineering, medical, and communications support may be the lifeblood of any military's ability to fight at the strategic and operational level,[7] but they are capabilities that are constantly under the microscope, and rightly so. Over-insured, inflexible, over-complicated, or short-sighted support plans only hinder the ability of a theater commander to conduct an operation, and there is no doubt that the involvement of the modern private sector has enabled us to add much greater efficiency and effectiveness to our many recent deployments. Many of our practices in the past have not utilized best business practice. This has changed, and we are the better for it; to use the jargon, our fighting power[8] has been enhanced. And that—as they say—is the bottom line.

THE OPERATIONAL-BUSINESS BALANCE

That all said, and while large aspects of expeditionary operations can be and now are handled by contractors, we—the military—do retain overall command and control, and a steel core of military capability continues to operate throughout the process, holding the whole together. Operational Imperatives dictate that there will be various but complementary roles for contractors, especially when the forces involved are engaged in war fighting as opposed to other types of deployment. The FRSA is certainly not necessarily a benign area, and it can often be a major target for the opposition. In the 1990–1991 Gulf Campaign, the FRSA was the target for numerous SCUD attacks, and the threat of terrorist/special forces attack was high. During the NATO deployment to Kosovo the SPOD in, and L of C out, of Thessaloniki was the target for demonstrations, riots, and brick throwing; port exits were blocked and trains were taken over by demonstrators—and this was within a NATO country! Ironically the British Army had almost lost its military rail capability, retaining only one regular squadron after the major reorganization of the mid-1990s; yet without that squadron we would not have been successful in the initial phases of the deployment through Greece and Macedonia, nor during the first two months in Kosovo itself, which included a derailment and injuries to the military crew. That is a lesson we don't want to have to relearn too often.

The business of moving military forces into a theater of operations and getting them ready for "action" at a so-called line of departure is known as the RSOI process—Reception, Staging, Onward Movement, and Integration. General Sir Mike Jackson, now the UK's Chief of the General Staff, noted in his Year 2000 Training Directive to the NATO Headquarters that he commanded at the time that "One of the most important and difficult phases of operations is actually getting the force to the Line of Departure. If this can be achieved satisfactorily, then the prospect of operational success is high."

One of the theater commanders' priority concerns is thus ensuring the success of the RSOI process. The sea and air approaches, the key land L of C, and the natural choke points on it may well be fought for and over; the maritime and air component commanders must be able to guarantee freedom of movement into theater, and the FRSA itself needs to be firmly commanded and controlled. And those deployed within the FRSA in the initial phases of the deployment need to be capable of turning their hands to any number of tasks, and be capable of protecting themselves; for as General Rupert Smith observed when commanding 1st UK Armored Division in 1990–91: "Casualties are the only certainty of any Commander's Plan."

Casualties throughout the FRSA and the Brigade Support Area are indeed a harsh reality of every deployment. Among everything else, they are heavy industrial areas and accidents are inevitable in, for example, container parks where operators are working in very austere conditions; these and disease and other non-battle injuries (DNBI) from local infections, traffic accidents, and so forth, all sit alongside "normal" battle injuries.[9]

But there comes a time when we can begin to pass over the supply of any one of a number of services, normally on some form of rolling handover program. The timing of that rolling handover is not clear-cut, for it is inevitably dependant upon the operational situation. When we deployed to Macedonia the aim was to move north into Kosovo as soon as the peace agreement, which was being negotiated in France at Rambouillet, was signed; our plan was therefore to hand over large parts of our support services quickly. Months later we were still planning forced entry options into Kosovo, while at the same time we were dealing with myriad security and other issues—not the least of which was the flood of refugees into Albania and Macedonia. Without regular military manpower we simply could not have coped with the 1999 Easter refugee crisis in either country, nor would we have had the agility to support high-tempo warfighting if 4 Armored Brigade and 5 Airborne Brigade had been called upon to act without an agreement. That all said, with operational tour intervals for our medics, logisticians, and engineers at around twelve months, there was no one keener than I to hand over these and other functions as soon as we could, so that this military manpower could return to the United Kingdom and prepare for the next deployment.

To assist in that process of handover we now make extensive use of in-place enabling contracts, and include contractors within our major planning exercises. Genuine partnerships are being developed, as too is the concept of "sponsored reserves," where private companies actually earmark nominated civilian personnel for deployment alongside the military, complementing our reserves. Our mobile weather teams, for example, deploy all around the world with us; for their size they are the most highly decorated unit in the military,[10] yet none of them are full-time military personnel, the majority working for local or national meteorological (met) outlets such as the media—the radio or television met stations.

I stress (if it needs stressing) that these contractors do not just work for the smaller military players like the United Kingdom. The stark truth is that not even the might of the United States can manage a conflict today in places like Iraq or Afghanistan, particularly concurrently. Its military has reduced from some 2.1 to 1.4 million since the end of the Cold War, leaving them with significant shortages in times of major commitments. They have found the private sector to be convenient, reasonably effective and, most importantly, affordable. Without this outsourcing the United States would have had to find a further division of regular, or more politically damaging, reserve or National Guard forces to deploy into Iraq and Afghanistan. Military body bags are emotive—dead contractors, only in it for the money, are perhaps merely unfortunate!

But it is, of course, not all sweetness and light. This remains a complicated business; CONDO staff are often paid more than regular soldiers, and their terms of service can often be better. The negotiating and letting of contracts can still be, indeed often is, both time-consuming and frustrating. Not too surprisingly, contractors do not want to move into uncharted territory, such as taking part in the initial moves into places like Iraq or Kosovo; and the security of contractors along with their status has become an important issue. The medical support of nonmilitary people in a theater of operations, for example, is tricky. The medical rules of entitlement are often far from ideal; civilians employed under CONDO are not necessarily entitled to use military facilities but, in places like Iraq, they often have nowhere else to turn.[11] Their presence also broadens the age and fitness range of the population at risk, presenting problems not normally experienced when dealing only with soldiers. Somewhat ironically, it is often CONDO nurses and doctors who provide the clinical capabilities needed, as well as the expertise in areas such as pediatrics, clearly useful when dealing with refugees.[12] But they cannot carry weapons and cannot (or at least should not) travel in military helicopters, so their flexibility is limited.

So to sum up thus far: There is nothing new about the military's use of private contractors. They have historically played a key part in military operations around the world and they continue to do so. And the reality today, whether we collectively like it or not, is that these contractors have made such serious inroads into the military business that it is no exaggeration to say that we could not deploy, sustain, or deliver military intent without them. We now meet our needs in a way that attempts to balance risk through both operational and business imperatives, and contractors are vital to delivering the latter. Partnerships developed in the United Kingdom continue through the Coupling Bridge and on into every theatre of operation. We retain a rapidly deployable, coherent military capability, but it lies alongside an integrated and reasonably well-balanced civil component. For initial entry, the core is military manpower, but it has the ability to turn to available contracted support, handing over non-core capabilities as quickly as possible. In the recent conflicts in the Gulf and in the Balkans, contractors were used in significant numbers during the move into theater and in preparations for operations once we had deployed. The provision of camps, both their construction and maintenance, telephones, routine air, road and rail transportation, including flights between the United Kingdom and the theater, bulk fuel, food, water, maintenance and upgrading of vehicle fleets and aircraft; all this and more were sublet to contractors, allowing the redeployment of the military capability back to the United Kingdom in order to be ready for the next deployment.[13]

The Emergence of the PMC/PSC

This all said, significant change emerged some time ago, notably over the last 10 to 15 years, but particularly since September 11, 2001. Security providers have mushroomed in countries all over the world in order to deal with the threat to civilian populations from hijackers and suicide bombers. Private companies are now employing hundreds of thousands in airports, hotels, and conference centers, primarily to conduct security checks on baggage and people. But governments have also allowed contractors to take on broader aspects of security, including combat and protection services. In places like Iraq and Afghanistan we have seen an unprecedented increase in both the scale and role of private sector companies, together with a change in the terminology— CONDO and CONLOG has been joined by PMCs/PSCs.[14] UK companies like Aegis, Erinys, Armorgroup International, Control Risks Group, and Global Risk Strategies are now contracted worldwide alongside others like the U.S. giants MPRI and Dyn-Corp, providing everything from civil-military coordination and force protection (including civil service guarding), pre- and post-conflict advisory and training services (including evaluation), to protective security and security consultancy (including demobilization and security sector reform [SSR]). Their impact on the humanitarian community players, previously largely limited, is now much more evident.

While numbers continue to change, there has been an increase from just one significant PMC/PSC in 1989 to more than ninety today. More than fifty foreign security companies are currently licensed to operate in Iraq. In the 1990–1991 conflict there was perhaps one private contractor for every fifty soldiers; the numbers today are closer to one in ten. The United States may be the largest coalition partner in Iraq, but PMCs/PSCs are easily the second biggest provider of capability, with anywhere between twenty and thirty-five thousand employees[15]—some Iraqis, some other nationals—more than twice the size of the UK military commitment.[16] As we put together the Office of Reconstruction and Humanitarian Affairs (ORHA)[17] to prepare to go out to Iraq it was clear that a great deal of our own support was going to be provided by PMCs/PSCs, and equally clear that any substantial reconstruction was going to have to be carried out by private contractors. ORHA's ability to communicate, our life and logistic support and all of our personal protection came from the private sector, and security for everything from the oil installations to the ministry buildings and embassies would soon rest in its hands.

Aegis—run by Tim Spicer, the founder of Sandline International, the defunct PMC that gained such notoriety in 1998 when it was accused of breaking UN sanctions in Sierra Leone—is now one of the major players in Iraq. Having turned to the private sector for wide-ranging support, the Americans found that they had no method of coordinating and tracking all the companies operating throughout the country; their solution was, to coin a phrase, to set a thief to catch a thief. The $300 million to $400 million worth of contracts let to Aegis enable tracking and preventative and protective security for all the nonmilitary players involved in reconstruction in the country, including the United Nations, and they do protect military personnel on a daily basis. With the freedom to carry weapons for close protection and escorting they can, and do, fight if necessary, although that usually only involves returning fire when attacked while they maneuver to extract themselves; when necessary they can even call for regular military backup. Taken as a whole, I suspect that many lives have been saved, both contractors and diplomats. Of note, and somewhat ironically, the contract includes running a hearts and minds campaign among the Iraqis, and around two hundred international, ex-military bodyguards and one thousand locally recruited Iraqis were also hired to run the security for the recent elections—and the reality that the protection of UN officials was put in their hands has not been lost on either Aegis or the others in the business.[18]

It must also be acknowledged that every day these people put their lives in danger; they face up to the prospect of being ambushed or blown up by roadside Improvised Explosive Devices (IEDs), and many (probably hundreds) have died or been wounded in the process. The majority are of course ex-military, so they know the risks; they also enjoy the buzz and they know the rewards. They are paid a relative fortune for their skill sets, whether as a chef or as a security "expert." Salaries can be, and often are, above $500 a day, several times what they would earn as regular soldiers. The typical "shooter" will earn $120,000—$150,000 a year (and ninety days' annual leave); the best-paid are certainly earning more than I am as a serving major general. And the stark reality is that reconstruction in places like Iraq would be making even less progress without them; the $24 billion program there was floundering badly as insurgents targeted both the infrastructure itself and those attempting to protect it. The coalition had nowhere near enough military power in place to tackle the insurgency, and they had nowhere else to turn other than the private sector to begin to rebuild just about every aspect of the infrastructure; power, hospitals, schools, water, and sanitation were all held together with chewing gum and chicken wire after sanctions and there was no way that the Iraqis were capable of rebuilding on their own. Because of the way the United States had treated the international community in the run-up to the military campaign, not many were prepared to help out with anything much. Some countries no doubt took great delight in seeing the coalition squirm, and although there were, and are, military and financial contributions from a number of others, the size and practical implications of their commitment was, and is, relatively limited.

The problem of course is the way that some of these companies operate, not just in Iraq but in places where the spotlight is not so intrusive. While the best use controlled defensive driving skills, the common image around the world is one of armored civilian vehicles packed with armed men, many with attitude problems, and brandishing weapons of every shape and size, escorting convoys and guarding and protecting both people and infrastructure. This shadow army appears to be largely unregulated and seemingly operates outside of the law. In Iraq, at one end of the spectrum, there have been a number of shooting incidents in which civilians have been killed or wounded, but more irritating[19] to most is the overall day-to-day influence of PSCs on ordinary Iraqi citizens and the aid agencies working to support them. Everyone is affected by these vehicles, which are being seemingly driven by maniacs, and the individuals who muscle their way around—and I write as one who has sheltered beneath their protective wings and been irritated and embarrassed by their approach.

THE MORAL COMPONENT

When assessing the professionalism of military/security organizations the British approach is a doctrinal one. In assessing fighting power we look first at what we call the physical component—what equipment does this organization have; is it the best, is it well maintained and supported, can it be delivered to where it is needed? Secondly, we assess the conceptual component—do these people understand how best to use the equipment; do they understand the nuances, do they have a sense of the underlying issues, know how best to bring the utility of their skills sets to bear on the situation? Thirdly, there is the moral component—how well are these people led; do they have a sense of the culture in which they are operating; do they have a sense of integrity, duty, justice, and righteousness; do they understand the laws of armed conflict, the Geneva Conventions—what is their "ethic," their underlying ethos? A widely known military maxim is that "the moral is to the physical as three is to one"[20]; I would certainly argue that this moral component is the most important of the three and, in the context of the PMCs/PSCs, it is the one that worries me the most.

There are no perfect military organizations; indeed many are far from perfect. But the best militaries recognize the absolute imperative of the moral component, which is why we take breaches of discipline so seriously. The alleged abuse cases emerging from Iraq sadly prove that even the very best fall short, but in the British—and many other—forces there is a robust disciplinary system in place to deal with these, thankfully infrequent, incidents.

And there are inevitably concerns about the ability of the private sector to mirror the highest standards demanded in any theater of operations, and to deal with those who fail to live up to them. I have certainly seen enough to be convinced that this is a serious issue, and there are enough stories around to give credence to those concerns. I have personally come across employees of various PSCs involved in the black market—selling fuel, cigarettes, and so forth—as well as seeing the disturbing reality of protection and prostitution rackets, rapes, and so on.

As the demand for security companies for work in places like Iraq and Afghanistan has skyrocketed, many new companies have emerged to grasp a share of the spoils; they have started from scratch and there are huge variations in the standards of recruitment and training. While many would argue that they prefer to work alongside the military, and indeed under our control, this is not the same as being a part of a common purpose, with unity of effort. And contracts are often let by governments seeking political stability through military solutions provided by organizations outside the normal circle—getting them to intervene in civil wars in the mistaken belief that PMCs/PSCs can bring some form of resolution to the conflict.

One of the more disturbing stories to emerge out of Iraq recently concerns the apparent suicide of a senior U.S. officer late last year (2005). An article in the *Los Angeles Times* on November 28, 2005, reported on the experiences of Colonel Westhusing, a leading scholar of military ethics and a full professor at the West Point Military Academy. He had apparently volunteered to go out to Iraq but was so upset by what he saw that he committed suicide. With a doctorate in philosophy—his 352-page dissertation was an analysis on the meaning of honor—Westhusing found himself confronted by corruption within a PSC that he was overseeing; they had seemingly cheated the U.S. government and committed human rights violations. The traditional military values of duty and honor had, he realized, been replaced by the profit motive.

At West Point, cadets are drilled in the strict moral code, not to lie, cheat or steal, or tolerate those who do; in 1979 they were themselves just emerging from a cheating scandal—I say again that no institution is perfect—and Westhusing lived through those days of restoring the cadets' own honor. He was selected as honor captain for the entire academy in his senior year, graduated third in his class, and became an infantry platoon leader; he quickly began to develop a promising career, returning to the academy to teach philosophy. Having deployed to Iraq, he found himself in January 2005 overseeing a PSC with a $79 million contract to train a corps of Iraqi police. In May he apparently received an anonymous four-page letter detailing allegations of wrongdoings: not just underhanded work practices to boost profits but also alleged witnessing of or participation in killings. Westhusing was said to become "sick of money grabbing contractors"; he wrote a note saying that he couldn't support a mission that led to such corruption, human rights abuse, and liars—he felt sullied and dishonored.

Interestingly Westhusing was considered by some to have been somewhat naïve in his thinking; and many would no doubt argue that he needed to recognize that morality couldn't outweigh the harsh realities of operations in places like Iraq. I will leave readers to draw their own conclusions, but would just point out that the events I described earlier in the Crimea of 1854 prove that there is nothing new here—cheating and corrupt contractors are a harsh reality.[21] And I for one would argue that we surely cannot accept anything less than demandingly rigorous standards if we are to attempt to hold the moral high ground on operations around the world. All government contracts now tend to be carefully supervised—but not all contracts are government-let, and the bottom line is that many of these private companies do not have particularly good reputations. There is certainly no exhaustive external monitoring regime in place to scrutinize the activities of the industry as a whole in the various operations they find themselves in.

SCRUTINY

There are only two pieces of international law currently in place; both relate to mercenaries[22] and neither would prove particularly helpful in anything but the starkest cases of malpractice. Ironically, the most advanced national legislation is in America; any U.S. company that provides any security-related service abroad must register and apply for a license, and seek government approval for any contract over $50 million. Within the United Kingdom, the 1870 Foreign Enlistment Act is almost impossible to enforce and, in 1976, the Diplock Report recommended its replacement—but nothing of substance emerged until a "Green Paper" was published February 12, 2002, as a result of a recommendation by the Foreign Affairs Select Committee.[23] This—really rather good paper—established the case for regulation and looked at six options: a ban on military activity abroad; a ban on recruitment for military activity abroad; a licensing regime for military services; registration and notification; a general license for PMCs/PSCs; and finally self-regulation—a voluntary code of conduct. The pros and cons of each option were considered, and the government called for views from members of Parliament, NGOs, companies, and anyone else interested in the subject. Further options followed but, as yet, no legislation has been enacted.

However, while the legislature continues to prevaricate some of those out on the ground are getting their act together in order to preempt government intervention. The better companies—like Aegis—do now have a system of self-regulation, with printed and issued "codes of conduct" and control measures such as rules of engagement. Most only work under contract for a legitimate government, and a business with a corporate identity and salaried staff back in the home base may be held accountable for its actions in an operation—and they certainly have to rely on their reputation for future contracts. The first director-general of a PSC "trade association"—the British Association of Private Security Companies (BAPSC)—has also just been appointed. Andy Bearpark is a senior British civilian humanitarian who has worked extensively in complex emergencies around the world. Most recently he worked as the senior reconstruction coordinator in the Balkans, before then moving out to join the Coalition Provisional Authority in Baghdad in mid-2003. He has now cajoled (bullied?) twenty-one UK-based companies to join him in developing a sort of ISO for this type of work; he acknowledges the shortfalls of the past, but argues that the "old days" of the 1980–1990s are gone.[24]

British security companies do certainly have a pretty good reputation, and not surprisingly they are very keen to maintain that
reputation. Bearpark's intention is to think through the distinction between the legal and practical implications of a PSC supporting the military and the role they play in supporting the
overall civil effort or actually performing rebuilding tasks (like
SSR) themselves. Alongside this is his intent to ensure that some
basic minimum standards are established, including training in
such things as the Geneva Conventions. This work is now beginning to move forward from its early stages; but there is much still
to be done before anything substantial—even approaching the
SPHERE standards—emerges.

WHERE TO FROM HERE? BECOMING
MORE EFFECTIVE AND ACCOUNTABLE

So, the reality is that these companies are out there, that they are
far from perfect, but that they are now so engaged in day-to-day
operations around the world that they can no longer be ignored.
The obvious question for the array of other nonmilitary players is
how they will respond to this reality. Many have already done so,
pragmatically accepting that the world has indeed moved on. Humanitarian workers now work in a far more difficult climate than
ten or fifteen years ago—and claims of neutrality, impartiality, or
independence no longer offer protection from warlords or terrorists; casualties among the NGO community have been mounting,
as they have been among the media and the other nonmilitary
organizations, and kidnappings are becoming commonplace.
There may be various reasons for this. It is certainly fair to say that
the clear distinction between the role of the military and the others in complex emergencies is becoming increasingly blurred,
and this hasn't helped. There has always been a role for the military in helping the local civilian community to deal with the immediate aftermath of combat, but until relatively recently that has
been on a local, tactical basis. Every British military unit would,
and still does, take great pride in helping "their" local village or
town, in any number of ways, raising money from contacts at
home or taking on local projects to help the local population

or both. Over the last decade or so this has become more of an operational-level business, and there can be no doubt that there is no longer "clear blue water" between the military and nonmilitary players. To be fair, quite a lot of progress has been made over the last ten years or so in our collective understanding of the need for the military and the humanitarian community to work better together, and this must continue to evolve, but more importantly I sense that there is an increasing demand for a far more joined-up and businesslike approach to the whole humanitarian response system. We need to understand why this is so.

Part of the reason is the historical failure of the IO/NGO community to deliver a joined-up effect. Sometimes this is because they have not been present at the crucial time in sufficient numbers to be able to deliver support; this may be for any one of a variety of reasons, but when it happens it can take them a long time to become effective—time the victims all too often do not have. My own experiences in the Balkans certainly opened my eyes to this.[25] But even when they are present, the efficiency of their delivery is increasingly open to question. Too often the major IO/UN agencies and many of the key NGOs are not structured to deliver either effective or efficient outputs coherently. Considered in pure business terms the whole community has grown almost exponentially over the last couple of decades. The worldwide response to recent humanitarian disasters—such as the 2004 Boxing Day tsunami and the 2005 autumn earthquake in Pakistan—was extraordinary, resulting in hundreds of millions of dollars being raised to help deal with the consequences.

And the work in support of the UNDP millennium goals, particularly those linked to poverty like the "Make Poverty History" campaign,[26] has generated a huge, bottom-up groundswell of support. Some of the better NGOs actually put out a call for people to stop sending them money for specific responses because they couldn't deal with the generosity being shown, but others have certainly taken in whatever has come their way. We are beginning to see the first reports and analyses showing how this money has failed to reach those it was intended for; and one thing is for sure, more such analyses will follow. Link this with the difficulties that many NGOs found—and continue to find—in Iraq, Darfur, and the Democratic Republic of Congo (DRC), and the sorry state of many other operations around the world, and my conclusion is that these "businesses"—because that is what they are[27]—are failing both their stakeholders and their shareholders, who are the victims and those who contribute their hard earned cash as supporters and donors.

To pretend that there is no emerging crisis of confidence is, I sense, akin to the way that many in the military refused to face up to the realities of everything that has been happening to us over the last decade or so. It is obviously far better to get on the front foot in order to drive the changes that are coming. Responding to complex emergencies, including natural disasters, is, by definition, a complex business; and in just the same way that we the military have had to recognize the benefits that the private sector can bring, so the nonmilitary players have to begin a serious analysis of how they too can harness—or leverage—those benefits. The establishment of a coherent and joined-up supply chain into the disaster area; moving the people and the humanitarian materiel into the country concerned; establishing the equivalent of an FRSA; coordinating the flow of materiel up from the APODs/SPODs; establishing the medical plan, the shelter plan—all this and more needs looking at critically to see how the overall effort can be delivered more effectively and efficiently. Some partnerships with professional private sector companies are beginning to emerge, but more needs to be done.[28]

And among and alongside the potential utility of CONDO or CONLOG, the community must consider the best way of expanding their engagement with the PSCs. This is clearly more controversial, but there is plenty of scope for closer relationships. And I say "expanding the engagement" and "closer relationships" because the reality is that there are already a wide range of linkages. Various parts of the UN, the ICRC, World Vision, and many others have already used private companies to protect their facilities and staff in places like Africa—even environmental groups deal with such companies to protect various endangered species from well-armed poachers. But, so far, these and other developments have taken place under a veil of silence, in an ad hoc way. It is time that changed.

This of course has to be done carefully. A first step—somewhat ironically—may well be to use suitable private consulting firms to analyze where we are and where we need to be; their knowledge of the wider private sector, and how it works, is crucial if well-meaning individuals and individual NGOs are not to be hood-winked. We also have to recognize that private companies are, to state the obvious, only in it for the money. Businesses have to make a profit, but if they can deliver a service that currently costs $100 for, say, $90, and yet still make a profit—and do it quicker and more effectively—then they deserve to make that profit; there is no immorality in that, as long as they agree to abide by some ground rules. Private companies need clear ethical guidelines that balance the simple intent of maximizing profits; contracts awarded within a normal competitive framework must ensure fair prices, oversight provision for issues like recruitment, and accountability, with contingencies for dealing with "rogue" employees. The vetting of particular companies is not easy, but an updated register/database of financially transparent firms with a good track record could be maintained by governments, an umbrella NGO/aid organization, or even the United Nations with appropriate oversight.

There are of course the obvious dangers, not least the proliferation of armed individuals, and each NGO will have to take a view on what is acceptable here. But those engaged in the most difficult operations around the world may well find that this is the only way of continuing. All too often those who are suffering most in these complex situations are the homeless, the internally displaced persons (IDPs), and the refugees, and they can then find themselves subjected to protection rackets, kidnappings for prostitution, as cover for gun running, and so on. I saw a great deal of this in the Balkans and it was a pretty unsavory business. Aid agencies not only have a duty of care to their employees but also a responsibility for the people they are working with and ultimately for.

So, in sum there is work to be done. The humanitarian community needs to face up to the reality that their work is becoming the focus for increasing criticism. The various agencies cannot avoid the need to become more professional and accountable; the media have already begun to home in on the way that the huge amounts of money raised are spent,[29] on the length of time it takes to make a difference initially, and on the long-term benefit the money buys. This, along with a reluctance to work in closer cooperation with others, including the military where appropriate, needs addressing. And the private sector has a part to play here, particularly in post-conflict work. There is much to be learned from the way that the militaries around the world have engaged with CONDO, CONLOG, and with PMCs/PSCs. We do need to recognize that there are clear distinctions between the role of PSCs operating alongside the military and their role supporting the civil effort—either protecting others or actually engaging in SSR in their own right; those distinctions can, and need to, be worked through. But professionalizing supply chains and using contracted support for security-related services is not the same as dancing with the devil. There are many advantages, which of course have to be weighed against the disadvantages, but on balance I sense that there is much to be gained; and I for one would urge closer engagement.

5

Looking Beyond the "Latest and Greatest"

Christopher Holshek

THERE IS A TENDENCY, in a world of increasingly ephemeral attention spans, to pay greater attention to the "latest and greatest" developments to generalize about a topic of current interest. Behavioral psychologists and economists call this the "availability heuristic." The well-publicized tensions between nongovernmental organizations (NGOs) and particularly the U.S. military in Afghanistan in 2002, culminating in the July 2004 decision of one of the world's prominent NGOs, Medecins Sans Frontieres (MSF), to withdraw after twenty-four years from Afghanistan, might suggest that civil-military cooperation in humanitarian crises is in a downward spiral. However, when the span of these relations is examined both horizontally across the globe and vertically through the post–Cold War era, a more assuring picture comes into view. By and large, civil-military cooperation in humanitarian crises is filled with numerous instances of relative success (including the unprecedented relief efforts after the Indian Ocean tsunami), suggesting they are not inherently problematic. A recent strategic workshop at the U.S. Institute of Peace noted that "interaction between humanitarians and militaries had deepened over the last decade to include formalized exchanges, coordination, and institutional development of centers and institutes. Indeed, an emergent consensus on coherence—coordination of intervention and humanitarian action—was emerging by the turn of the millennium."[1] Nonetheless, the difficulties experienced by both the military and NGOs in "post 9/11" international force interventions, such as in Afghanistan and Iraq, have evinced serious challenges to the present and future of this increasingly crucial relationship. An overview of how these relations have evolved would not only provide some perspective to this issue, but point to some ways ahead.

Since the end of the Cold War, the relationship between the military and the civilian organizations providing relief services in the wake of natural or man-made disasters or conflicts can be described as maturing. While the 1990s were by no means a halcyon era in this regard, demand for the services of both civilian and military providers of humanitarian services grew exponentially. During that time, some clear trends with impact on this relationship had emerged, as summarized in the concluding report of the Challenges Project, sponsored by the Swedish National Defense College and related organizations:

> One obvious change in peace operations over the last decade has been an increase in the numbers and disciplines of contributors: international and national, governmental and nongovernmental, and military and non-military. The inability, however, of this broad, diverse and complex set of players to conceive, plan and work together in managing a crisis and implementing a peace plan, despite the massive commitment of financial and human resources, is a major challenge in crisis management and modern peace operations today. On some occasions, civil and military elements have worked together constructively and harmoniously, but on others the inability to achieve an appropriate level of cooperation has seriously weakened the overall effectiveness of the mission. The reasons are many and, although experience varies, the all-too-frequent instances of inability to cooperate willingly, to coordinate effectively and efficiently and to pursue common objectives collectively and professionally are sometimes referred to as the "Civil-Military Cooperation Issue (CIMIC) issue."[2]

Beyond the mere proliferation of players, however, civilian relief organizations grew increasingly more capable of taking a greater role—even the lead—in humanitarian relief operations. Better resourced, more professionally staffed, and more operationally adept, they have been able to take on the roles and tasks that the military has performed, more or less, by default. They have also developed their own coordinating structures, often in conjunction with the United Nations or a lead agency such as UNHCR, or with international or intergovernmental organizations (IOs or

IGOs). In many cases, the relationship between these lead organizations or consortia and many of the especially smaller NGOs are contractual or subcontractual in the sense of market specialization in relief or predevelopment services. This capability and sophistication has been good news, but it has led to the growing need for the military to better understand and enable civilian organization activities, as these organizations demand a greater say not so much in the international political decision-making process, but in related operational decisions on the ground. This has complicated matters even further for the military.

Further, NGOs now appear in many more forms, including the indigenous NGO, which tends to take over the brunt of relief activity, either supplanting the international civilian relief groups in contractual or subcontractual relationships, or as competing organizations, as the situation matures. In addition, many (especially indigenous) NGOs, are sponsored by (or affiliated with) political and religious organizations, thus blurring the distinction between an NGO and an advocacy or activist group, and thus making it much more difficult not only to define what an NGO is, but whether these NGOs in particular can truly claim impartiality, neutrality, and independence. (This is why it is very often instructive to investigate the money stream of donor sources of an NGO in determining its aims and interests.) And what of those NGOs, more established and having a record of adhering to the principles that should afford them their special status, that choose to collaborate with, albeit for good, practical reasons, less impartial, neutral, and independent civilian organizations? Has their impartiality, neutrality, and independence in this process been compromised? These questions have further exacerbated the challenge of civil-military cooperation.

As for the military:

> Just as we must ask *which civilians* form the civil-military relationship, it also matters *which military forces* are involved. Some militaries bring international political baggage. Accepting troop contributors from interested regional actors or major powers may increase the odds of military effectiveness at the expense of political impartiality. Secondly, militaries have different orientations toward society. Some have been segregated from society and oriented toward defense against uniformed adversaries on a defined battlefield, as was

the U.S. military during the Cold War. Other militaries have more recent experience with counter insurgencies and other internal control functions.[3]

The military has maintained relative dominance—beyond leadership and management training, organization, and logistics—in operational coordination and synchronizing structures and methodologies, particularly in information management. The United Nations, as an overarching civilian coordinating instrumentality, has steadily improved since the initial implementation of the "Report of the Panel on United Nations Peace Operations," better known as the "Brahimi Report." Parallel with the growth in competence of civilian relief organizations has been the growing ability of the military to synchronize military and nonmilitary elements in these increasingly dynamic and complex situations, albeit sometimes reluctantly, mainly at the hands of specialized military personnel. In the United States (and now the United Kingdom), they are called civil affairs officers (CA); among other NATO and most other countries, civil-military cooperation (CIMIC); in the United Nations, civil-military coordination (CM-Coord); and so on. Depending on national policies and military doctrinal cultures, civil-military cooperation could mean different things to different militaries. CA, for example, has an expansive menu of mission-functional areas "across the full spectrum of conflict" in support of the global strategy of the United States, whereas NATO CIMIC doctrine, in an attempt to coordinate civil-military action among numerous national militaries, is more restricted to direct support of a military commander's mission with reference to a specific mandate, and in the UN context it is more obtusely interpreted. This has correspondingly complicated matters even further for civilian organizations trying to work with the military.

The Challenges Project also notes that "the complexity of interdependence between civilian military is not simply because both communities are engaged in all functional categories of peace operations, but due to a number of other complicating factors"[4]:

- As mentioned, the plethora of organizations in number, type, and status, as well as their activities in a given mission area;

- The relative impact of progress or failure in one activity on another (among them, security operations on humanitarian relief actions);
- Changes in the roles and capabilities among players at various times in the intervention;
- Obstacles, misunderstandings, and dilemmas (discussed below) impacting civil-military cooperation and coordination, some derived from fundamental differences in corporate culture and others from circumstances;
- The ability and willingness of each community to appropriate resources, personnel, money, and technology to civil-military cooperation and coordination.

Beginning with Kosovo, however, there was an additional complication that would come into greater play following the 9/11 terrorist attacks on the United States; namely, the simultaneity of security and peace operations:

> In the 1990s, the UN Secretary-General's "An Agenda for Peace" implied that modern peacekeeping followed a sequence: if conflict prevention failed then one moved on to various means of peace-making; once there was an agreement to pursue a peaceful solution then traditional methods of peacekeeping could be applied; and finally, once peace had taken hold, peace-building could begin . . . The reality of today's operations, however, is that there is essentially no such tidy sequence. Conflict prevention, diplomatic peace making, peace enforcement actions, classic peacekeeping, peace-building and nation-building (development) are often all taking place simultaneously. In addition, humanitarian assistance operations have been required in addressing the consequences of these recent conflicts.[5]

More than any other complicating factor, it was the concurrence of security and peace operations that would cause the greatest rub between NGOs like MSF and U.S. forces, particularly in Afghanistan. In places like Afghanistan (and later Iraq), the simultaneity of security and peace operations means less than permissive environments for the conduct of humanitarian relief operations. The major difference between pre-9/11 humanitarian relief in conflict areas and post-9/11 operations is that relief workers, being much more in "post-conflict" situations, grew used to operating in relatively permissive environments for humanitarian relief. Working under more hostile conditions was more the exception than the rule. Following 9/11, this relationship has (so far) been much the reverse. In short, peace operations, to include humanitarian relief, have become a considerably more dangerous business for the military and civilians alike. In 2003, there were more fatal attacks on humanitarian workers than ever previously recorded. This has seriously encroached on what is known as "humanitarian space":

> As defined by the European Commission's Directorate for Humanitarian Aid, "humanitarian space" means "the access and freedom for humanitarian organizations to assess and meet humanitarian needs." Humanitarian principles, including preserving the humanitarian nature of operations, independence from political and military actors, impartiality, neutrality, and non-discrimination, are essential to humanitarian actors. However, at least some agents of violence in African refugee camps exploited humanitarian intentions, changed relationships with camp communities, and other political and military actors, and degraded physical security.[6]

Or, as former U.S. Deputy Assistance Secretary of Defense for Stability Operations Joseph J. Collins put it: "In today's world . . . the military aspects of a problem and the humanitarian aspects of a problem are wrapped together like a pretzel, and it's awfully difficult to unravel. We often find ourselves today in situations where, on the cusp of a military operation, we're also putting ourselves in the middle of a humanitarian crisis."

In response to the greater use of special operations forces and methodologies by U.S. forces, among them the appearance of nonuniformed troops conducting unconventional missions in their hunt for terrorist groups in Afghanistan, many NGOs—a good number working in the country and region long before 9/11—issued strong protests to these methods, fearing they compromised the neutrality of NGOs and, in blurring the ostensible distinctions between combatants and noncombatants, endangered NGO personnel working with or in proximity to, for example, CA forces attempting to "win hearts and minds" through humanitarian actions and in attempts to coordinate civil-military humanitarian responses.[7]

A December 2002 policy brief by the Agency Coordinating Body for Afghan Relief (ACBAR), representing over ninety NGOs working in Afghanistan, articulated their concerns to the Coalition Force strategy of deploying Joint Regional Teams to enhance security and promote better coordination and delivery of assistance. While the NGOs "welcomed the shift in Coalition focus to the establishment of a more secure environment in which reconstruction can take place," they also were concerned that "using military structures to provide assistance and reconstruction support will both prematurely deflect attention from Afghanistan's deteriorating security situation and also engage the military in a range of activities for which others are better suited." ACBAR substantiated its points by articulating its first concern that "(1) long-term impact will be sacrificed for short-term political and military dividends, (2) communities that oppose the current government may get different levels of aid than those who support the government, (3) communities in conflict areas may receive different levels of aid than those in areas considered stable and (4) the military will aim to use NGOs as 'force multipliers' to achieve political or security-related ends."[8]

In arguing its second concern, the ACBAR briefing notes that the "average cost of keeping a U.S. soldier on the ground in Afghanistan is $215,000 per year," while "the average cost of an aid worker in Afghanistan is less than a tenth of that cost, largely because the vast majority of aid workers are Afghans, not expatriates." The briefing also suggests that "(1) military expenditures on assistance activity could go much further in the hands of assistance professionals, and (2) because those expenditures will be counted as a contribution to the assistance on Afghanistan rather than as an internal expenditure of the military, this commitment will substitute for, rather than supplement, the commitments that the donors have already made to help rebuild Afghanistan."

Finally, the briefing argues perhaps the crux issue (considering the previous two concerns have been brought up by NGOs in pre-9/11 operations); namely, whether civilian humanitarians are put at physical risk due to the relief and reconstruction activities performed by military forces under hostile conditions:

> Local populations on the ground often cannot or will not distinguish between soldiers and civilian aid workers engaged in humanitarian and reconstruction activities. Military participation in

assistance may significantly enhance antagonism towards humanitarian professionals and the risks that those the military chooses to disengage from its reconstruction efforts, NGOs will be required to take over and will be perceived as agents of the larger political and military strategy as a result. While military-led assistance may be short term, the impact on community perceptions of civilian humanitarians may be lasting.[9]

In addition to having the military focus exclusively on security missions, the ACBAR briefing recommends that the military "should not engage in assistance work except in those rare circumstances where emergency needs exist and civilian assistance workers are unable to meet those needs due to a lack of logistical capacity or levels of insecurity on the ground," and if it does engage in such activities, that they should fall under civilian leadership, be documented through a "transparent accountability mechanism," and accountable to a "code of conduct agreed upon between the military and representatives of the civilian assistance community." Most importantly:

> The military should take the necessary steps to ensure that communities, policy makers and the general public do not confuse military- and civilian-implemented assistance. In this regard, (1) any civil-military coordination should take place in civilian-managed demilitarized locations (no arms, etc.) separate from existing NGO-only coordination locations and (2) the military should be transparent with respect to its security and political objectives in particular assistance interventions and should demarcate its assistance accordingly (soldiers should wear uniforms at all times etc). At no time should the military refer to its engagement in assistance as "humanitarianism" or to NGOs as "force multipliers" as both such misnomers blur the distinction between civilian- and military-led interventions . . . The military should articulate their rules of military engagement in circumstances where they are also providing assistance.[10]

Along with a position paper prepared at the behest of many NGOs by the UN Office of the Coordinator for Humanitarian Assistance (OCHA) to the Secretary-General, who in turn provided it to the U.S. Ambassador to the United Nations, the U.S. NGO coordinating group, InterAction, in an April 2, 2002, letter from the heads of sixteen major American relief NGOs, expressed their concerns to the U.S. National Security Adviser.[11] Then, in a May 2003 conference in Washington DC, they addressed as a main topic the relationship between the military and NGOs, expressing similar concerns. Retired Ambassador Jim Bishop, in reinforcement of the ACBAR concerns, pointed out: "There have been incidents where NGO personnel have been injured, raped. And when the military started engaging in retail humanitarian activities, dressed indistinguishably from humanitarian workers except for pistols bulging out of their pockets, that further compromised the independence of NGOs and put them at risk, as Afghans began to assume the NGOs were military personnel." The Pentagon's response to this was, having already ordered soldiers back into uniforms in the spring of 2002, to create Provisional Reconstruction Teams (PRTs) to create a more coordinated U.S. military and civilian interagency response for stability and reconstruction in outlying areas in Afghanistan, including military CA personnel and civilian representatives from governmental agencies, mainly the U.S. Agency for International Development (USAID) and Office of Foreign Disaster Assistance (OFDA), but not NGOs.[12] More familiar coordinating mechanisms such as civil-military operations centers (CMOCs) were employed.

While some NGOs had little issue working with the PRTs or CMOCs, others maintained their objection to military conduct of humanitarian relief per se, among them MSF. In July 2004, following the murder of five of its aid workers, MSF announced it would withdraw from Afghanistan under protest, its main arguments articulated in a *New York Times* editorial:

> Relief workers are being murdered at an alarming rate because of a perceived lack of neutrality, because they are regarded as extensions of a donor nation's political and military agendas . . . the neutrality of all relief workers employed by nongovernmental organizations in the post-Sept. 11 world was being compromised. . . . The demand on relief agencies to shed that protective cloak of neutrality—despite the dangers to those in the field—has never been more aggressive than it is today. . . . Unless the United States, the key donor nation, publicly espouses the position that relief work is neutral, and unless the Bush administration makes it clear that those saving lives in the field do not follow a donor nation's

political and military policies, other sources of donations might dry up. Nations that frequently augment American contributions may understandably be reluctant to donate the billions of dollars and personnel needed for humanitarian efforts. And more civilian relief workers are going to get killed in their service to humanity.[13]

The civil-military denouement in Afghanistan is a good example of what the Challenges Project calls the three basic challenges affecting civil-military cooperation—described as "obstacles, misunderstandings, and dilemmas":

> The first is that there is a series of fundamental obstacles, which, if not understood or dealt with, can seriously impede the ability of the two communities to work together . . . [and] include major differences in culture, mandates resources, levels of authority and experience, as well as problems of personality (in leadership) and functional areas of responsibility. . . . Secondly, over time and based upon simplistic assessments and experiences, a number of misunderstandings have arisen (and have unfortunately gained unwarranted credibility) on the part of elements of one or the other communities . . . [including] "military forces are a manpower tool," rather than being a force tailored to a mission, "NGOs can be tasked," "the military is there to support civilian operations," "only one organization can be involved in a specific function," "once military support to civilians is given, it should continue," and "the military needs more training" . . . whereas in the eyes of the military a great deal more civilian education and training is desperately needed. Thirdly, a number of dilemmas confront both communities, in that there are differing views and approaches to a number of issues yet each can be considered "technically correct." While these obstacles and misunderstandings can generally be addressed through education, training, and better dialogue there are a number of fundamental differences confronting military and civilian contributors to modern peace operations.[14]

Among these dilemmas is that, while civil-military cooperation is essential to the success of either community, civilian interaction with the military risks compromise of the time-honored principles of humanity, impartiality, independence, and neutrality. In understanding these dilemmas, and finding a way through the thicket of issues in civil-military cooperation in humanitarian relief operations in general and under semi- or nonpermissive conditions in particular, it is helpful to reorient through examination of the essential characteristics of the two communities.

Regardless of the level of progress in civil-military cooperation over the years, there are key differences in the *modus operandi* of military versus civilian organizations. While the military normally focuses on reaching clearly defined objectives through linear operational (planning and execution) progressions with given timelines under a unified command and control structure, civilian organizations are concerned with a process of fulfilling changeable political interests through a fluctuating sequence of dialogue, bargaining, risk-taking, and consensus-building.[15]

The military and many government bureaucracies, particularly at the agency level, tend to be more doctrinal and programmatic than the United Nations or nonpublic groups, although the UN Department of Peacekeeping Operations promulgated its own confidential "Handbook on United Nations Multidimensional Peacekeeping Operations" at the end of 2003. NGOs, on the other hand, are rarely large enough, consistently staffed enough, and have the overhead resources to develop and implement doctrine for which they perceive to have little need. In addition, "in an era when donors and the media are increasingly focused on the bottom line and tend to rate humanitarian organizations by what percentage of donations goes to the ultimate beneficiaries, the need to explain and justify administrative costs is a pressing concern."[16]

British Army Maj. Gen. Timothy Cross, in an earlier publication in this series, provides an excellent detailed analysis of the differences between military and civilian organizations in humanitarian relief fundamental to the corporate cultures:

> Any operational deployment has a number of "lines of operation"; the military line is alongside the political, diplomatic, legal, economic, media, and humanitarian lines. To be effective, military commanders must face up to the challenges of shattered societies as well as direct military threats. They need to remain focused on their primary imperative, that of establishing a secure environment to enable the other lines to be developed, but balancing the various frictions is not easy. . . . But taken to an extreme the military can be too "task" orientated, becoming over-controlling, autocratic, and critical; the individual is held to be subservient to the greater good. State focused, with legitimacy coming from the state, the military

are, by definition, political servants and are neither neutral, impartial, or independent. Too often we can forget individual needs and close our minds to others' views; often our head rules our heart.[17]

Cross lists the strengths of NGOs as: being principled in humanitarianism, which is the basis of their legitimacy; knowledgeable in having served in many countries and skilled in their work; committed to the longer-term, which is often the nature of such operations; networked with other organizations and locals, much more adept at "relationship-building" than the military; linked to the media and thus able to command a moral imperative for humanitarian intervention; and enhancing the role of women.

Their weaknesses, however, often lie in their lack of material resources, the inability to respond quickly to changing conditions, their overemphasis on single issues and inability or unwillingness to see the "big picture," and rivalries with other organizations, military and civilian, often seeing them as competitors:

> The NGOs exhibit softer, more manageable cultural traits than the military; traits that make them, generally, less confrontational and, generally, fairly effective in multicultural environments. There is rooted in their souls, a "blood line" divide, which was often put there in their early years and which many struggle to cross in their search for moral and ethical virtues and a "what I stand for" doctrine. Nonetheless, taken to extremes, they can be self-indulgent, too focused on their particular human issue and, living within a "rights-based" culture, they can be resentful of control, morally arrogant, and blind to the dark side of individual human nature; often their heart rules their head.[18]

There are thus considerable differences between the nature and modus operandi of military and civilian relief organizations—differences that cannot be eliminated, but perhaps harmonized through mutual acceptance and a careful balance between humanitarian space and civil-military integration. Beyond focusing on differences, the nature as well as the need for civil-military cooperation in humanitarian relief can be well illuminated by comparing and contrasting these communities in terms of comparative advantages and disadvantages when it comes to providing relief and development services to affected populations:

Although civilian organizations have taken the lead in crisis response and "nation-building," the military maintains certain comparative advantages which complement the operational shortcomings of much of the civilian peace operations community. These advantages include, for example: decision-making; staff coordination; planning and organization; consequence, crisis and transition management, as well as other forms of problem-solving; logistics management; information operations; and above all, training. Beyond its primary role of securing the peace operations environment, the military can play a vital role in leveraging the success of the civilian peace operations community. This is particularly true in the early phases when civilian organizations are not as well-deployed and resourced in the field as the military, yet at the very time when certain actions, taken or not taken, can have long-lasting impact on the legitimacy and effectiveness of the international presence. This, paradoxically, is in the direct interests of the military and their sending states in order to minimize the military's role—i.e., in supporting the "exit strategy" and reaching the "endstate."[19]

Particularly in the sense of the last sentence above, military and civilian intervention elements have become more codependent for their own successes than ever before. The seeds of both confrontation and cooperation in civil-military relations in humanitarian relief extend well before 9/11; if anything, the more dangerous and complex environments in Afghanistan and Iraq have demonstrated to experienced soldiers, diplomats, and aid workers an even greater need to find more practical means to work together and bridge their more principled differences:

It should not be forgotten that many NGOs were born out of the suffering caused not just indirectly, but directly, by military forces around the world, both ill-disciplined and unprofessional national armies and "rebel" or irregular forces. Nonetheless, the principles of independence, neutrality, and impartiality are usually tempered with a recognition that there is a "bottom line," as they face up to the conflicts between positive principles and negative imperatives—not to legitimize rebel movements, not to contribute to the war effort of either side, not to submit to government controls that interfere with their ability to fulfill their humanitarian mission. Recognizing that the very process of fulfilling the humanitarian

imperative can mean that both neutrality and impartiality are compromised, and that their involvement does influence a conflict,
their approach is to "minimize" rather than "do no harm."[20]

Or, as the UN Department of Peacekeeping Operations' "Handbook on United Nations Multidimensional Peacekeeping Operations" explains it:

> Humanitarian assistance has always been grounded in the idea of
> providing aid based on the consent of the government or govern-
> ments involved. This model was effective when wars were between
> States and space could be created for humanitarian organizations,
> such as the International Committee of the Red Cross (ICRC), to
> assist prisoners of war and others in need. In the internal conflicts
> of today, however, the dividing line between civilians and combat-
> ants is frequently blurred. Combatants often live or seek shelter in
> villages, and sometimes use civilians, even children, as human
> shields. In some cases, communities provide logistic support to
> armed groups either voluntarily or under compulsion and become
> targeted as a consequence. . . . Humanitarian assistance never oc-
> curs in a vacuum and is never simply a matter of the delivery of
> food or medicine. The way in which assistance is designed and de-
> livered, especially the selection of local partners and intermediar-
> ies, will almost invariably have important political consequences.[21]

Thus, while it is important for the military to understand the principles under which (legitimate) NGOs operate, it is likewise important for these NGOs to understand that their involvement has
an unavoidable political context. If anything, because of the
emerging realities explained earlier, IOs and NGOs are now more
politically relevant—or at least are perceived to be—than ever.
Thus, while NGOs and other civilian relief organizations should
never abandon their time-honored principles of humanity, impartiality, independence, and neutrality, which set them apart from
other members of the intervention community, they must also
temper their adherence to these principles with a certain degree
of pragmatism in application, in order not to defeat the purpose
for which they came to begin with:

> In any case, inasmuch as military community needs to better under-
> stand and accommodate the ways of the civilian community whose
> success in peace operations is essentially prerequisite, civilian orga-
> nizations and their practitioners in peace operations—the majority

of whom have no military experience—must likewise be prepared to work with the military, operating from its side of the Clausewitzian continuum, this time between politics and peace. Nevertheless, "the natural reluctance of governmental and nongovernmental agencies to be seen as working with the military in complex emergencies has diminished in recent years, and NGOs in particular are finding that a collaboration can benefit all parties."[22]

Even before 9/11, terrorists, insurgents, criminal organizations, and many other informal power structures against the international intervention that can be called "spoilers," particularly in areas where culture and religion shape the dialogue, often have little to no interest in NGOs improving life for indigenous populations—unless they can take credit for it or at least not have it perceived that they rather than outsiders are responsible. If the spoilers cannot co-opt or gain advantage from the presence and activities of NGOs, they will do everything or anything necessary to frustrate them—from intimidation tactics to kidnapping or even killing their personnel. Because the spoilers are often most interested in the status quo or status quo ante, they resent the presence and activities of relief and development organizations that help people to move toward and become more oriented on the future, regardless of their association with the military or any other government organizations. Moreover, NGOs and other "change agents" come with information and perspectives (such as the role of women and public education) that present competing ideas to the orthodoxy of many spoiler groups, helping to connect these hitherto disconnected societies to the world outside.

It was therefore no accident in Iraq, for example, following the bombing of the UN compound in Baghdad in August 2003, that many relief workers were killed, kidnapped, or otherwise dissuaded from continuing to be a force for positive change in that country. The brutal kidnapping, in October 2004, and eventual murder of Margaret Hassan, Director of CARE International Iraq, who long lived and was popular there, was a clear indication of this "spoiler" intent. In military terms, this evinced a deliberate campaign to attack the "operational center of gravity"—the presence, willingness, and ability of these "change agents" to continue the process from local dependence on the military and other "occupation" instrumentalities to more sovereign control of political and economic destiny, a key feature of the "exit strategy" of the military. In short, by attacking NGOs and other civilian relief and development groups—again, often regardless of their relationship with the military—the spoilers are attacking the military and the political cachet it represents and at least the perception of legitimacy now so central to their operations. The presence of NGOs and other change agents helps to legitimize this process of change—the more it looks like the whole world has come to help a distraught population, the more legitimacy the international intervention has. This essential by-product of the presence of NGOs has been one of the main reasons why the military sometimes—and whenever, incorrectly—terms NGOs as "force multipliers." The error is not so much in recognizing the reality of this legitimizing factor, but in assuming that is a reason why the NGOs are there.

The military, however, is not alone in its clumsiness. In a rejoinder to the MSF arguments for quitting Afghanistan publicized in *The New York Times* in August 2004, Cheryl Bernard, a scholar with the RAND Corporation and wife of the U.S. ambassador to Afghanistan, points out that "the decision was made for the wrong reasons, on a premise about humanitarian aid that no longer holds up to political reality"; namely:

> It's a different world out there, and unless they want to get out of the aid business altogether, they'll have to come to terms with it . . . The new generation of terrorists does not spare unarmed humanitarians. They do not leave clinics, schools and other benign civilian projects untouched: They destroy them especially, because they want civilians to suffer and reconstruction to fail. Fear and backwardness are a kingdom they can rule; healthy, secure and prosperous populations have no use for them. This means that humanitarian aid workers are not neutral in the eyes of the terrorists; rather, because they work to make things better, they represent a threat. . . . Whoever supports progress, stability and the well-being of civil society is the enemy. In this deeply regrettable new situation, security, development and aid are parts of an inseparable whole, and until stability is achieved, humanitarians will have to operate under the cover of arms—or not at all. . . . An objective assessment of the facts would lead organizations like Doctors Without Borders to demand more military presence, not less; closer cooperation with the military, not a separation of spheres.

Alternatively, they will have to withdraw not just from Afghanistan, but from most of the conflicts of the 21st century.[23]

The question, therefore, should not be whether there should be civil-military cooperation in humanitarian relief, even in the least permissive of operational environments, but how. Again, the "Handbook on United Nations Multidimensional Peacekeeping Operations" provides a good point of departure:

> The military component will not normally be structured, trained or funded for the direct delivery of humanitarian assistance, which is a civilian task. The military is more likely to be asked to provide a secure environment in which humanitarian assistance can be delivered successfully or to provide security and protection for humanitarian relief operations. This may take the form of ensuring freedom of movement, convoy escorts, protection of humanitarian personnel and storage sites, among other assistance. The military component often, however, has assets and capabilities, such as transport and other logistical support that are useful in a humanitarian effort. Use of military assets for humanitarian tasks should be coordinated by an appropriate civilian authority as part of a coordinated plan of emergency relief. . . . Military contingents also undertake humanitarian activities on their own initiative, using their own resources. Some governments consider this humanitarian dimension an essential part of their peacekeeping contribution and, often, an important factor in mobilizing national support for the military deployment. Humanitarian projects undertaken by the military can contribute significantly to improving relations with the local population and the parties to the conflict, thereby increasing security and building consent. These activities should be based on the international humanitarian objectives and policy framework in the mission area and avoid duplication of effort with humanitarian agencies. It is vital that the initiatives help build local capacity and be sustainable in the long term.[24]

Fortunately, much has already been written on the ways and means that military and civilian organizations can cooperate— and much more needs to be written. Nonetheless, beyond the Challenges Project report, any discussion of civil-military cooperation in humanitarian operations should include an exploration of the following areas:

Security. While security is primarily the military's job, it is not exclusively their concern. On the one hand, this mission may have a much wider application for the military than either community is at first willing to admit, especially in less permissive environments. That is because sometimes the military falls into the trap of security becoming an end in itself, rather than as an enabler to the broader goal. On the other hand, relief agencies not only have an increasing stake in the security situation in conflict-affected areas, but also a greater impact on stabilization:

> To the extent that combat operations are prevalent or persistent, the lack of a secure environment limits, and may prevent, the deployment and effectiveness of civilian assistance providers. The resulting void in relief and reconstruction assistance hinders military efforts to eradicate insurgent forces. Should coalition forces concentrate on establishing a secure environment so that civilian relief and reconstruction efforts can flourish, or is it necessary to use military resources to fill the void in civilian assistance in order to pacify hostile territory? . . . In non-permissive environments, military forces may be the only source of assistance, straining its capabilities and creating tensions with the civilian relief and reconstruction community.[25]

Often, in the immediate period following a conflict or similar crisis, there is a vacuum of civil control of many basic public functions, which the intervening military force has no other choice to fill (or the spoilers will) until competent civilian relief and reconstruction organizations are in place. The performance of law and order, training and buildup of police forces, development or repair of essential political, economic, and communications and transportation infrastructure, governance operations, and so on may be necessary to initiating a virtuous cycle of security and relief and reconstruction in the most critical period—the first few months. Freedom of movement, for example, is as important to security operations as to humanitarian relief. At least early on, the military will need to be involved more directly and robustly in humanitarian relief, providing themselves, securing civilian relief personnel and resources, such as humanitarian relief supplies, convoy escorts, clearing mines, and unexploded ordnance, and so on. In any case, any military involvement in these traditionally nonmilitary areas should be done with a view to "civilianize" and "localize"—that is, turn it over to international or, ultimately, local change agents for service delivery.

In this respect, the military should look at how it can be a "multiplier" to civilian relief capability and efforts and not how these organizations can be co-opted into security operations. In this respect, the role of the military should be seen as "enablers," because the success of change agents is prerequisite to the success of the military. This is in keeping both with the military's quest for an "exit strategy" and the view of civilian organizations' view of the longer-term intent to empower locals. This enabler–change agent role relationship is the crux understanding to solving the security-relief conundrum and maintaining the delicate balance between the military and civilian interveners. Above all, whether through general international agreement or a situational ad hoc arrangement, both communities need to come to a formal working operational definition of the terms "humanitarian" and "security" in order to better delineate roles and responsibilities and maintain humanitarian space.

Security, for example, has both physical and psychological dimensions, as well as combatant/noncombatant, humanitarian, economic, political, national, and local public elements. While the military may rely on more physical means to provide security, civilian agencies such as the ICRC depend on their transparency and neutrality to be able to work among all sides of a conflict. The Red Cross or Red Crescent on their vehicles may have greater protective value than the armor plating of a seventy-ton tank. Who can contribute what to a safe and secure environment must be clearly understood and respected by all players in the intervention, regardless of mission and operating principles.

Information. Information transparency is the engine of civil-military cooperation, in both directions. While NGOs often have knowledge of the local culture and community leadership, socio-psychological conditions, and humanitarian needs assessments, the military is privy to information on the security situation and threats to safety such as mines, infrastructure assessments, weather, topography, and so forth. Information management and database sharing, from the *Kosovo Encyclopedia* project to the Afghanistan Information Management Service or AIMS (http://www.aims.org.af), have made great strides in, for example, logistical and air-traffic coordination in the past few years. A number of information-sharing initiatives are being monitored and prompted by the U.S. Department of State's Humanitarian Information Unit (http://www.state.gov/s/inr/hiu/).

Still, there is much progress to be made in Web-based and other discreet methods of information-sharing, particularly considering every organization's tendency to work with its own systems and information, the "information-is-power" psychology that pervades many organizations seen to be in competition with others, and the military's sensitivity to information and thus operational security and the habit of classifying information that may not require classification. It should be universally agreed upon, for example, that GIS-based technologies should be used jointly by military and civilian organizations for common information-sharing engines and databases. Because of the sensitivity of certain information, such as regarding spoilers, mines, and other critical elements NGOs may encounter, civilian organizations need to understand that providing the military such information, especially on a voluntary basis, may serve their interest in helping the military create a more secure environment, the military in turn must view civilian organizations only as sources of information—never as intelligence. Despite the clear value of civilian organizations as sources of operationally exigent information, particularly in what the military calls "human intelligence" (HUMINT), more important to stability, antiterrorist, and counterinsurgency operations, both communities must establish, in advance, clear rules of engagement on the collection, dissemination, and attribution of such information for eventual intelligence purposes—the more discreet the exchange, the better.

Coordination. Beyond virtual means of civil-military information exchange, specific physical coordination nodes, often built by the military, are necessary to facilitate the most efficient and effective use of humanitarian relief resources, to the benefit of the affected population. This not only avoids the issue of "five organizations fixing the same school house while five other school houses go unfixed," it helps to minimize the military's direct involvement in humanitarian relief, helps collectively prioritize projects, takes advantage of shared information in support of decision-making, and most importantly, enables civilian organizations to more quickly take the lead in humanitarian relief, mainly because it provides an overhead capability many (especially smaller) civilian relief organizations lack in terms of resources and management expertise to put together. It also often helps mitigate a common problem in humanitarian relief areas, which can simply be called "assessment fatigue."

From the point of view of the recipient of aid, there is nothing more frustrating than watching countless organizations, civilian and military, show up to assess—rather than address—their needs before aid finally arrives. In this respect, there is no quicker way to delegitimize even the most well-intentioned relief efforts, and not just for a few. Whether these coordination nodes are called— "CMOCs," "humanitarian information centers," or whatever—is secondary. The deployment of liaisons from the major NGOs to the U.S. Central Command headquarters in Tampa, Florida, prior to Operation Enduring Freedom, while producing mixed results, served as an interesting precedent to enable deconfliction of civil-military issues in the planning and preparation phases, as well as to provide the civilian relief community the opportunity to exercise its advocacy in reminding the military of its humanitarian obligations, for example, in targeting.[26] Beyond that, it suggests the idea of civil-military cooperation and coordination preventative actions—before the outbreak of a crisis.

Among these actions could be capacity-building among regional organizations such as the African Union. The most important thing, especially for the military, is that the civilian organizations not only show up at civil-military venues, but take control of the coordination effort—the sooner, the better. In addition, both organizations need to be disciplined about personnel designated to play a liaison role. For the military, this should be civil-military specialists (CA, CIMIC, etc.); for relief organizations, it should be designated liaison personnel, preferably with a military background or a background in working with the military, to represent one or many organizations. This not only minimizes confusion, but protects both communities from under- or over-commitment. As with security and information, clear lines of coordination, through a commonly agreed understanding of respective roles and responsibilities, are even more important in hostile or semi-permissive environments, and as any businessperson knows, always with an eye to the market:

The division of labor between civilian and military institutions at the international level involves not only determining roles of multilateral militaries, but also those of civilians of international and non-governmental organizations. Finally, societies attempting to rebuild after war will be making their own decisions about the division of labor between civilian and military institutions as they transform their own security sector. It is imperative that, as external implementers seek to provide war-torn societies space to make such transformations, they do so with care to the example they set in the process.[27]

Logistics. Next to security and information, this is the most practical—and most benign—area of civil-military cooperation. In fact, as the situation progresses, the majority of issues between military and civilian relief organizations are (or should become) logistical. Better shared resourcing not only enables more effective civilian-led relief, but minimizes the resources the military has to draw from its core security operation—mitigating "mission creep." Nonetheless, the military may need to realize the quickest and most effective way to get civilian relief activities up and running effectively is to provide an initial surge of logistical support effort. Logistical information-sharing tools have vastly improved the ability of military and civilian organizations to work together. And logistical support and especially logistical information-sharing is perhaps the most discreet way the military can enable the success of change agents like NGOs in a low-key, less visible manner with less risk of compromising (at least the perception) of NGO independence, neutrality, and impartiality. Notable examples include AIMS, the Humanitarian Logistics Software developed by the International Federation of Red Cross and Red Crescent Societies in collaboration with the U.S.-based Fritz Institute (http://www.ifrc.org), or the Worldwide Humanitarian Assistance Logistics System Handbook developed by the U.S. Institute for Defense Analyses (http://www.ida.org). In addition, logisticians—or logistically versed operators—from both communities should be central members of the civil-military planning and coordination cast.

Training and Education. As mentioned before, one of the greatest comparative advantages the military maintains is in professional development, due to the tremendous value many militaries place not just in training and education, but in lesson-learning. In the U.S. Army, for example, an officer can spend as much as 40 percent of his career going to school. Unlike most civilian relief organizations, the military can and must afford the overhead. While IO/NGO personnel training and education should be seen as an "allowable expense" by both its executive and donor boards, the military (and other government agencies), again in the role as an "enabler," as a matter of programmed budgeting, should open the doors of many of its institutions to civilians to professional development courses, seminars, and events, especially those dealing with "humanitarian operations," civil-military cooperation, coordination, security, information-sharing and management, logistics management, and so forth. This is enlightened self-interest, not just in improving the capacity of these organizations to more quickly espouse roles the military (and other government agencies) would ultimately rather have civilian relief (and development) organizations take on.

Moreover, their presence—prior to operations—is a coeducation value, for operators and not just executives. It helps improve cross-institutional understanding, deconstructs often long-held stereotypes, and ultimately improves civil-military and interagency cooperation and coordination and reduces the learning curve while operators must focus on the problem at hand, while critical time is going by, in addition to feeling out their implementation partners. Once this is in progress, it also enables selective collaboration on training and capacity-building of regional and local organizations, leveraging localization, and allowing local players to more quickly become stakeholders in the peace process and thus mitigate the threat of spoilers.

Institutions such as the UN Department of Peacekeeping Operations Best Practices Unit (http://www.un.org/Depts/dpko/lessons/) and the International Association of Peacekeeping Training Centers, or IAPTC (http://www.iaptc.org), can play major coordinating roles as a repository of operational lessons as well as training and education opportunity maps worldwide, respectively. Institutions such as the Institute of International Humanitarian Affairs should redouble efforts to host information seminars and problem-solving oriented workshops to allow executives and especially operators in the civilian and military communities to come together and inform each other on their views of civil-military cooperation and respective strategic and operating principles, as well as capabilities and limitations, in order to mitigate obstacles, misunderstandings, and dilemmas—before the intervention takes place and precious time and credibility is lost on both sides. In addition, it is high time the United States led the way in the establishment of an interdisciplinary and civil-military training and operational development center. . . . The focus of such a center would be on developing and exercising methods and modalities of operational-level peace operations cooperation and coordination. Improved information-sharing regimes, such as a global, interagency and civil-military coordination website based on GIS technology, or deployable coordination software programs and databases, could be one set of deliverables.[28]

Beyond all this, it should never be forgotten that "institutions do not play roles, people do":

> We can promulgate all the information and education in the world, but the face-to-face coordination of two to eight people is irreducible. This NGO/military relationship is about people. The ones controlling the operation in theater are the most important linchpins in the entire endeavor. Good people matter—they must be selected carefully.[29]

There has already been a great deal of discussion, study, and work on the way ahead in civil-military cooperation and coordination in humanitarian relief operations. As the Challenges Project suggests, "there are four main actions that can be taken in order to improve civil-military relations." These are:

> . . . firstly, to begin by building on shared values and concerns between the civilian and military communities; secondly, to address the fundamental challenges set out above (the obstacles, misunderstandings and dilemmas) through, in the main, better training and education; thirdly to consider a basic set of principles for better cooperation and operational coordination for adoption by principal international organization and arrangements, UN agencies, and major NGOs; and fourthly, to work at both the strategic (headquarters) level and the operational level to improve civil-military cooperation and coordination, and also to improve civil-civil cooperation and coordination.[30]

The January 2005 U.S. Institute of Peace (USIP) strategic workshop on "Humanitarian Roles in Insecure Environments" (referenced earlier), segueing from an earlier seminar hosted by the U.S. Army Peacekeeping and Stability Operations Institute (PKSOI) at the Army War College in Carlisle, Pennsylvania[31] (also present at the event), identified the following recommendations that, to a large extent, coincide with those of the Challenges Project, albeit more concretely, namely:

- Promote military commanders' understanding of humanitarian provider norms and imperatives.
- Establish a process for inputting humanitarian feedback to update military doctrine and training.
- Establish ongoing liaisons from major IOs and NGOs at regional combatant command (i.e., theater military) headquarters for planning and deconfliction.
- Have the military adapt (de)classification procedures for enabling civil-military information sharing.
- Create a common set of metrics for all aid assistance agencies and organizations together, under a lead (preferably civilian) organization for information management.

In addition, a number of guidelines, references, and tools have existed or are emerging to promote civil-military cooperation and coordination. Although far too many to mention here, among these are (beyond those already mentioned):

- The UNHCR's "Handbook for the Military on Humanitarian Operations," in circulation since January 1995.
- The U.S. Institute of Peace's *Guide to IGOs, NGOs, and the Military in Peace and Relief Operations,* first published in 2000 and about to undergo major revision. This is probably the best single-source document of its kind.
- "Guidelines on the Use of Military and Civil Defense Assets to Support UN Humanitarian Activities in Complex Emergencies," produced by UN OCHA, which has since been augmented by the UN Steering Committee on Humanitarian Response Guidelines of June 2004.
- Web-based tools such as the Relief Web (http://www.reliefweb .int) and the Sphere Project, Humanitarian Charter, and Minimum Standards in Disaster Response (http://www.sphere project.org).

- The Register of Engineers for Disaster Relief (RedR)—http://www.redr.org.
- Military doctrine publications, such as the U.S. Joint Publication 3–07.6, *Joint Tactics, Techniques and Procedures for Foreign Humanitarian Assistance,* August 15, 2001, or the U.S. Army's Field Manual 100–23–1, *Multiservice Support to Humanitarian Assistance,* October 31, 1994.
- Organizational codes of conduct, such as the International Committee of the Red Cross's "Code of Conduct for the International Red Cross and Red Crescent Movement and Non-Governmental Organizations in Disaster Relief" (http://www.icrc.org).

The USIP strategic workshop, in recognition of the plethora of such references and guidelines, has proposed the establishment of a working group, most likely to be led by the new Department of State Office of the Coordinator for Reconstruction and Stabilization, in coordination with the Humanitarian Information Unit, to at least catalog all these references for easier access by all players. It still, however, does not address the issue of some sort of overarching, civil-military rule set. For that reason, a UN interagency group, in cooperation and coordination with the military staffs of UN members states, should devise a "Universal Code of Conduct Between Civilian Organizations and the Military in Humanitarian Relief" that outlines not only a set of overarching principles in civil-military cooperation, but details specific guidelines in civil-military coordination in security, information and intelligence, coordination, and logistics.

Beyond having the power of international norm, this document could help both communities understand and mediate what to expect and not expect from each other in humanitarian relief situations in permissive to nonpermissive environments, and considering both man-made and natural disasters as well as conflict situations. In addition, it would make it more difficult for spoilers to interfere with the process of humanitarian relief because it would not only explain the inherent right of legitimate international players to provide humanitarian relief, but more clearly spell out why spoilers are in violation of humanitarian relief principles more universally accepted. In addition to the Challenges Project, the ACBAR briefing, the ICRC, and many of the guidelines and references mentioned above, the Code of Conduct could be based on the so-called "Mohonk criteria for humanitarian assistance in complex emergencies," drafted in the 1990s, but never fully implemented.[32] Once drafted, it would be presented to the UN Secretary-General for submission to the General Assembly for adoption and promulgation.

With all the talk about "paradigm shifts" in the civil-military relationship in humanitarian actions, the basis of the civil-military imperative in these situations, years before the situations in Afghanistan and Iraq made them center-stage, was already recognized:

> Operating to the principle of altruistic self-interest allows each community to more properly assume its comparative advantage. Each community has something unique to offer. NGOs bring humanitarian expertise, a familiarity with the affected area, and sustained commitment. The military brings an infrastructure that provides communication, logistics, and security. In its most simple form, the equation works like this: the military's infrastructure leverages the NGOs into collaboration which the NGOs provide the military with their ticket home. In other words, NGOs are willing to participate in collaboration and eventual coordination because of the need for a comprehensive effort, not to mention that the military will sometimes move their relief supplies and personnel for free. The military, on the other hand, needs to transition to civilian agencies in order to withdraw quickly—something to which both sides agree.[33]

More than anything else, civil-military cooperation should be an exercise in managing expectations. The following is an example of what this could mean in practical terms. With regard to realistic expectations, the military should expect civilian NGOs to:

- Protect their operational independence. NGOs normally do not accept any obligations other than those of their supporters.
- Adopt a neutral posture among the parties to the conflict, thereby securing a degree of protection in a "white hat" mode.
- Operate in dangerous areas assisting innocent civilians at risk.
- Possess limited capabilities compared to the military—security, transportation, communication, and so forth.
- Deploy early and stay longer than the military—these are not short-term missions for civilian organizations.

Similarly, NGOs should expect the military to:

- Act under the direction of governments that exercise strong control over their armed forces' operations.
- Stabilize the security situation within their limited capabilities.
- Protect their own personnel first, then those of the host country's civilian organizations.
- Avoid overcommitments, because the military's rules of engagement will not allow it to go too far.
- Terminate its operations and depart when the security situation appears stable.[34]

While the challenges to civil-military cooperation in humanitarian relief are greater than ever, due to the more complex, difficult, and dangerous operational environments facing both military and civilian organizations, the risks and rewards, likewise, at a higher level, are increasingly intertwined between these two communities, who have become more codependent than ever to achieve respective and collective success. If the interventions in Afghanistan and Iraq have demonstrated the limits of civil-military cooperation in humanitarian relief in non- or semi-permissive environments, the widespread international and multilateral effort to provide assistance to the victims of the Asian tsunami is showing its potential. Much has been achieved and much has yet to be achieved. The key will be improving understanding between the two communities and establishing ground rules for cooperation and coordination.

Above all, civil-military cooperation in humanitarian relief should be about managing expectations, within and between these organizations and with the affected population itself. The nirvana of compete integration and unity of effort between the two communities is just that, but it is also not necessary. Often, it is about mutual understanding of the principles and missions that define their presence and operations, looking for common aims and interests. Even if you agree to disagree, it may, as a minimum, be about getting together in order to stay out of each other's way. Coordination on the practical issues of security, information management and information sharing, coordination mechanisms and methods, and logistical matters should be the greater area of concentration, and will help balance out the thornier issues of philosophical or even political differences. As in business, the customer (i.e., the recipient of humanitarian relief) should be king, and therefore have the greatest common priority. One thing is clear—failure in civil-military cooperation means not just the failure of one or the other, but the failure of all and the suffering of many.

6

Not If . . . But When and How?

Larry Hollingworth

> Some analysts consider the merging of humanitarian, political, and military roles and goals inevitable, practical, and desirable. Others believe that in the attempt to bring political, military, and humanitarian objectives within the same framework, there is a danger that humanitarian objectives and principles will be compromised. Still others take the pragmatic approach to civil military cooperation, negotiating the more contentious "gray areas" on a case-by-case basis.[1]

ON FRIDAY AFTERNOONS at the International Diploma in Humanitarian Assistance course, there are group presentations. The relationship between military forces and humanitarian assistance agencies is a regular subject for discussion. This chapter is partly written from the results of many a Friday afternoon session and also from reading and listening to senior writers and speakers on humanitarian affairs. It is not always easy to credit individuals with thoughts and spoken words expressed in conferences; I hope my colleagues will forgive me for this omission.

It is my intention to examine the relationship between the various military groups and the principal humanitarian organizations working in natural and man-made crises, both in inter- and intrastate situations. I will concentrate on the emergency phase of response. I will not dwell upon the greater picture of non-humanitarian civil-military cooperation, but I will touch upon it.

It is exceedingly rare not to find national military in a crisis area. They are the first-line response of the government to situations beyond the day-to-day scope of their authority. The national military will patrol the streets, deploy checkpoints, and, depending on their training and discipline, will help or hinder the operation. Relief agencies will need to establish some rapport with their commanders. This may include applying for permits to operate and authority to travel. Access may be denied or restricted. Depending on the scale of the operation and the international involvement, pressure may be placed on the military commanders by national authorities to cooperate with the relief effort.

More and more intrastate conflicts predominate, and here the national military is only one factor in the equation. One is compelled to deal with opposition forces who themselves may represent more than one faction. In some situations, one also has to deal with local warlords with their own armed groups who may or may not be loyal to the central government and who may or may not have their own local agenda, legal or illegal.

National humanitarian agencies, and those international agencies whose mandates demand that they work in combat areas, will necessarily have to create a modus operandi that accommodates dealing with local armed factions. Such action may well challenge their principles. More purist or pious international agencies that object to working with the military can choose other crisis areas in which to operate.

In an interstate conflict, where there are at least two distinct military factions, humanitarian agencies face a challenge to their impartiality with every turn of events. It is to be noted that there are current crises that involve the armies of four or five bordering nations. In such circumstances those agencies willing to work with the various military plead for a negotiated humanitarian space in which to operate. Some critics liken such negotiated humanitarian spaces to a vacuum, which ignores the realities of the situation and compromises a fundamental principle of the humanitarian imperative, the right to provide aid.

Amazingly, some agencies that find subtle and tortuous ways to salve their consciences when dealing with internal and neighboring military aggressors have grave difficulty dealing with the military in an international response. The more sophisticated and efficient the international military, the greater the difficulty humanitarian agencies often experience. Their pain is slightly eased if the international response is mandated by the United Nations and, preferably, wears the blue beret. Nevertheless, the pain increases to a chronic level if they perceive the military engaging in "humanitarian" tasks, regardless of the color of the soldier's headgear. The implication is that the provision of humanitarian aid is exclusively the domain of humanitarian agencies and that the role of "the military" precludes its involvement in the provision of aid.

However, even the most antimilitary of agencies usually accept that in the earliest stages of an emergency response, especially one of great size, the military has an important role in the provision of logistical support. Time and time again it has been proved that no one agency or conglomeration of agencies has the logistical response capacity of sophisticated armies. In every recent major emergency the establishment of an adequate bridgehead, be it airport, seaport, railhead, or roadway, has required military support. This support clears and lengthens runways, provides air traffic control, clears harbors, repairs roads and bridges, and provides mechanical handling equipment, trucks, helicopters, and manpower. Moreover, it provides all these in strength and in a short time frame. In essence, the military takes the strain while the aid agencies respond within their capability.

Ms. Sadako Ogata, then the UN high commissioner for refugees, in a press conference regarding Kosovo on April 20, 1999, was in no doubt of the need for military assistance:

> This emergency has already shown that traditional responses are not sufficient. It (the refugee exodus) is much bigger and much faster than other outflows. We need help to transport relief supplies; we need help to set up more camps. We will continue to lead the operation but we urgently need more contributions of the kind that only the military and civil protection units can provide.[2]

General Joulwan, Commander-in-Chief, U.S. European Command (CINCEUR), and 11th Supreme Allied Commander Europe, was well aware of the importance of the military contribution when he said in December 1998: "The military becomes the court of first resort. It simply takes too long to put together an ad hoc civilian structure to deal with the immediacy of the conflict prevention requirement."[3]

But does "the court of first resort" compromise the work of the normal standing sessions? The Humanitarian Practice Network

(HPN) thinks it might. "It is essential that the two roles: —impartial humanitarian assistance as a response to an urgent and inalienable right, and peace operations with their inevitably partial and political mandates—are kept separate."[4]

If the military and the humanitarian agencies are kept separate, how do they cooperate? In the best of operations the military will attend humanitarian aid agency coordination meetings the moment they are established and, to be fair to the aid agencies, these meetings are usually up and running in the early hours of response. The military reports what it has done and what it intends to do, and in the experience of this writer, listens to input from the coordinators of the aid agencies. Frequently the military will be requested, or will volunteer, to bring in equipment, materiel, food, medicine, and personnel belonging to the aid agencies.

In more recent emergencies it is the next phase that causes the most animosity. It is a problem of demarcation. As the agencies arrive and deploy, many do not expect to see the military either ahead of them or behind them carrying out "humanitarian" tasks: helicopter deliveries, air drops, civil affairs activities, hearts and minds campaigns, soldiers repairing roofs on clinics, replacing windows in schools, military doctors holding clinics in villages, stocking pharmacy shelves, military engineers repairing water pipes, installing latrines, erecting tents, establishing kitchens. This participation, this "cross-dressing" is anathema to many agencies and provokes a loud cry of "Stop! This is our job. The emperor is wearing our clothes."

Is this a valid complaint? Do civilian humanitarian agencies have an exclusive right to provide aid? The provision of humanitarian assistance is not a new phenomenon. Those who work in the humanitarian assistance field are not pioneers in a new profession. Euripides in 431 BCE was concerned at the plight of those in exile. "There is no greater sorrow on earth than the loss of one's native land." There have been armies since millennia before the birth of Christ. They have fought, killed, raped, and pillaged throughout their history. They have also established garrisons, reconstructed villages and towns, built roads and wells. They have enforced peace and kept peace. They have responded to earthquakes, floods, and famines.

Who are soldiers? Who are civilians? No one is born a soldier. All soldiers were born civilians. Some civilians become soldiers; most soldiers return to civilian life, some soldiers become humanitarian aid workers.

Does the military have a right to deliver aid? "According to International Humanitarian Law(IHL), the primary responsibility for the material welfare of a civilian population in a conflict zone falls upon the military forces in control of the area."[5]

Is the provision of "material welfare" by the military "humanitarian"? "Assistance provided by a military force or a special section attached to it can hardly be described as 'neutral.' But it has an obligation to provide for the basics for all civilians under its control. This assistance is quite legitimate and cannot be dismissed as non humanitarian by relief agencies."[6]

Is "humanitarian intervention" a new phenomenon? "States have been intervening for the purpose of humanitarian assistance for at least two centuries. Who they protect and how they intervene to do so have both changed. States now entertain claims from non whites; non Christian people . . . and they will do so now only multilaterally, with authorization from an international organization."[7] But this was prior to the 2003 Iraq war! "Humanitarian intervention has evolved over time focusing first on military action to rescue one's own citizens in other states, then expanding to include the protection of citizens of other states, and is now eclipsed into 'responses to complex humanitarian emergencies.' This new term is a conscious attempt to create legitimate space for more kinds of actors in these situations than just militaries."[8]

Who are the beneficiaries of intervention? "Before the 20th century virtually all instances of military intervention to protect people, other than the interveners' own nationals, involved the protection of Christians from the Ottoman Turks. In the post 1945 period, humanitarian intervention has concerned military action on behalf of non-Christians and non-Europeans or both. And since 1989 several large-scale interventions have been carried out claiming humanitarian justifications as their raison d'etre." Examples cited are "Iraq following the Gulf war; United Nations Transitional Authority in Cambodia; the large-scale effort in Somalia; the deployment of UN and NATO troops to protect civilians, especially the Muslim population primarily from Serbian forces in Bosnia; NATO's campaign in Kosovo Yugoslavia."[9]

Finnemore challenges the interveners' humanitarian motives with some sharp questions:

> I want to know what it means to them to be humanitarian. What action does that entail or not entail? . . . what kinds of claims prompt a humanitarian intervention and what claims do not? I want to know the extent to which, and the ways in which, humanitarianism competes with all other forms. I want to know what complements other kinds of incentives States might have, to intervene or not to intervene.[10]

David Rieff is very clear about military humanitarian intervention:

> Even assuming the British and the French are prepared to fight a war in the name of securing humanitarian access for aid workers, they would still fight that war so as to win it. And to win it, as in Afghanistan, they would first make the humanitarian situation worse. All wars do. That is why imagining that just wars can be joined with humanitarian imperatives is delusional and antihistorical.[11]

Jane Barry and Anna Jefferys of HPN raise a relevant and specific issue when they state that in the decade of the 1990s only in three operations—northern Iraq in 1991, eastern Zaire in 1994, and Kosovo in 1999—did the military directly deliver humanitarian assistance.

Nothing stirs up some NGOs more than the mention of direct aid delivered by the military. But, before they have opened their Web site to scribe their views, a pen has already been dipped into the vitriol. Rieff has noted,

> The objection of MSF and indeed, Oxfam, MDM and other mainline NGOs, to the American relief airdrops during the war in Afghanistan was never that the United States had no right to drop food packages. Rather, the relief agencies insisted that the Americans must not claim that this humanitarian activity was anything more than window dressing, or that somehow the humanitarian and military objectives could be talked about in the same breath.[12]

Rod Lyon notes that there are three distinct ages of modern Western civil-military relations:

> The first age is essentially . . . the era of total war. This age begins with the American Civil War and spans a period of about 80 years from 1860–1945. It is the age of mastering expertise associated with

mass warfare. The second was the age of the Cold War and covers
1946 to 1990. It is characterized essentially by the doctrine of deter-
rence, limited war and the non-use of force. The third age dates
from about 1990 and covers that period during which the Western
military has increasingly been pulled towards operations other
than war.

He maintains that "the 1990s were characterized by the use of
force for humanitarian intervention rather than for the waging of
great power war, for the protection of indirect rather than vital
interests. Humanitarian missions took on the flavor of social welfare operations.[13]

Lyon relates a recent Iraq anecdote both amusing and telling:

The Australian Defense Organization, (ADO) pointed to the important role that ADO personnel played in advising the Central
Provisional Authority (CPA) on a range of issues: helping to develop new financial governance arrangements: interfacing with the
economic and other policy advisers within the CPA, which is the
de facto government, on the rule of law, and on improvements to
detention systems. The ADO obviously did not think it odd that
Australian forces have advisory responsibilities in policy areas in
which the military plays no role domestically in Australia!

He asks, Is it possible that we are seeing a drift away from the idea
that military professionalism is simply about the management of
violence?[14]

The Marshall Plan is worth remembering; General Marshall
won the Nobel Peace Prize in 1953 for his efforts in the rebuilding
of Europe. The military contributed greatly in ways that today
would clearly be defined as humanitarian. Marshall, in 1943, had
set up a civil-affairs division of the U.S. Army. "Peace and security,
economic prosperity and stable democracy are interdependent.
We have to recognize that the democratic principles (moral
strength of the gospel of freedom and self respect for the individual) do not flourish on empty stomachs." Deserved credit has
been given to the humanitarian initiative of General Marshall:
"The golden age of civil affairs was the occupation of Germany
and Japan after the end of the Second World War. Civilian experts
in uniform participated in the efforts to reconstruct societies and
economies, which had been devastated by war. The function was

situated in the army reserves, and it receded until it was energized by use in counter insurgency operations in Vietnam."

In 1625 Hugo Grotius wrote in *De jure belli ac pacis* on when "humanitarian" intervention was warranted:

> Yet where a Busiris, a Phalaris or a Thracian Diomede provoke their people to despair and resistance by unheard of cruelties, having themselves abandoned all the laws of nature, they lose the rights of independent sovereigns, and can no longer claim the privilege of the law of nations. Thus Constantine took up arms against Maxentius and Licinius, and other Roman emperors either took, or threatened to take them against the Persians, if they did not desist from persecuting the Christians. Admitting that it would be fraught with the greatest dangers if subjects were allowed to redress grievances by force of arms, it does not necessarily follow that other powers are prohibited from giving them assistance when laboring under grievous oppressions. For whenever the impediment to any action is of a personal nature, and not inherent in the action itself, one person may perform for another what he cannot do for himself, provided it is an action by which some kind service may be rendered. Thus a guardian or any other friend may undertake an action for a ward, which he is incapacitated from doing for himself.[15]

Let us move on more than three hundred years and look at a more recent definition: "Humanitarian intervention is the threat or use of force across state borders by a state or group of states aimed at preventing or ending widespread and grave violations of the fundamental human rights of individuals other than its own citizens without the permission of the state within whose territory force is applied."[16] The "intervention" part seems to upset few people. But the coupling with "humanitarian" upsets many. To be humanitarian, does a response need to answer the call for food, medicine, shelter, and water? Or is a humanitarian response answering the call for freedom and democracy? Is it even more encompassing and easier if the response is to defend "human rights"?

Tanguy has stated that "we must agree to talk about humanitarian intervention when referring to civilian action; military intervention when referring to military action; and to forget the fallacious slogans of military humanitarianism and military humanitarian interventions."[17] Terry, another MSF writer, notes:

"Humanitarian action is more than a technical exercise aimed at nourishing or healing a population defined as in need. It is a moral endeavor based on solidarity with other members of humanity."[18] Forster of ICRC clearly supports these views:

> If a military deployment is presented as being mainly humanitarian that is not the way it will be perceived, neither by the groups who oppose the military presence nor for that matter by some sections of the population. It would be helpful to introduce a change in semantics by avoiding labeling as humanitarian, or mainly humanitarian, those multipurpose operations that besides providing assistance to the population pursue other objectives such as controlling a territory or gathering intelligence.[19]

UN Secretary-General Kofi Annan suggested "the term 'humanitarian' in 'humanitarian intervention' be dropped or confined to non forcible actions." He continued by further defining his vision of humanitarian: "Humanitarians among us are those whose work involves saving lives in imminent danger, and relieving suffering that is already acute. They are people who bring food to those threatened with starvation, or medical help to the injured, or shelter to those who have lost their home, or comfort to those who have lost their loved ones."

While some authorities welcome what has been called "militarized humanitarian intervention," others take quite the opposite view. "I see military humanitarianism, like humanitarian intervention itself, as a contradiction in terms. . . . as a matter of principle and practice, humanitarian action is—and should remain—first and foremost civilian in character."[20] Rieff concurs, but with qualifications:

> But to argue for military intervention on political grounds is not the same thing as arguing for military intervention on humanitarian grounds. It is a perversion of humanitarianism, which is neutral or it is nothing. This is not to argue that NATO, or the South African Defense Force or the Japanese navy, if it is so inclined, cannot perform humanitarian missions. Relief agencies do not have a monopoly on aid the way the ICRC has a monopoly, elaborated in international law, on administering the Geneva Conventions in the field."[21]

Accepting that "humanitarian action" is vital, and putting to one side for the moment who is to do it, let us move on to an equally relevant question: where it is to take place?

According to many agency textbooks, humanitarian action needs "humanitarian space."

> At its minimum, it requires establishing and maintaining an environment in which humanitarian agencies can work effectively to assist those who need their support. Such an environment is one where the key principles of neutrality and impartiality are the cornerstones of assistance. It is also an environment where assistance is not a tool of war but is based on need and reaches people no matter what side of a conflict they are on, regardless of military and political action. . . . Humanitarian space exists when combatants respect humanitarian principles. It is an environment of relative security in which civilians are entitled to respect for their lives and their moral and physical integrity.[22]

Another writer notes that "many humanitarians are concerned that various military actors have gradually encroached into what was traditionally regarded as humanitarian space, imperiling the humanitarian principles of neutrality and impartiality. Others are concerned that in some cases, military actors, by undertaking humanitarian tasks, politicize and devalue the humanitarian 'brand,' endangering their security and their ability to deliver assistance."[23]

Neutrality and impartiality are qualities easier realized by agencies than by the military. Furthermore, outside the UN system, many NGOs feel no obligation whatsoever to follow the authority of either the United Nations or the international community. Some refuse most emphatically to deal at all with military authorities.

For anyone who wishes to throw out neutrality and impartiality a warning:

> Neutral and impartial assistance is subject to extremely strict conditionalities laid down in IHL. If a belligerent has reason to suppose that any relief is being diverted or abused by the other, or turned to military advantage in any manner, or the other belligerent party or the humanitarian agency is refusing to allow third party inspection or monitoring of the supplies, then that belligerent can withdraw consent for the relief operation to continue. (The federal

Government of Nigeria insisted on this with respect to the ICRC operation in Biafra, and when the Biafrans refused to agree to these terms, the ICRC was obliged to close down its program).[24]

But for many there is an inevitability of compromise. "Humanitarians can question the legitimacy or wisdom of particular military actions but once they have been instituted they can find themselves working in complex military environments."[25] And the warning:

> Humanitarian agencies have still not fully established the appropriate mechanisms for relations with all of these new players. It would be a mistake to assume that these actors will all automatically share the views of humanitarian agencies on the delineation of roles in humanitarian operations. . . . military players may be more concerned about the rapid deployment of personnel, equipment, and supplies and less intent on ensuring that the right perceptions are created on the ground.[26]

Tauxe defined the ICRC's position:

> The direct involvement of the military in the humanitarian domain gives rise to several paradoxes which merit careful consideration. The ICRC views humanitarian action as being governed by the principles of impartiality and non partisanship and is therefore convinced that it must be conducted independently of political and military objectives and considerations. . . . ICRC's humanitarian operations are inherently non coercive, that is they must be accepted by all and can never be imposed by force. The deployment of the UN Protection Force (UNPROFOR) in Bosnia-Herzegovina helped countless civilians and saved many lives, but also contributed to the militarization of humanitarian assistance.[27]

Tauxe cites, however, acceptable examples of ICRC/military cooperation:

> In the ICRC program for the release and transfer of persons detained, the NATO led Implementation Force, IFOR, provided the security and logistics in handover areas as specified in the ICRC plan of operation. The presence of IFOR units at checkpoints along the inter entity boundary was essential for ensuring the necessary security framework. At the same time, IFOR guaranteed full respect for ICRC's independence. ICRC delegates regularly participated in NATO military exercises and training courses, notably

with the aim of helping to improve the knowledge of international humanitarian law among NATO troops and familiarizing them with humanitarian issues. . . .

Bosnia-Herzegovina, Kosovo and East Timor showed there is much scope for constructive interaction and cooperation between the ICRC and the military when they are working alongside each other. However, they must be distinguishable not only in substance but also in appearance.

The military can render invaluable humanitarian services without turning itself into a humanitarian enterprise. Such is the case when there is a severe shortfall between the demands for relief assistance and the resources available from humanitarian organizations to be committed quickly to sustaining civilians. Humanitarian organizations may also use military assets such as tents, communication equipment, or military aircraft for the delivery of humanitarian aid in operations that remain under the entire responsibility and direction of the humanitarian agencies.

The ICRC firmly believes that effective and comprehensive crisis management calls for good working relations, constructive dialogue and cooperation among the civilian and military entities involved. The ICRC is convinced that the purpose is not to merge the activities of the military with those of humanitarian organizations but rather to identify points of contact at which interaction may be consolidated in a spirit of complementarity.[28]

Wright, the coordinator of the UNHCR response in Bosnia and Kosovo, observed:

There is a continuing evolution in the relationship between humanitarian actors and the military during peacekeeping missions and during missions which involve military support for humanitarian operations. There is a long-standing tradition of military forces assisting civilian actors. The military are after all, recruited from civil society; they remain members of civil society when not in uniform. During national emergencies, the military are called upon to assist in maintaining law and order if the situation exceeds the response capacity of the police. In these circumstances as well as during their use in conflict they remain responsible to their civilian masters: their government.

The 1994 Oslo guidelines provided a mechanism for the consensual use of military and civil defense assets. The cornerstones of humanitarian action are humanity, neutrality and impartiality. Humanitarian action is the mandated responsibility of civilian organizations. This is not to say that there should not be a military role in

humanitarian action, but to reinforce the widely held view that a
military role should be exceptional. It should be used only when
there are insufficient civilian resources to provide life-sustaining
relief, and should be handed over to civilian actors who are professionals in their line of work as quickly as possible.

Most civilian humanitarian actors have come to understand that
standby civilian capacities are currently unable to respond effectively to a Goma or Kosovo scale humanitarian emergency. As a
result, military support in such situations has come to be seen as
vital to avoid a large scale loss of life, despite the possible compromise the involvement of the military entails for the impartiality of
humanitarian action.

It remains essential for humanitarian actors to have unrestricted
access to the vulnerable, especially to ethnic minorities. In extreme
cases, convoys of relief items need escorting and relief supplies
need guarding. Vulnerable individuals may themselves require
physical protection. While this may appear to be more appropriate
as a police role there is little doubt that the creation of a democratic multiethnic police force takes several years after such an internal conflict.[29]

Furthermore, as Helton noted,

Violence and the degradation of public security in emergencies has
led to a rise in the involvement of the military. These mixed security and humanitarian operations have included relative short term
successes like Haiti, and consensus failures like the ultimate outcome in Somalia. Cooperation has been close in some venues like
Bosnia and largely absent in others like Rwanda.

Many lessons were learned. While the military should not normally be the direct provider of aid, military and political cooperation and coordination can be essential to address humanitarian
needs. The role of the military has varied in settings from providing
logistical support to deployment of ground forces with peacekeeping mandates under UN auspices—East Timor or Sierra Leone—or
peace related deployments under some other rubric such as
NATO—Bosnia or Kosovo or Coalition Forces in Iraq. There is
often now a plan for a military element in such operations to address security issues. Indeed public security and logistical support
from the military has proved indispensable to civilian humanitarians in many international crisis responses.[30]

Nicholas Morris of UNHCR, in his reply to a stinging critical
attack on the agency's performance in Kosovo, countered:

"UNHCR requested NATO assistance after careful thought. The agreement with NATO explicitly recognized the primacy of the humanitarian organizations."[31] As a result of their experiences in former Yugoslavia and Rwanda, UNHCR proposed the concept of "service packages." These were eight packages—from the provision of aircraft to the supply of domestic fuel, each package to be provided complete with management services. The intention was that donor governments would provide from earmarked sources, mainly, but not exclusively, from the military. The proposal stockpiled some of the early rounds to be fired in the war in the defense of neutrality and the desirability of nonmilitary, nonbilateral donations.

An analysis of a number of case studies prepared for the United Nations noted that "each crisis pits the same institutions (the United Nations, governments, NGOs, the Red Cross, and Red Crescent movements) against the same protagonists (government and insurgent groups, civilian and military officials) in a continuing effort to find solutions to recurring problems (i.e., the obstruction of humanitarian access, the manipulation of relief, inequitable economic relationships, the absence of viable and accountable local structures)."[32]

If military and civilian agencies have to work together, what should be the ground rules? The question "Who is in charge?" must be answered clearly and precisely. General Joulwan, with decades of experience of command, is clear that:

> The military can be under the control but not under the command of civilians. . . . The establishment of a civilian military implementation staff . . . is the key to the effective use of diverse organizations and resources. A clear mandate of authority must be promulgated by an organization with the standing and clout to make such a mandate legitimate. . . . The leadership role may shift over time.

But civilian military cooperation in Bosnia has introduced a new issue:

> Perhaps the overarching lesson gleaned from the first two years of conflict prevention operations in Bosnia-Herzegovina is that the military, no matter how effective and how efficient it might be, cannot by itself create the conditions for lasting peace. The daunting challenges of building the kinds of institutions and processes that

underlay agreements, and indeed are the very heart of conflict prevention, are far beyond the capabilities of any military. The military
can bring about an absence of war; the military cannot bring about
an enduring peace.[33]

A 2004 report on the Iraq war observed that:

While there are differing nuances in assessments of the situation
most humanitarian actors agree that the Iraq crisis has resulted in
a dangerous blurring of the lines between humanitarian and political action and in the consequent erosion of core humanitarian
principles of neutrality, impartiality, and independence. Serious
compromises from which it will be difficult to disentangle have
been made. The bombs directed against the UN headquarters in
Baghdad, and against the International Committee for Red Cross
a few days later, have added a tragic element to widespread fears
and concerns about the future of independent and effective humanitarian action. Agencies are also split within and among themselves as they struggle with the contending pressures of principles
versus institutional survival. Well established NGOs, particularly
those based in the United States, have faced stark choices and arm
twisting from their governments as well as competition from less
principled quarters in the community, "for profit" contractors and
the military. Very few US NGOS could afford to say no.

No one in the global humanitarian assistance community (who
attended the conference) was prepared to express the view openly
that "we should not be in Iraq, that we should let the Occupying
Power deliver on its IHL responsibilities and sort out the mess it
created." Conversely the view taken by some that "we have no
choice but to be there" obscures a wider range of options that did
exist and deserves consideration. This is not the first time that the
lines between humanitarian and political action have been blurred.
Afghanistan and Kosovo provided a foretaste of unpalatable pressures on humanitarian action. And from Angola, Timor and points
in between, humanitarians have functioned in highly politicized
landscapes. Many believe that the Iraq crisis represents a new level
of . . . intrusiveness on the humanitarian enterprise differing not
only in degree but also in kind from its predecessors.[34]

Ben Hemingway, then international relief and developments
programme officer for Iraq, offers a similar view:

One year has passed since the start of Operation Iraqi Freedom.
The year has taken both the coalition forces and the NGO community on a path far removed from the anticipated separate missions

of humanitarian relief and military operations. Instead, it became evident that the mission of the NGOs and the coalition units deployed to Iraq were at least deeply intertwined if not closely connected. Iraq is not the first instance of this alignment of armed forces and NGOs. Throughout the world NGO representatives stand side by side with the US military in places such as Afghanistan, Iraq, Haiti and Liberia. To build better communication with, and understanding of the NGO community the Special Operations Training Group of the first Marine Expeditionary Force contacted Interaction in early January seeking NGO representatives willing to conduct basic NGO training at Camp Pendleton in California. The training was part of the 15th Marine Expeditionary Unit preparation for deployment to the Gulf later this year. In five days of training, representatives from the International Rescue Committee, the Centre for Excellence in Disaster Management and Humanitarian Assistance, the US Army War College and International Relief and Development, covered topics ranging from basics in understanding non-governmental organizations and international organizations to international relief co-ordination structures and field negotiation techniques.

But all is not sweetness and light among the NGOs.

Increasingly there has been discussion among NGOs as to the appropriateness of accepting funding from the US government in Iraq and Afghanistan. The concern ranges from basic conflicts with core precepts of NGO conduct and in the extreme, fears of becoming complicit in the militarization of humanitarian assistance. The Afghan incident of the "Provincial Reconstruction Teams", consisting of soldiers in civilian attire (who) conducted community development and reconstruction activities, blurred the lines of distinction between NGOs and the military."

And there is more:

Without the security and support provided by the Civilian Provisional Authority, working in Iraq would be exponentially more difficult and precarious. Questions concerning the ultimate control of relief and reconstruction activities in Iraq circulated throughout the NGO community in the lead up to the conflict. If there was ever to be a challenge to the fundamentals of NGO conduct, this seemed to be it. Some NGOs chose to opt out of the relief and reconstruction programs in Iraq citing the possibility of Pentagon oversight as a breach of the core values of NGO conduct. Other

NGOs decided that their interests were more closely tied to the badly needed relief they could deliver to the people of Iraq. Even the United Nations took the unprecedented step of setting out principles of interaction with the Provisional Authority.

A humanitarian operation using military assets must retain its civilian nature and character while military assets will remain under military control. The operation as a whole must remain under the moral authority and control of the responsible humanitarian organization. This does not infer any civilian command and control over military assets. Humanitarian works should be performed by humanitarian organizations. In so far as military organizations have a role to play in supporting humanitarian work, it should, to the extent possible, not encompass direct assistance, in order to retain a clear distinction between the normal functions and roles of military stakeholders. Direct assistance is the face-to-face distribution of goods and services.

The differentiation of civilian humanitarian and military roles is essential for a number of reasons. The military is an instrument of its nation's foreign policy. Humanitarian assistant organizations are not. Humanitarian assistance organizations are not and must not be mistaken to be instruments of any nation's foreign policy.[35]

Sean Pollick, a Canadian army officer, offered a succinct, if simplistic, explanation of military involvement:

We in the military do not have the resources or the expertise to provide food and shelter to a population for any extended period. We cannot provide employment for refugees, we cannot provide people with individual protection and we do not have the expertise to nurture a stable government. The civilian agencies, each according to their specialty, do. The military have to realize that we are dependent on the success of the NGOs in their humanitarian mission in order to end our commitment and go home, just as the NGOs are dependent on us to provide at least a minimal level of security so that they may start to accomplish their mission.[36]

Pollick makes a telling point on coordination. "The sheer number of NGOs is staggering in and of itself. In Kigali there were 109 operating out of the city. While in Bosnia, a 1996 estimate placed the number of NGOs at 1700." His sting is in the tail of the sentence. "The sheer number is a complicating factor, as is the uneven quality of the NGO's encountered."[37]

There are situations in which, mainly for security reasons, independent humanitarian actors do not have access to those affected by conflicts and in need of life-saving assistance and protection. The only alternative may then well be the provision of assistance by the military themselves.

The genie is out of the bottle. The military now have a chest full of medals earned from missions which have included humanitarian aims. They have performed well and have had satisfaction from their results. Furthermore, at some time in many of these campaigns, they have led the humanitarian response. At other times they have benefited in ways, both military and moral, by closely supporting the welfare of those under their sphere of influence.

Governments that contribute troops enjoy the reflected glory of the success of their high-profile, well-reported military endeavors. They also enjoy the fact that the cost of their military contribution, while charged to the crisis, remains within their own budget and coffers.

The civil humanitarian response faces more challenges, not fewer. The scale of recent crises is larger than before. The initial logistic need is greater than before. The actual money received to respond to the crises does not match the money requested. There is little hope of finding funds for resources to match and replace those provided by the military. If the aid agencies are not self-sufficient then they need the military logistic cavalry waiting for the bugle call.

Humanitarian actors work in environments where the essential tasks of delivering the most vital of life-sustaining commodities is challenged by armed groups. How much of a role is the military expected to play in securing the environment for humanitarian access and in protecting both the deliverer and beneficiary of aid? Respect for humanitarian space, principles, emblems, and staff is diminishing. The personal security of all actors in a crisis area is now a major factor. Agencies famed for keeping their distance from armed persons now employ security staffs who carry weapons. If the humanitarian space is not there does this mean that neither is the humanitarian imperative? Does the imperative override the need for space?

Is it true that the "humanitarian" cornerstones of neutrality, impartiality, and independence are chipped and weatherworn, that they no longer hold upright the humanitarian edifice? To some organizations are they talisman to be held onto for sentimental reasons, for others are they the relics of an age passed? For a few are they still the rocks upon which their principles lie?

Jacques Forster very precisely weighs the key words: "There is general agreement that humanitarian assistance must be impartial. It need not necessarily be independent and neutral. Assistance can be undertaken by governmental institutions or by NGOs acting on their behalf by intergovernmental organizations or by NGOs that do not hesitate to take sides in a conflict."[38]

As Forster knows so well, even those most committed to their principles can be targeted and attacked. The Baghdad headquarters of both the United Nations and the ICRC were bombed.

> The attacks represent a global rejection of humanitarian actors who are perceived as part of a coalition representing the enemy. They are seen as representing Western values. The attacks represent a determination to disable civilian population in order to fuel the resentment of the population against those perceived as unable to reestablish law and order and basic vital services. In that perspective agencies whose action tends to improve the lot of the population both in material and psychological terms are seen as going against such objectives. In Iraq and Afghanistan the ICRC could be perceived as contributing to the efforts to stabilize the situation and be rejected for what it does. The attacks represent a determination to clear a region of all foreign presence in order to control it more effectively. Attacks against humanitarian staff are meant to indicate that all foreign institutions whatever their areas of concern as well as national staff are no longer secure.[39]

Political will and major donor funding ultimately decides, for most agencies and organizations, where they work. They can follow the big money and accept the conditions, find private funding and follow their mandates and principles, or choose to work in an area where there is less funding but fewer conditions attached. They can therefore choose to work with the military, or choose not to.

The media has a strong influence on the political will and the placement of funds. It has a strong influence on the reaction, response, and performance of agencies and organizations. Politicians, donors, and humanitarian actors are sensitive to the opinion of the media. From the initial headlines demanding to know why the aid community is not there, to the headlines asking what they are doing there, to the headlines asking why they are still there, aid workers are under the lights of the camera and the gaze of the print journalist. The media interviewers and observers will vary from those with knowledge of the minutia of humanitarian laws and principles to the pragmatists, some of whom are more gung ho than the incautious marine. Aid agencies can choose to work with the military or not, but they better know well the reasons for their choice.

Remote management—national staff in country, international staff out of country—has kept programs running in Iraq during dangerous times. Is this a model for the future? Is national staff running national programs with remote control the final step before we really implement total capacity building? Or will the need to liaise with the military be the stumbling block as national staff refuse to associate with military, national or international, for fear of reprisal?

Will there ever be an efficient UN Rapid Reaction Force? Will it have a component tailored to a role in support of humanitarian intervention? Will this component wear a uniform and be armed? Who will it report to? Will purist agencies like it any better? Will David Rieff be right? "Soldiers who are competent enough to fight the Taliban or Yugoslav Federal Army or the Somali warlords are not going to do what relief workers want. Instead they are going to expect that relief workers will do what they tell them to do."[40]

What is the status of the civilian "for-profit" companies proliferating in crisis areas? Many of them have "security" as their main task. Some are as heavily armed and at least as well provisioned as traditional, national military. Is it easier for aid agencies and organizations to work with these fellow "civilians"? Do they compromise our humanitarian principles? Are these "ersatz" military? Are they more dangerous and less accountable than the "real" military? Who funds them? Are they the same donors that fund humanitarians? Look at the logistic support tasks carried out by civilian contractors in Iraq. Ask how long before the commercial companies introduce a humanitarian directorate to their security and logistic support pillars. Will the humanitarian aid world, as we know it today, end up only with the tasks the commercial companies consider nonprofitable?

I have no doubt that these players will take a greater role as each future crisis occurs. I also have no doubt that they will be run with a ruthless business efficiency and will appear to be cheaper and more cost-effective than the current humanitarian response provided by the major agencies. However, I suspect that they will not wish to operate everywhere. They will prefer to be in places where they know they can apply a business plan, enhance their reputation, and make a profit.

The question for the future will not only be whether we wish to work with the military of governments, but do we wish to be involved with private security companies recruited by governments to provide security on the territory where we will operate. If we have shown reluctance to work with state-controlled armed actors who may be both neutral or impartial, how will we take to private armies who are neither neutral nor impartial but are motivated by profit? Furthermore, how will we view our relationship with private humanitarian companies who will be funded from the same sources as ourselves, recruit personnel from the same pool as we do, but who will pay more and may offer greater job satisfaction? As a pragmatist, if they get the job done, if they provide the needs of the beneficiary, I will be happy. They will never be neutral, they may be impartial, they certainly will be independent.

If the easiest course for the immediate future is civil-military cooperation, how can we achieve harmony between the two choirs? How can we get them to sing from the same song sheet? How do we build up mutual respect? Are we to talk about a two-track system, which cross-fertilizes through briefings, meetings, and courses, or do we favor a single track where we have joint headquarters, liaison officers, joint training, and exchange appointments? Do we confine the integration to logistic functions? Who will fund this training? I am reminded of the quote of General Briquement: "The international community is generous with its mandates but not with its resources."

If the military continue to do "humanitarian work," to whom will they be accountable? How transparent will they be? What will be their benchmarks of success? Can we establish a new humanitarian symbol and an enforceable international law, with severe penalties for nonacceptance and noncompliance, that permits humanitarian aid agencies and organizations access and safety? What are the views of the beneficiary? Will a study prove that the beneficiary has a horror of aid delivered by the military, or a horror of no aid? Is humanitarian aid delivered by humanitarians like organic food—pure and unadulterated? Will the beneficiary help to implement respect for the benefactors and their agents?

"We have seen a bigger and more effective partnership with military forces, both national and foreign, than I can ever recall, they have lent their aircraft, helicopters, naval vessels, search-and-rescue teams, logistical support and air traffic and ground handling teams."[41] So observed Jan Egeland in the early days of the response to the 2005 tsunami crisis where the cooperation between the military and civilian response was excellent and considered to be a model to be followed.

However, since the tsunami the world has seen the ever more successful response to the earthquake that hit both the North West Frontier Province and the Azad Jammu Kashmir region of Pakistan. The initial response was provided by local authorities and local military forces. International aid very quickly followed. But the real success of the operation began with the establishing of a Federal Relief Commission (FRC) that was commanded by a Pakistani military officer and that coordinated the efforts of the Pakistani military, and the Pakistani civil authorities with the international and national aid communities. The process was facilitated through the UN initiative of introducing "cluster" decision making groups that were attended by both national and international civilian and military actors. In fact, many of the observations noted above were put to an almost optimal practical test in the 2005–2006 Pakistan earthquake where I served as Deputy Humanitarian Coordinator with the UN Office of the Coordinator for Humanitarian Affairs. A careful review of this experience offers optimism for future humanitarian crises.

When a thoroughly professional, highly trained Pakistan Army officer (General Nadeem, chapter 7) began his appointment with the FRC, which directed the Pakistan official response to the earthquake disaster, he met, listened to, and questioned the key players in the humanitarian response teams, both national and international. His military quickly observed the concerns and fears of a community with which he had few prior dealings. He took the time, effort, and patience to look at the response requirements from the viewpoint of the professional aid workers. He and his colleagues were quick to adopt to the jargon and acronyms of the aid community. They read agency handbooks, quoted SPHERE standards, and attended cluster coordination meetings.

In the forward field locations near the epicenter of earthquake damage, the local military general met daily with the UN Office for Coordination of Humanitarian Affairs (OCHA) area coordinator. The dialogue centered on humanitarian issues. The generals were well prepared; they knew the mandates of the UN agencies, the roles of the organizations, and, before long, the capabilities and limitations of each. Equally, the aid coordinators learned the ranks and tasks of their new partners. The staffing and material strengths of the military were an eye-opener to the civilians, while the paucity of aid world personnel was an unexpected shock to the military who, especially, could never come to terms with the high turnover rate of humanitarian staff.

In each of the forward hubs, OCHA deployed a civil-military coordinator. They were either retired military now working full time for OCHA as civilians, or service personnel loaned from contributing countries to OCHA. They were a great success, particularly in the early stages of the operation where they were able to set up in each of the hubs an operations room with excellent briefing maps that impressed all visitors, especially the military. It has to be said that each of the civil-military coordinators brought with them a respect and maturity that helped in the efficient setting up of these offices and in the promotion of a team spirit. They all were flexible in their roles and turned their hands to any task. Naturally they were good allies to their military counterparts.

The Pakistan earthquake response was chosen as the pilot for the much-vaunted "cluster" coordination process. This was an attempt to move away from purely sectoral responses to crisis. In essence, and by definition, it was non-UN concentric, giving equal participation to all actors with an interest in the subject of the cluster (logistics, shelter, camp management, food, education and nutrition, water and sanitation, protection, health, communications).

Each cluster had a designated head of cluster who chaired the meetings and had the added responsibility of being the "provider of last resort." The FRC nominated a military or a civilian member to each of the clusters. They acted as the interface between the FRC and the cluster and, as such, were the counterparts of the OCHA civil-military coordinator. In addition the FRC designated a Pakistani military officer with UN experience to serve at the meetings of the heads of cluster. These FRC-cluster representatives reported directly to FRC, providing the two senior generals (Farooq and Nadeem) direct flavor of the mood and gossip within the clusters.

Our usual natural interlocutors, the civil authorities, were also part of the FRC. There was never any doubt that they were under the leadership of Generals Farooq and Nadeem. To be fair to the senior executives from the earthquake area, they had lost staff, offices, and resources in the disaster and needed time to recover before they could take the strain of assuming full responsibility for their regions. This meant that we, the aid community, in the earlier stages dealt more with the military than with the civilian authorities. It also meant that we needed to place a higher priority on capacity building even if it was only providing much appreciated administrative support to the offices of the civil authorities.

I saw no agency shun or avoid contact with the military and likewise the military included elements of the aid community at even their highest strategy meetings. On both sides there was an open office policy. It was possible to meet the highest members of each community with little formality at short notice. This was assisted greatly on the side of the aid workers by the fact that the military with which we dealt were in uniform but never armed.

Aid workers traveled with Pakistani military, soldiers flew on aid agency helicopters. NATO provided a very useful contribution including engineer support to clear the roads and an aviation fuel farm that kept both the civilian and military helicopters in the air.

Monitoring and assessing teams at high altitude were a mixture of international and national aid workers with Pakistani military. Vital health workers and medical facilities, both military and civilian, were provided by the international community and coordinated by the World Health Organization in cooperation with the Ministry of Health and through the FRC.

This was a natural disaster. We were not at odds with, or at risk to, any fighting groups or factions. Security was not a concern. There was no issue of neutrality, impartiality, or independence. The common enemy was the weather and it proved to be a weak adversary, thus contributing more to the success of the operation than much of the aid delivered.

Overall, the military-civil cooperation in this complex humanitarian crisis worked because it was directed from the top echelon of the military. It also helped that the Pakistan Army is a sophisticated, disciplined, and reasonably well resourced body and that one of its members, a general, is running the country! I left Pakistan with a folder full of applications from military personnel for places on aid-worker courses or requests for jobs with aid agencies.

I know of no aid workers who have resigned and joined the military. I know of an increasing number of military that have joined the aid world, some in senior grades. Many of them have brought experience from more than one peacekeeping operation. They have no qualms and no difficulties in dealing with their ex-colleagues. Nor do they seem to have had any problems integrating with their new ones.

I am sure that, as the melting pot of aid response includes more ingredients, the majority of constituents will lose their rigid packet labels and that the resultant thicker soup will better sustain the beneficiary. I am equally sure that a few purist organizations will stand away from the fire and vigorously defend their Spartan approach and continue to uphold values of a previous age.

For me, personally, being a humanitarian aid worker is no longer a vocation, it is a job. It is a complicated, difficult, and dangerous job with awesome consequences on the lives of the recipient. It is a job that requires the highest standard of training. It has remarkable similarities with the military and close parallels with the commercial world. I close with a further quote from the

HPN paper with which I began, and that I hope will not offend too many of our colleagues in uniform: "UN and NATO peace-keeping missions are currently present in less than a third of the 50 or so countries in conflict in the world. Humanitarian agencies, by comparison, are active in most."

7

The 2005 Pakistan Earthquake

Nadeem Ahmed and Andrew MacLeod

PAKISTAN, OCTOBER 8, 2005—early morning. School bells ring, children crowd into rural classrooms in mountaintop hamlets. They hope the school day will be fun and the homework short. Impoverished towns and villages kick into daily life. They anticipate business in the bazaar, or bargains in the shops. Indian and Pakistani soldiers stare down their barrels to eye each other across the Line of Control. *They* hope the peace process will continue. "Situation normal" was the right phrase to describe that day.

Just after school started that Saturday morning, a massive earthquake struck, 7.6 on the Richter scale, shaking the earth for approximately a minute, destroying four hundred thousand homes, damaging two hundred thousand others. Five hundred medical facilities, most government buildings, many roads, bridges, electricity supplies, water services, sanitation facilities, all things wiped out in that minute. Three and a half *million* people became homeless; thirty thousand square kilometers were affected. Thirty-five thousand school children were killed. An equal number of adults in towns also died. Seventy-three thousand gone, as many severely injured.

In terms of scale, a greater territory was affected than that affected by the Asian tsunami. There were more injuries, although less deaths. The terrain, rather than flat and coastal, was mountainous and rugged. The weather, rather than temperate and tropical, was Himalayan, threatening and lethal. The freezing temperature of the mountainous winter was less than two months away. Predictions of massive second waves of death caused by infection, starvation, and cold were realistic and frightening. Disease could be expected, calamity was thought certain.

While billions of dollars were donated to support the tsunami victims, funds given for Pakistan earthquake relief were slow and scarce. The international relief community was partway through a process of self-examination following poor coordination and massive duplication of effort seen after the tsunami. The Humanitarian Response Review (HRR) had come up with some recommendations, but they were yet to be endorsed let alone implemented.

Faced with a massive catastrophe without precedent in modern times, many times larger in impact than Hurricane Katrina, the Pakistan government, nonetheless, had to react. Expectations were bleak and the task was huge, yet less than six months later the government of Pakistan, with the support of the Pakistani people, international agencies and organizations, and foreign volunteers, was able to declare relief operations over. The second wave of deaths had been avoided; deaths from the cold were less than those recorded for the previous year. No one starved to death, no disease breakouts occurred. Just under a million tents were distributed, nearly four hundred thousand emergency shelters were built, water supplies were rebuilt, and the closed areas of Kashmir were opened to foreign assistance. In less than six months the Pakistan government, with the help of the international community, was able to say, "Job well done, now let's look to rebuild."

This chapter reviews the bases for success, considers some of the realistic lessons learned, identifies areas for improvement, and suggests positive examples for future emergencies. One was paramount: cooperation is king. If one concentrates on the overall success of the operation, one can miss the many opportunities for improvement and progress that come from looking into the details and the process. Yet if one concentrates on small details, one may forget the success by becoming bogged down in small-scale issues regarding process. Lessons learned must be based not only on what went wrong and why they went wrong; they must also be based on what went *right* and why.

SEARCH AND RESCUE WITH EMERGENCY RESPONSE

In any natural disaster of this size, in any country in the world, a stable government turns to its military for immediate response.

Given that the earthquake struck and affected both Pakistan-controlled *and* Indian-controlled Kashmir, including across the Line
of Control (still an internationally recognized cease-fire line between two nuclear powers technically at war), it was natural that
both the Indian and Pakistani military were mobilized.

Although it took some days to reestablish full command and
control mechanisms to replace senior, middle, and junior level
commanders who died in the earthquake, the Pakistan Army was
able to respond in the initial days depending on the strength and
ability of remaining personnel. The forces were activated for
search and rescue for civilians and soldiers alike, to assess damage, and secure the frontier, which had been brutally fought over
in previous years. In those first few hours and days, as communication links were out of order, as command structures had been
decimated and key personnel wiped out, order had to be restored, law and order enforced, and most importantly, thousands
upon thousands of medical emergencies had to be dealt with.

At General Headquarters level, the senior commanders became
more and more aware of the size and scope of the disaster as
information flowed in from village after village. The Joint Chiefs
convened meetings to coordinate a response, mobilize forces,
and analyze the continuous flow of new information. It soon became clear that this crisis was too big for any country to handle
alone. While some have criticized the Pakistan Army for its "slow"
response in the first few hours, the forces were largely functional
within three or so days—this compares very favorably to other
natural disasters in other parts of the world, most recently after
the Hurricane Katrina in the United States, and in the 2004 tsunami–affected countries.

INTERNATIONAL COORDINATION

One factor missing in the Pakistan government initial response
was a functioning National Disaster Management Authority
(NDMA). The President and Prime Minister recognized this de-
ficiency and created a Federal Relief Commission (FRC) within
the first week after the earthquake. The government of Pakistan's

Department of Economic Affairs in conjunction with the Ministry of Foreign Affairs had been historically the focal point for dealing with foreign organizations and NGOs. A senior bureaucrat was designated the principal focal point to assure national and international cooperation and coordination.

INITIAL UNITED NATIONS AND INTERNATIONAL MOBILIZATION

The duty officer in the UN Office for the Coordination of Humanitarian Affairs (OCHA) was awakened at 5:30 A.M. on Saturday, October, 8, Geneva time, and informed that a massive earthquake struck ten kilometers underground approximately one hundred kilometers from Islamabad, the capital of Pakistan. By 8:30 A.M. the duty officer with the head of the Emergency Services Branch and other senior staff were all in the second floor office of the United Nations' European headquarters, Palais des Nations in Geneva.

In the early stage of a natural disaster, especially one of massive scale, accurate information is usually scarce, yet assumptions and actions need to be made. After this earthquake it took two weeks for information to flow from the outer reaches of the affected area to allow authorities to appreciate the full scale of the disaster. Yet from the very first days it was apparent that assistance would be required from outside of Pakistan. A UN Disaster Assessment and Coordination (UNDAC) team would certainly be useful, as a major earthquake, close to population centers, was obviously going to pose difficult and complex challenges.

Three key factors helped. Firstly, Pakistani officials who had been trained in the UNDAC system were informally sought out and asked if assistance would be requested by Pakistan. Secondly, a preexisting standby agreement with the government of Switzerland was activated to provide rapid transport for a team if it were to be requested. Thirdly, a potential UNDAC team was identified from preexisting rosters, members put on four hours notice to move, and personnel and institutional preparations begun.

By the middle of that Saturday afternoon the President of Pakistan officially requested the United Nations to mobilize support,

including the UNDAC team, which arrived the following morning, merely twenty-four hours after the earthquake. Only one
other team, the Turkish Red Crescent Society's search and rescue
team, reached this affected zone as quickly.

Pakistani Civil Defense officials, specifically those trained by
UNDAC, met the arriving team and organized internal transport
to the key affected region. The UN country team organized office
space and coordination meetings with UN agencies and key international NGOs previously present in Pakistan. The UNDAC
team's rapid arrival, with Pakistani government and UN in-
country support, allowed for the immediate establishment of an
onsite coordination center in Muzaffarabad, the city closest to the
earthquake epicenter, a welcome center for international humanitarian assistance volunteers at the Islamabad airport, and a functioning coordination office in Islamabad. The three structures
quickly became the international focal points.

The UNDAC team's other initial tasks were also critical; they
had to establish communication links back to UN OCHA headquarters in Geneva, and to act as the information focal point to
international search and rescue teams, donors and NGOS,
through the online Virtual OSOCC (onsite coordination center).
One simple, but critical, task was the creation of the first situation
report (sitrep) to be sent to headquarters and published both on
the Virtual OSOCC and on Reliefweb. In the early days of a large
emergency such as this, it is the UNDAC sitreps that are a primary
source of information for many actors.

On the first day of deployment, October 9, another critical decision was taken. It was decided by the UNDAC Islamabad core
team that the sitrep should be written using a simple format based
on the Humanitarian Response Review Cluster recommendations
(see box). This decision was the basis for implementing an unauthorized, experimental, but largely successful humanitarian
response.

Within forty-eight hours the UNDAC team followed the first
sitrep with the decision to issue a rapid Flash Appeal. Although
the Flash Appeal is well known to donors as a rough and ready
initial guide to the costs of a relief operation, it can sometimes
take weeks to issue, hence hindering initial donor support.

Humanitarian Response Review

Following the tsunami, and what all international actors saw as a poorly coordinated relief effort, the Inter-Agency Standing Committee (IASC) asked UN OCHA to establish a review of humanitarian response.

Through the summer of 2005 a wide-ranging consultation process involving all key actors formulated a series of recommendations. In essence it was recommended that humanitarian response be divided into nine sectors or "clusters," and for a global "cluster lead" to be made responsible and accountable for coordinating the subject matter of each cluster. The nine clusters were:

1. Health
2. Food and Nutrition
3. Water and Sanitation
4. Logistics
5. Camp Management
6. Emergency Shelter
7. Emergency Telecommunications
8. Protection of Vulnerable Groups
9. Early Recovery

A cluster for "education" was considered but rejected.

The HRR recommendations were finalized in September and due to be put to the IASC at the December 12 meeting. In between the September recommendation and the December meeting was the October earthquake.

The Flash Appeal was based on the clusters identified by the HRR process. All NGOs, international organizations, donors, and interested parties that were represented in Islamabad crammed into a small meeting room at the World Food Programme office in Islamabad. At this meeting a draft guideline for a Flash Appeal was distributed, a short description of the "cluster process" provided, and cluster leads appointed based on the HRR recommendations. With little guidance, no terms of reference, and no background to draw upon, these lead agencies were asked to rapidly pull together draft projects for consolidation into the Flash Appeal.

Within twenty-four hours of the decision to draft the appeal, initial proposals had been formulated, and emergency response projects totaling $2.6 billion were brought back to a general coordination meeting for finalization. In a spirit of coordination and urgency, representative agencies analyzed each cluster, removed duplications, and lowered unrealistic expectations of what could be achieved in six months. They devised a "rough and ready" Flash Appeal for a six-month emergency response totaling $266 million.

While the first sitrep and the Flash Appeal may reflect routine administrative issues, they highlight a crucial question: how would the international community coordinate and interface their relief operations with government structures and institutions? As the Flash Appeal discussions were underway the senior UN official in the country, Jan Vandemoortele, arrived in Islamabad. He quickly established his leadership, deciding to rely heavily on UNDAC advice, and accepting that the cluster recommendations of HRR would be implemented for this natural disaster response.

This decision had a number of critical ramifications. Firstly, a new and experimental approach would be used for what was quickly becoming a larger and more complex humanitarian response (larger and more difficult than the tsunami response). Lead agencies had neither trained their cluster coordinators nor budgeted for the positions. Agencies had little institutional knowledge of the structures, and basic tools, such as terms of reference and guidelines, simply did not exist. Clusters created first for the sitrep and then for the Flash Appeal now made a permanent mark on the relief operation. The clusters were formalized, leaders appointed, and coordination structures and mechanisms were put in place. Although experimenting with a new approach for a large emergency has its drawbacks, the alternative of using the previous discredited system was not a viable alternative.

Two key institutions developed. The UN country team group convened regularly to discuss UN administrative issues. The cluster heads forum brought together all cluster coordinators, the UN resident humanitarian coordinator, and Pakistan government representatives, and met under the chairmanship of UNDAC and made most major strategic decisions.

One forum was missing—that being a broader NGO/UN heads of agency meeting. Inadvertently, the creation of the "cluster heads forum," and its decision-making role, left UN/NGO heads of mission either sidelined or reduced to only administrative roles. Later in the emergency the head of Oxfam's Kashmir operation summed it up as follows: "My operation people have somewhere to go. My food person can go to the food cluster, my health person to the health cluster—but where do I go?" She was right. Under this new model, where would the two hundred or so heads of agency or organization get to input their *strategic* rather than technical input? The answer to that question remained unknown, right until the end of the operation. The challenge remains for non-UN NGOs to find for themselves an effective coordination mechanism so that they can more effectively "plug into" government and UN coordination mechanisms.

In hindsight some have questioned the decision to implement the clusters approach in the Pakistan earthquake crisis. However, UNDAC team members and the humanitarian coordinator took the best pragmatic option. After all, what was the choice? On one hand the previous methods, which had been discredited in the tsunami crisis, and led to the HRR, could have been used, or these new recommendations, that were thought to be better, could be tried, even if not previously tested. After the relief operation was over most commentators, from the NGOs, the United Nations, and the government of Pakistan, could point to some systematic errors and room for improvement based on the cluster choice. All agreed, however, that it was a better response than normal, at least as far as humanitarian coordination was concerned.

Where the cluster experiment really proved its worth was in the relations of humanitarian workers with the military. The military's Medical Corps could liaise with the Health Cluster, the Logistics Corps with the Logistics Cluster, and so on. As time went on the critical personal relationships between the cluster coordinator and the Pakistani civil or military counterpart became key. Also, the humanitarian coordinator and chief of operations/cluster coordinator were able to strengthen personal relations with the federal relief commissioner and the FRCs head of military wing. These personal relations allowed for the creation of the key group—the Strategic Oversight Group, as shall be discussed more below.

The early deployment of the coordination team was a critical factor in the effective operations of international search and rescue teams. The fact that Pakistan had within its military structure people who had been UNDAC-trained, and personally knew the UNDAC members, was also of great benefit.

The early request by Pakistan was a key critical decision. It is better to call for assistance, and then send it back if it is not needed, than to have aid arrive too late. It is even better to have standby agreements in place for rapid deployment, rather than trying to organize it on the spot and off the cuff. Strong personal connections are just as important, if not more so, as institutional connections. Joint training and exercises in emergency response are vital to building personal connections. This includes bringing the army and international humanitarian organizations together before crises occur. It is also important for the United Nations to recognize the benefit of personal relationships and have deployment times adjusted to maximize the benefit from these connections. Key personnel movements and changes later in the operation proved to be frustrating for Pakistani officials.

THE FUNDING CRISIS

Midway through the second week after the earthquake, after the first meeting between the cluster heads and the FRC focal points, but before the launch of the National Action Plan, a crisis meeting was called. The Flash Appeal had been launched but no funds were coming in. UNHCR had expended almost all its emergency reserves, as had the WHO, UNICEF, IFRC, and other major organizations. A small group from these agencies met to discuss each cluster area; priorities were reexamined and advice generated. A plan called "Winter Race" was recommended, as was a contingency plan for the funding shortfall. This informal group drew up contingency plans that would have seen the complete withdrawal of the United Nations from operational work, restricting itself to technical advice only, and asking for the Pakistan authorities to fund the vital UN helicopters out of available bilateral funds. With money running out, and the United Nations maybe winding back, it was thought that the net humanitarian benefit would come from "humanitizing" the military's planning process.

Without the benefit of assured, available funding, other decisions had also to be taken. In conjunction with the UN's Emergency Relief Coordinator, an aggressive media strategy to raise awareness of the funding situation was begun; a countdown of days left for helicopter funding, then less than seven, was made public, as was a call for tents, tents, and more tents. A revised Flash Appeal was generated, based on new information and assessments, now putting the cost of the relief operation closer to a staggering $560 million. Money started to flow but only just in time.

BEYOND WEEK TWO

In any emergency, in any country, the first two weeks are haphazard at best—and Pakistan was no exception. By the end of the first week multiple international search and rescue teams were on the ground, augmented by Pakistan military, coordinating in a haphazard way, but with strong direction by local military commanders and the UNDAC OSOCC in Muzaffarabad.

Logistical problems were a mounting nightmare. Roads were not just cut or blocked, many mountain sides had collapsed, meaning that roads were not damaged, they were simply gone—and for all intents and purposes ceased to exist. Helicopters were vital. The Pakistan military stock of helicopters was insufficient to deal with the massive needs, even augmented by U.S. military support. The United Nations had been able to deploy a handful of helicopters, but poor donor response meant that few could be leased. Early estimates assumed a need for over one hundred helicopters—which would make this the largest helicopter aid airlift in history.

While local military, international, and spontaneous national groups were doing all they could for emergency medical evacuation, aid deliveries, and rescue, what was missing was a strong central direction. Given that no functioning national disaster management authority existed, and given that the military was set up to deal with conflict and not aid, the urgent need for the newly created FRC grew. In the meantime the army had to step in. Two organizations not used to cooperating are an active military and a skeptical humanitarian world—especially in sensitive zones.

Prior to the earthquake, only a handful of foreigners were allowed by Pakistani authorities into Pakistan-controlled Kashmir. The Line of Control was sensitive, with major exchanges of artillery between India and Pakistan a fairly frequent occurrence. Most major governments, including the United Kingdom, the United States, and Australia (the national homes to many aid workers), had travel advisories recommending against travel to Kashmir. The North West Frontier Province of Pakistan, which shared the force of the earthquake with Kashmir in almost equal measure, was known as conservative, and by some was thought to be a potential hiding place for Osama bin Laden. Travel advisories also recommended against foreign travel in this zone. The military were understandably hesitant to open up controlled areas to a host of poorly regulated and loosely aligned foreigners as part of a large and disparate group known as "aid workers."

Aid workers, for their part, often have deep institutional mistrust of the military. In many countries, "army" does not mean "professional organized force"; rather it might describe a twelve-year-old boy, drugged, and carrying a Kalashnikov. Although this was clearly not the case in Pakistan, many aid organizations find it almost impossible to work closer than "at arms length" with the military. Also the requirements of earmarked funding, mandates, and principles of neutrality and independence mean that many organizations, and many individual aid workers, have never worked, nor ever wanted to work, with the military.

Given that the earthquake occurred in two sensitive, contested areas, and given the institutional hurdles that often exist between the aid world and the military world, the outlook for cooperation and coordination might certainly have been expected to be bleak. How different reality was. The UNDAC team expanded in the first two weeks, establishing forward "humanitarian hubs" (consciously *not* called "UN offices") in Muzaffarabad, Bagh, Battagram, and Mansehra—each with a civil-military liaison officer provided by OCHA in Geneva. The objective here was to increase and facilitate interaction between the military and the civilian world at the field level.

At the headquarters central level the United Nations designated an experienced civil-military liaison officer to facilitate contacts with the Pakistani military, and the newly established FRC. Concurrently the military chiefs of staff were becoming more aware of the size of the disaster and sought out further humanitarian assistance. A critical meeting was held at the start of the second week of the crisis, when the Director General of Military Operations convened a meeting of key generals and UN representatives led by OCHA.

There was a frank and open discussion in which both sides shared their fears for the size and scale of the disaster, and the concerns that it would be beyond the scope of all to deal with. Surprisingly, honestly, and strongly, the Pakistani military shared with the United Nations their belief that they did not know what to do. This was a critical moment.

The UN experts defined the number of helicopters and amount of logistical support that could be brought to bear, subject to funding. UNDAC outlined the health, water, and other aspects that could be delivered, and together the military and United Nations began to feel that results could be achieved. The Army realized it could work with the aid workers, and the aid workers realized they could work with the Army—although both sides would be put on steep learning curves on how each other worked, and where the limits to the relationship would be established.

A series of meetings between key actors on both sides allowed the military to learn the history, ethos, and mores of the aid community, the meaning of "earmarked funding," the fundamental principles of the Red Cross movement, why MSF broke from ICRC, and why the UN agencies are often each other's largest competitors. In essence the "dirty laundry" of the aid community was shared, in order for the military to understand where the strengths, weaknesses, and boundaries of the relationships would lie. Critically, also, the HRR process was explained, and the experimental nature of the natural disaster response mechanism being tried was openly stated.

On the military side similar information on strengths, weaknesses, and capacities was shared, as was the nature of the nascent

FRC, including its draft proposed structure and interface proposals. It was decided that perhaps the cluster structure put in place by UNDAC might also serve the FRC well. Through such exchanges at a senior level a series of strong personal bonds developed between cluster focal points.

Another critical partnership developed out of those early meetings. Three key actors, the Pakistan Army Air Wing, the UN Helicopter Air Service, and the U.S. Navy combined to formulate the Air Operations Cell (AOC). Each of the air assets was combined into a common pool, tasked by its particular capacity, the cargo it carried, and where it needed to go. The AOC was a great success throughout the relief operation. This, according to all actors, was a "first." Never before had a home military, foreign allied support, and the United Nations worked so well in the delivery of air support. As helicopters became more and more important, and more became available, air coordination became critical. Eventually over one hundred helicopters filled tight valleys making air traffic control difficult, and also making the best use of air assets an ongoing challenge.

What started off on paper as two unlikely allies, humanitarians and military, developed the potential to become a strong team—but with two strong provisos: the disparity of funding, and some personal mistrust between individual military and humanitarian personnel. The second of these worked out over time, with a lot of effort by the Pakistani leadership to "sell" the humanitarians to the military, and by UNDAC to "sell" the military to the humanitarians. While bonds were strengthening centrally, military and humanitarian actors worked increasingly well at the field operational level. The cluster coordination mechanism put in place at headquarters was replicated in the field hubs with all parties seeking to work through the natural distrust that military had with humanitarians, and vice versa, until strong relationships were built.

OPERATION WINTER RACE

Three weeks after the earthquake the initial search and rescue phase was winding down. Hope of finding new survivors decreased. The coordination mechanisms were beginning to work.

A National Action Plan was launched by the FRC but an enormous problem loomed: there were 3.5 million people without shelter and only 30 days before the Himalayan winter was due to strike. High-altitude villagers were beginning to migrate down the valleys, and it was important to stop them or large camps would coalesce around destroyed urban centers. With little flat land to spare, camps would have huge population densities, disease would spread, and thousands could die. If on the other hand people stayed in their villages, they would have no home, no food, and no chance of survival. Thousands could die. Then came "Winter Race," an unexpected gem.

Winter Race, or its variations, came from three sources, one from a UN volunteer, one from the Pakistan military, and one from a former U.S. Navy Seal who was wandering the hills helping people rebuild emergency shelter, "one warm room" to survive the winter.

When the relief operation began most tents were not "winterized." A "winterized tent" is one that is specially designed with extra protection and flaps for the cold; the Chinese make the best. The world simply does not have many winterized tents. Almost every available winterized tent was sent to Pakistan, but there were still not enough, not nearly enough. Half a million tents, minimum, would be needed; less that forty thousand were thought to exist. The Chinese government increased production of winterized tents and donated fifty thousand to Pakistan, but that still left hundreds of thousands of families, over two million people, without adequate shelter. Although people could survive in the lower altitudes with a non-winterized tent, those at high levels were in deep peril. They either stayed where they were, in danger, or moved to overcrowded camps, and faced other perils.

A young Pakistani volunteer at the UN Emergency Coordination Center came to the chief of operations and complained that "you are not using our brains." Several ideas were offered as a solution to the high-altitude homeless problem. One was Paniflex, a Pakistani product used for advertising billboards. This product is a heavy duty plastic that advertising is fused onto, and discarded once the advertisement has run. It could not be recycled as advertising, but it could be used as an emergency tent covering! In the early days of the relief effort one would fly over the earthquake-affected region and be confronted by advertising for anything from soap to motorcycles.

The best idea was reconstruction of "one warm room" from the rubble of people's collapsed houses. When the mud, wood, and lime houses collapsed, wood tended to still exist, as did much of the corrugated iron sheets from roofs. They may have been bent, but they were not destroyed. An unattached former Navy Seal presented his models and descriptions of emergency "one warm room" concepts to the interagency core group. A pilot trial was begun with a helicopter sent into a village to do a rapid assessment of the housing material needs, then call forward a second helicopter with equipment and personnel. The second helicopter would offload material and demonstrate the building of one "A-frame" house that could house a family and be architecturally more stable in the area prone to aftershocks.

The group believed this a feasible project, but did not hold high hopes as it was thought that at best, five thousand shelters could be built before the harsh winter descended and the race would be lost. The Pakistan Army meanwhile had also come across the concept and was testing it with Army Engineers and the Pakistan Architects Association.

Pakistani steel mills churned out hundreds of thousands of roofing sheets, thousands more were imported, and thousands even came from India after special import exemptions were granted. Twelve engineer battalions, three hundred Pakistani volunteers, and hundreds of international efforts were assigned to help. What began in the mind of a frustrated Pakistani volunteer was taken to the United Nations and improved, taken again to the military, and improved more, shared with the international community as a whole, and instead of ten thousand shelters, Pakistan constructed in several months nearly four hundred thousand emergency housing units.

The result was startling. The feared flood down the valley stopped. Indeed some people left camps and went home up the hills. The consequential massive overcrowding did not happen, the disease outbreaks did not occur, the second wave of deaths did not hit. The importance of what was dubbed "Operation Winter Race" cannot be overestimated. The whole concept is demonstrative of how much can be achieved by coordination and sharing of problems and ideas—not just mere information exchange.

By the time November came to an end the overall operation was taking shape. The FRC was up and running and the UN cluster system was functioning both in the field hubs and in Islamabad, though things were not easy. The operation may have been "working," but it was only working because people, Pakistani civilians, military and internationals, were all working long and arduous hours, and for those in the field they were doing so in very tough conditions.

While the "big picture" was looking good, the details were not always as good. Communication flows needed fixing, terms of reference needed writing, administrative details needed tightening, and, as always, the "information beast" of UN headquarters needed feeding.

Communication flows and information gathering and analysis was one aspect of the operation that never ran well: neither for the government nor for the internationals. Yet this fact did not result in an under-delivery or an under-servicing of the population in need. Particularly for UN agencies that had to submit extensive data to headquarters, silence was a difficult message. Baseline data simply did not exist; a comprehensive village list did not exist; rapid information assessment and coordinated analysis were often not possible. Yet other than for headquarters units that desired, rather than required, such precise information, this lack did not result in poor delivery.

As it turned out the key assumptions that were made in the very first Flash Appeal meeting in the first forty-eight hours were good assumptions that stayed relevant right through the relief stage: 3.5 million people affected, around 500,000 houses destroyed over an area of 30,000 square kilometers. Three months after the earthquake the relief operation was on track. Hard work was being done, and still needed to be done. Aid was being delivered, and a feeling of optimism was starting to creep in. The biggest fear became complacency.

A Strategic Oversight Group (SOG) had been put in place within the FRC that oversaw all operations. The SOG were the senior Pakistan, UN, and major donor representatives; they co-opted subject matter experts depending on the agenda items.

The humanitarian operations and military operations were so interlinked that at the strategic level there could no longer be any meaningful division between the military operation and the humanitarian operation. It was one.

SOG, important though it was, was downplayed and not often mentioned. It did not appear in sitreps or in reports back to headquarters. Many people did not know of its existence. It was thought that many players, both military and civilian, would have been uncomfortable if it were known how closely the strategies were linked. Thus many at the field level would point to a "military hospital here and an NGO hospital there," seeing the separation. But at the strategic level both hospitals were known, approved, and needed.

Both institutional and personal bonds had been developed at senior and at field level, so that most people knew who to turn to in order to solve most problems. OCHA was functioning well as the focal point to the military commanders in the field and headquarters, and cluster coordinators knew who the focal points were in military and civilian structures.

Beginning the Transition

Experienced UN and humanitarian staff are painfully aware that, at the end of relief operations, a lull often occurs before the recovery and reconstruction phase begins. Aid workers leave an emergency zone, contacts and momentum is lost, and the humanitarian impetus to coordinate is replaced by a dysfunctionalism in planning. Such predictable problems were discussed openly with government interlocutors, as were the shared concerns that the Earthquake Reconstruction and Rehabilitation Authority (ERRA) did not seem to be making adequate headway in preparing the ground for recovery, to maintain the best of the system that had worked so well. As early 2006 progressed and the end of relief operations were in sight, planning for post-relief continued. Given that the relief effort in Pakistan was experimental in its development of the cluster approach, the transition would also therefore be experimental.

This relief operation had been enormously successful. It was the right decision to experiment with the cluster approach as a joint experiment between the government of Pakistan and the United Nations. The success could have been even better if certain things had been different. We see the following as critical:

1. A National Disaster Management Authority must exist in advance. It must participate not only in national exercises and meetings, but also in international fora. It should also deploy to assist in regional or international emergencies. While a small to midlevel disaster may be able to be managed by the NDMA alone, large-scale crises need international assistance. If individuals within institutions know each other from exercises or operations elsewhere, and if an NDMA had existed, the hard work and time lost in the first three weeks could have been avoided or reduced.

2. The cluster approach, undertaken as a trial in an ad hoc way, nevertheless worked. The detailed problems identified in real-time evaluations and reports should be taken on board. Lessons learned on what went *right and why*, not just what went wrong, should also be conducted.

3. National sovereignty remains king. While independence for NGOs is critical in complex emergencies, cooperation is required in natural disaster response. In countries with functioning governments and militaries, NGOs should not be too hesitant in working with the military.

4. The success of this operation was largely due to the openness of the Pakistan military, even in its most sensitive region, along the Line of Control. In this operation senior generals, ministers, aid officials, and donors all had each other's private cell numbers and were always welcome. No issue could not be raised, discussed, and solved.

5. Cooperation in natural disaster response goes beyond information sharing. It needs to include joint assumption making, joint analysis, and joint planning. The aim should be to create one unified response, where possible. For NGOs it means a relaxation of norms. For government and military it requires a strict dislocation of relief and aid from any political or military objectives.

6. Above all the military and humanitarian worlds can work together, so long as they share with each other their weaknesses, and use each other's strengths to compensate for those.

Part 3
Post-Conflict Issues

8

Protecting Societies in Transition

Geoff Loane, Lois Austin, and Pat Gibbons

Introduction

THE END OF THE COLD WAR has resulted in an increase in the number and complexity of wars and political emergencies.[1] While many conflicts have been brought to a conclusion in terms of the cessation of active hostilities, it is difficult to find an example of a society that has progressed to a desirable level of peace and stability. Instead, states tend to experience a period of stasis that features a number of characteristics that include an uncertain political institution, an economy skewed by the war effort, a fragmented society/societies with limited social capital, and continued suffering and need for protection.

In essence, once active hostilities have ceased, a form of internal turmoil and discord continues. The period of time following the end of open warfare and leading into relative stability and peace (or in some cases reverting to conflict) is considered to be a period of transition.[2] Many of the societies currently undergoing this "transition" have filled the global media for significant periods for all the wrong reasons. On an international or media interest level these same societies have now faded to insignificance despite probable violation of human rights and continued human suffering at different levels.

This chapter examines the role of humanitarian nongovernmental organizations (NGOs) and international humanitarian organizations[3] working with and in societies in transition. The following areas are presented:

- An analysis of the background to current thinking on state failure,[4] collapse,[5] and reconstruction;

- A thesis on the evolving scope of the NGO and humanitarian sector given its status in the hierarchy of external stakeholders, including an outline of two conceptual frameworks for working with societies in transition
- The legal institutional model
- The social development (assistance) model, and
- A practical example that combines these models as applied by the International Committee of the Red Cross (ICRC) in Serbia and Montenegro.

STATE FAILURE, COLLAPSE, AND RECONSTRUCTION

The state concept can be characterized as a territory and its people organized under an effective government, with associated social institutions. "Statism" is a Western concept that has its origin in the 1648 Treaty of Westphalia when, following thirty years of conflict, agreement was reached to carve up Europe into a number of territorial entities and the de jure state was born. The state concept has become a global norm and the reference point for global economic, political, and cultural interaction. State formation continues as a work in progress for all of the approximately 190 states that are recognized today.

The primacy of statehood is mirrored in the associated concept of "sovereignty" that confers the government of the state with supremacy of power and authority over its territory and people. This universal state project has been facilitated by global processes, somewhat linked to conflict, including:

- colonialism—as tens of millions of mainly Europeans settled all over the world, especially in the United States;
- industrialization—as improved technologies enhanced the governance function (where technologies existed);
- the dissolution of empires at the end of World War I and the formation of new states in Central, Eastern, and Southern Europe;
- the end of World War II, which brought an end to the colonial era and the establishment of dozens of independent states in Asia, the Middle East, and Africa;
- the end of the Cold War, which signified the end of an era shrouded in the fear of global war between the two superpowers and the promise of a new world order; and

- since the end of World War II, the U.S.-sponsored UN system, which reflects the collective will of the community of states to enshrine, defend, and promote statehood.

Every habitable corner of the globe has claims of sovereignty by one or more parties.[6] The majority of relatively young and de jure states have been granted their independence, often following protracted struggles.[7] Efforts by authorities to earn de facto status have frequently proved difficult, often resulting in conflict and violence, death and destruction. Increasingly, however, while some states strive for sovereignty and self-determination, others are embracing the global project and find themselves collaborating with regional neighbors aimed at enhancing their global economic advantage. The net effect of this global project is a sharing of decision making on issues of not only economic but social and political relevance and the ultimate compromising of sovereignty.

State Failure and Collapse

The late 1980s and 1990s will be remembered as the period of uncompromising sovereignty. The Cold War fostered this thinking as the two superpowers supported states against internal and external conflict in return for political allegiance.[8] Few could have foreseen the problems that were to emerge with the ending of the "second world" and the difficulties that were to extend to almost every part of the globe in the 1990s. The decade that commenced with initial visions of a pluralist global society working towards peace and harmony will be remembered as one of growing global inequalities, enhanced vulnerability, and continued exploitation.[9]

Between 1957 and 1996 there have been a reported 127 cases of state failure, with the highest rates of state collapse happening since 1990.[10] Many, although not all, of these cases were marked by conflict. Failed states can be found on every continent.[11] There are suggestions that failed states pose threats to security and world stability and they are sometimes considered as destabilizing for their neighbor states, regional stability, and ultimately peace on a global level.

Many analysts conclude that state failure and its results will dominate the world this century. As previously noted, state failure and collapse is usually followed by a period of transition of indeterminate length, which leads either to relative stability or peace or in some cases a return to conflict and strife.

State Reconstruction

The international community has grappled with different approaches to support failed and collapsed states. The preferred approach tends towards "state reconstruction."[12] State reconstruction is rarely served in an à la carte fashion; however, it invariably includes the following stages:

- arranging for a halt in active hostilities through "agreements";
- encouraging "national dialog"; and
- organizing multiparty "elections."

Analysts contend that this is a Western approach that seeks to progress favored political, economic, and cultural philosophies. While it has been relatively successful in arresting active conflict in warring states, this success rarely advances to the desired ends whereby the "reconstructed state" demonstrates the characteristics of a Weberian state[13] with its institutional splendor. Instead the result may often be a state in transition failing to serve its people.

Grouping all exogenous stakeholders in state reconstruction as the "international community" risks conferring a false sense of approach, interest, and working methods on this diverse group. At the risk of overgeneralization, this disparate grouping, the components of which all have to operate in a shared environment, can be reduced to three categories namely:

- Multilateral actors who focus on the establishment of a private sector and resumption of commercial and productive activities;
- Governments and the Development Assistance Committee (DAC), who tend towards the statist view, focusing on institutions of governance;
- International humanitarian organizations (including NGOs), which are more inclined to social welfare and human rights. Some of these agencies are increasingly dependent on donors

and provide a safety net for donors to escape the post-conflict situation.[14]

Not all Western states share the same enthusiasm for state reconstruction. A small number of Western states continue to reinforce their hegemony over multinational organizations, and they in turn set the agenda for governmental and nongovernmental stakeholders. This reality must premise all approaches and models to working with societies in transition.

There is a variety of motivations leading countries to interfere in the affairs of others and there is little doubt that the outcome can be both positive and negative, or both intended and unintended. Traditionally these interests were deemed to be associated with economic exploitation; however, increasingly global security concerns are forwarded as primary reasons for intervention. Following the September 2001 attacks on the World Trade Center and the Pentagon, there appears to be global political support to link aid and security aimed at reducing the potential for regionalized insecurity that may result in a resumption of violence and increased threats to peace and stability.[15]

The reconstruction process that takes place during the transition phase is assumed to begin with the cessation of active conflict. This period is frequently labeled post-conflict. The term post-conflict can be somewhat of a misnomer given that transition periods are sometimes marked by a lull in violence and can in fact provide an opportunity to take stock for a next phase in the conflict. Transition phases, which will be of varying duration, can be marked either by a return to widespread violence or progress to peace and stability. The latter of these two is obviously more difficult to define but it may be signaled by free movement of displaced people back to their homes; an obvious reduction in the military spending in the country and demobilization of soldiers; recognition that reconciliation is in the offing; social integration and access to state benefits; and a semblance of normality returning to the political economy.

Approaches to State Reconstruction

In order to analyze how the transition process can be supported it is necessary to gain some understanding of the state reconstruction process, the typical roles played by the "international community" in this process, and their recognized strengths and failings in the reconstruction process to date.

Ottaway[16] forwards two broad approaches for state reconstruction based on an analysis of efforts to rebuild collapsed states in the 1990s. They are the "Donors' Approach" and the "Internal State Reconstruction Approach." Most state reconstruction includes elements of both. Table 1 contrasts typical features of both approaches.

The external approach has proved very costly with the largest part of these monies going to peacekeeping, administration, and consultants that invariably focus on establishing social institutions. The donor community is in a position to use methods other than raw power to maintain order such as the threat of hostile action or economic incentives. However, it must be remembered that, while donors have the capacity to establish organizations, they are relatively powerless when it comes to ensuring the transformation of these organizations to institutions. On the other hand those driving the internal approach frequently lack the resources to transform the raw power into acceptable social institutions.[17] It should also be noted that external actors cannot force change and are to a certain extent dependent on transformation from within the society undergoing reconstruction.

Table 1 suggests that the biggest challenges in both approaches are establishing commitment from the international community and the acceptance of the citizenry. Ottaway advises that one cannot begin the restoration process with the establishment of institutions, but rather by generating a minimum level of authority, which will invariably involve the use of force. The problem is that the international community is rarely prepared to commit to a protracted period allowing for the development of social institutions. Instead, what results is premature institution building, something that is regularly associated with social engineering. Most analysts would regard social engineering as highly problematic and question the existence of a normative framework for democratization and a neoliberal agenda. The very instrument that provides for democratic legitimacy, namely the "election process," is no substitute for accountability.[18] This accountability provides the mechanisms for people to see that the evolving system is accessible and accountable.

Table 1. Characteristics of External and Internal Approaches to Reconstruction

External Approach	Internal Approach
Focus on rebuilding institutions	Focus on reestablishing power
International community drives process	Military men and politicians drive the process
Aim is to reconstruct de jure state	Aim to construct de facto state
Very costly	Lack resources
Biggest challenge to move from imposed order to stable institutions	Biggest challenge to move from imposed order to stable institutions
Often quick withdrawal	Often reluctant to share their newfound power

Source: Adapted from Ottaway 2002.

Lack of commitment to the transition process on the part of donors frequently results in their early exit. There is a tendency for donors to commit funds to the process, which encourages a culture of projectism, which is typically short-term and not consistent with the concept of institution building. There is often fierce competition among NGOs for this funding, which in turn militates against any real coherence in devising an agreed strategy among implementers. Local NGOs (LNGOs) are frequently lost to the system. The relationship between international NGOs (INGOs) and LNGOs is complex and varied, and it mirrors that of the donors' organization and INGOs. INGOs frequently seek to empower their local counterparts and encourage them to be accountable and transparent in a manner typical of the way they are treated by donors. The result is a one-way accountability system away from the citizen.

The need to assess and address the problems faced by states in transition is essential. In order to have any effect the approach has to be multidimensional with participative responses at many different levels—security, economic, social, governance, and legal reconciliation.

THE TRANSITION ENVIRONMENT—THE SCOPE AND ROLE OF THE HUMANITARIAN SECTOR

The effects of conflict are numerous and far-reaching. While a detached view of the periods of transition that follow active hostilities and possible humanitarian responses are frequently analyzed at the state level, it is also essential to remain conscious of the effects of war at an individual and human level. It is these effects and these individuals that humanitarian organizations have to strive to address in the most effective manner possible during the transition phase.

Humanitarian organizations have a crucial role to play in transition situations as it is often the most vulnerable sections of society that are at risk of "slipping through the net" and not receiving the requisite protection and assistance to allow them to rebuild their lives. This risk of being "left out" is often a result of the group to which people belong (detainees, internally displaced persons [IDPs], refugees, civilians, etc.) or because they are deemed inappropriate for certain types of assistance. The effectiveness of work carried out at all levels and with all sections of society in transition periods is vital, but it is the work of humanitarian organizations, which touches individuals at a palpable and human level. Humanitarian agencies have a fundamental role to play in transition situations alongside and sometimes in conjunction with other actors.

There is a growing body of literature pertaining to the role that can and should be played by governments, the DAC, the World Bank, and private-sector organizations in transition situations in order to provide support for economic restructuring, reform of judicial systems, support for the establishment of functioning social security networks, and governance support. This chapter aims to build upon the work carried out in relation to the role the humanitarian sector can play at such times and, more specifically, the important connection between protection and assistance responses and activities of humanitarian organizations.

Given the increase in the number of countries in transition that has been seen in the last fifteen to twenty years, the longevity of transition periods and the risk of increased human suffering and hardship that frequently occurs at such times, the input of experienced humanitarian organizations is essential. As already stated, the transition phase is intricately linked to the conflict, and therefore the role of the humanitarian actors, who invariably play a key role in providing protection and assistance in time of conflict, spills over into the transition phase.

The change of situation from active hostility to transition requires humanitarian organizations to adapt their approach and activities accordingly. As has been mentioned, the characteristics of transition periods differ depending on various factors in the lead-up to the transition phase. Humanitarian agencies need to be conscious of what has happened prior to the onset of the transition phase in order to identify needs efficiently and address those needs appropriately. This is particularly true in the initial stages of periods of transition that are frequently marked by a fragile stability that may lead to peace but can also lead to a resumption of hostilities.

The transition period is viewed as a period for peace building to be fostered. This crucial process of post-conflict reconciliation is generally of major concern for most transition stakeholders, but not necessarily humanitarian organizations, due to the essential principles under which they operate, namely neutrality and independence. Peace building, reconciliation, and societal transformation remain the responsibility of other stakeholders, not least the communities themselves and national authorities. However, the work of humanitarian organizations can contribute to this process. Agencies working in such situations should be aware of the work being done by others in this regard in order to ensure that their efforts are not counterproductive. For example, humanitarian agencies must ensure that their activities do not have a negative economic impact and do not aggravate existing social tensions. Understanding the obstacles to peace in each context is essential in order that humanitarian actors can tailor their response to needs appropriately.

The last fifteen years has seen a change in the environment in which humanitarian organizations have to function. This environment marked by complex political emergencies and protracted crises has presented new challenges for aid organizations in their drive to respond to needs. During the Cold War, relief agencies were relatively alone in their neutral and impartial stance to the limited conflicts that dared activate in the shadows of the super-powers. The change in world order in the aftermath of the Cold War presented the United Nations with the role of adjudicator or mediator in the new conflicts of the 1990s as the threat of nuclear war lessened. It adopted a compromise view of nations, in effect introducing a third party to the conflict whose aim was to bring a peaceful solution to hostilities. However, the process of seeking peaceful solutions to conflict has proved rather more difficult than first envisaged (because of the conflicting roles of states as party to the conflict as well as being members of the international community), as has the associated process of protecting and assisting vulnerable populations in complex emergencies and post-conflict situations.

The introduction of a peace paradigm, with its associated tripartite nature, invaded the space of relief agencies and brought with it a new politic. The growth in the demand for relief encouraged development agencies, especially those with a presence in war-affected countries, to intervene in conflict areas—something not witnessed previously. Much is written of the negative effects of adopting development principles in relief, including bringing the relief effort into the conflict, complicating issues of security and protection for victims and aid workers alike, politicizing relief and using it for leverage, and diminishing humanitarian space.[19] The complexity of the relief operations has become blurred for all parties, not least the victims of the conflict.

Characteristics of the Transition Phase

The word transition as used in this context refers to the transition between war and relative stability and not any continuum from relief to development nor indeed is it to be confused with transition from a traditional to modern society. For reasons previously offered, it is naive to believe that a transition period will be void of hostility, disharmony, and problems. Characteristics of the immediate transition period include varying degrees of persistence in security risks and continuation of war economies and the necessity for security forces (albeit with a renewed mandate). Donors will invariably view the transition phase with a degree of caution.[20] Every situation is different and will contain unique contextual peculiarities. Other reasons for differences include the diverse causes of conflicts, the varying methods of warfare employed in conflicts, and the level and nature of external intervention.

There are, however, a number of features that are common to most conflicts, which lead into transition situations, including:

- Regional variations in the way the state territory experienced the conflict resulting in the need for a range of responses based on real needs;
- The majority of civil conflicts and an increasing number of international conflicts result from poor development, although the conflict itself may be "sparked" by any number of distinct events. Increasingly the need to address the root causes of the conflict is recognized;
- The effects of conflict are strikingly common and almost without exception include displacement of people, destruction of property, disintegration of social systems, and a high level of distrust among and within the local population;
- Different social groups are affected in different ways by the conflict. Certain groups, like displaced persons, children, women, disabled persons, and older people, are affected differently during conflict and they need to be targeted for special attention in the transition period; and
- Emerging authorities will require assistance to provide their citizenry with the security, representation, and welfare required to regain the trust and confidence in the governance system.

Conceptual Frameworks for Working with Societies in Transition

A number of models of intervention can be inferred from both the approaches to state reconstruction outlined earlier and from analyzing favored strategies used in the conflicts of the 1990s. Two such models in which the work of humanitarian organizations can be visualized can be labeled the "legal-institutional (protection) model" and the "social development (assistance) model." Both these models can be applied in periods of transition.

The legal-institutional (protection) model is characterized by a number of features, including:

- A concern with legal entitlements as determined by national and international law, together with the mandates of international agencies and NGOs;
- An overwhelming focus on the humanitarian concern for states rather than the deeper political, economic, and social causes of the conflict; and
- An emphasis on categorizing people, such as refugees, internally displaced persons (IDPs), de facto refugees, and so forth.

This model has a number of strengths, including the fact that it sets standards for states to ascribe to and often obliges these states to honor various bodies of law at both national and international levels. The model implies a commitment from states to adhere to the standards set out in international humanitarian law (such as the Geneva Conventions of 1949) and human rights law. This is particularly important in contemporary global society where there is a lack of global governance evidenced in the lack of coherence within the international community. One of the most effective tenets of this model is that its roots are found in laws and legal instruments that are subscribed to by states across the globe. The model therefore demands accountable behavior from these states.

There are, however, some limits to the model in that it merely recognizes a particular point in time and does little to address either the root causes of the problem or, indeed, the consequences of future developments.

There are also difficulties associated with categorizing people or groups of people and, if applied on its own, this model can risk fomenting existing divisions and exacerbating raw tensions between groups. In categorizing specific groups there can also be perceptions of some groups gaining disproportionately. The legal entitlement is often restricted to specific aspects of a targeted groups' existence, namely their basic needs. It does not allow for the full gamut of needs and wants.

The social development (assistance) model is based on the concept of people-centered social development that assumes that development is essentially a process through which the capacity of people is enhanced to empower them to realize their preferred life choices.[21] This is a universal concept of social development that equally applies to all societies, regions, local areas, communities, families, and so forth. It remains a key challenge for all societies, but none more so than the growing number of societies commonly labeled as post-conflict or in transition.

The description of this model is premised on the understanding that a model is not a blueprint but rather a framework to be adapted to suit given situations. The logic of the model is that one must fully understand the background and context of the conflict, including political and institutional factors, social and cultural factors, the geography and physical infrastructure of the territory, and associated economic factors.[22] Stakeholders should have an understanding of the predisposing factors to the conflict and the realities of the conflict in economic, political, and social terms. Failure to address these predisposing factors may result in their subsequent resurrection and contribute to a return to violence.

Cox[23] presents a framework for the social development model that combines elements of both the external and internal approaches to state reconstruction already outlined. He proposes a phased social development agenda. The immediate goals[24] include:

- an end to active conflict and peacekeeping for an interim period;
- the return of displaced persons and assurance of their reintegration;
- demobilization of soldiers and their reintegration into society; and
- beginning the reconciliation process.

The immediate needs of the population in the transition phase vary and any strategy must be based on the needs of the area and the available resources. This social development strategy requires an integrated approach that works to an agreed agenda.

Identified Needs

Different humanitarian agencies will have different roles to play in transition periods depending on their mandate and skills. However, the needs of individuals, communities and society at all levels must be addressed simultaneously to achieve the above tasks or goals. The most common needs include:

At the individual and household level:

- Security guarantees;
- Shelter of a suitable quality;
- Food, working towards self-reliance;
- Access to appropriate services (health, sanitation, education); and
- Opportunity for gainful employment.

At the community/local level:

- Sense of community;
- Mutually supportive atmosphere and joint activities;
- Income-generation activities;
- Rebuilding community focal points;
- Establishing appropriate networks and gateways for decision making; and
- Strengthening the capacity of local representatives.

At the national level:

- Law and order, representative police system, and functioning judiciary;
- Basic services including water, electricity, and so forth;
- Appropriate political system that is transparent and accountable;
- Economic system that includes banking facilities, credit facilities, and investment opportunities;
- Political system in place that encourages representativeness; and
- Physical infrastructure, including roads and bridges.

All of these are common to state reconstruction; however, the sustainability of the reconstruction process largely depends on ensuring this process is contextualized and that communities are motivated to enhance the relevance and appropriateness of the intervention effort.

Humanitarian organizations and NGOs have a clear operational role to play at the individual, household, and community levels. At the national level, input from governments, the DAC, and other key international bodies is essential in order to support and guide states through sensitive transition periods. However, humanitarian organizations should also maintain a consciousness of activities at a national level as well as building up relationships at this level that may positively impact their local- and household-level activities.

Both protection and assistance needs have to be addressed at all three levels. It is necessary for humanitarian organizations to accept that there can be no homogenous form of assistance (be it protection or material assistance) that can be provided to all those in need.

Different populations during the various stages of the transition phase may need diverse forms of assistance. For example, one portion of the population may be in need of direct food assistance while another part of the population would benefit from livelihood support. Some sections of society may be in need of certain protection guarantees, such as those being detained by the authorities or IDPs, while others are not. Protection needs may be varied and can include ensuring that adequate conditions of treatment are in place for detainees, that IDPs and refugees are able to return safely to their place of origin (or at the very least to be ensured of security in their temporary abode), that those whose vulnerability is linked to the conflict are materially assisted and have their livelihoods protected in order to assist them in becoming self-sufficient again, and that those who have lost contact with family members as a result of the conflict are able to trace their missing relatives and be reunified with them. Protection can also be provided in terms of trauma support and counseling and through the provision of support in terms of guaranteeing legal protection.

There are fundamental differences between the emergency ethos, which frequently centers on "doing for" a population, and the development ethos, which stresses the need to empower the population and therefore "do with" a population. While most commentators agree that all societies combine elements of both, the transition period is significant in that it is associated with a shift from a state of lack of control to one of increasing control over one's environment.

Table 2 identifies appropriate actors that should participate in satisfying the needs at all levels for a society in transition.

Table 2 provides an ideal scenario and one that needs to be adapted to suit a given situation. This approach is very much based on the principles of partnership and participation and requires a level of cooperation that is very difficult to achieve especially in the immediate aftermath of conflict.

Table 2.   Main Actors and the Principal Actions
at Two Different Societal Levels

Societal level	Who should be involved	Coherent actions to be taken
Individual, household, and community/local level	The entire population, including the most vulnerable, local authorities, NGOs and humanitarian relief/development agencies, relevant ministries working at local level, and elected representatives.	Baseline study of the situation on the ground to include economic, social and political data; identify the needs and wants of the population with their participation; agree on an *x*-year strategic plan for the local area; establish representative structures to manage and coordinate activities; and provide appropriate training to all parties to the process.
National level	Government, multilateral institutions, representatives from NGOs, trade unions, and employers.	Strengthening social institutions in line with the culture of the country, providing transparent and accountable structures, encouraging dialog between all parties to the conflict, and agreeing on operational mechanisms within and between social institutions.

The Role of Humanitarian Organizations

Two different frameworks for working with societies in transition have been proposed and an outline provided of which areas the different levels of societies in transition may need addressing. The way the conflict has been conducted and its resultant effect on the population will influence what kind of response humanitarian organizations can deliver in order to be operational and effective in transition situations.

What follows is a guide of the specific forms of assistance that may be needed at a household level and at a community level, which can be provided by humanitarian organizations active in the protection and assistance sectors.

Defining the most appropriate form of response will depend on many factors, including what stage of the transition process is being experienced (initial fragile stage, stability, near peace, brink of return to conflict) and who the intended recipients are

Table 3. Protection and Assistance Activities

Sector*	Activity
Protection	• Visits to detained persons • Tracing of missing persons • Providing communication links between separated family members • Reunifying separated relatives • Trauma support and counseling • Legal support (access to rights) • Security
Assistance	• Provision of essential and basic commodities such as food, household items, and hygiene products • Access to clean water and satisfactory sanitation conditions • Provision of adequate healthcare • Provision of shelter • Access to education • Economic and livelihood support[25]

*There is sometimes a blurred boundary between what constitutes protection and what constitutes assistance. This paper does not propose that the above categorizations are definitive—they serve only to provide guidance.

(IDPs, host population, community groups, detainees, women, children, wounded, traumatized, etc.). A transition phase is an indeterminate period of time in which a number of different approaches to protection and assistance can be implemented.

Experience has shown that program diversification is often the most effective way to reach and benefit a broad section of the population in need. An example of this can be seen through the activities of the ICRC in Serbia and Montenegro.

The ICRC in Serbia and Montenegro

Following the collapse of the Yugoslav Federation in 1991, the Federal Republic of Yugoslavia (FRY) was involved in ten years of armed conflict and experienced nearly a decade of internationally imposed economic sanctions. Conflict was not seen on the actual territory of Serbia until the NATO bombing of FRY, which took place from March to June 1999.

As a result of the conflicts, Serbia and Montenegro had to accommodate some 700,000 refugees who fled the wars in Croatia and Bosnia-Herzegovina from 1991 to 1995 and an additional 230,000 IDPs who left Kosovo after June 1999. The large number of refugees and IDPs imposed a large burden on the public services of Serbia and Montenegro, which were already in decline due to the overall economic and political crises being faced by the country.

Serbia and Montenegro are deemed to have been undergoing a period of transition since the end of 1999 until the present day.

The ICRC has been present in Serbia and Montenegro since 1991.

ASSISTANCE
Material needs

- Following the NATO bombing campaign of 1999, the ICRC established an assistance program providing food and hygiene to all IDPs who had fled Kosovo to Serbia and Montenegro. This direct material assistance program continued well into the transition period to a gradually reducing number of IDPs until the end of 2003.

Economic support

- In 2001 the ICRC launched an income generation program, also in favor of IDPs, to run alongside the material assistance program. The beneficiaries of the income generation program, while still considered vulnerable due to their status which was compounded by the fact that they were living in a country that was (and still is) in a phase of transition, were considered to be less vulnerable than those receiving food and hygiene assistance. The income generation program provided vocational training, trade and agriculture grants, and micro-credit opportunities in order to provide beneficiaries with the opportunity to be self-supporting.
- By 2004 the food and hygiene assistance was stopped and the most vulnerable among the IDP population became beneficiaries of a cash assistance program, which was run in conjunction with the Ministry of Social Welfare. One of the program aims was to try and ensure inclusion of the beneficiaries in the state social welfare system.

Strengthening of systems and infrastructure support

- In 2001 the ICRC launched a comprehensive program of assistance and reconstruction of the primary health care system in one of the municipalities in Serbia. The program targeted an area with a high percentage of IDPs but the resident population were also able to benefit.

PROTECTION
Missing persons and detainees

- In an effort to address some of the protection needs of the population, the ICRC continues to liaise with government ministries, local authorities, international institutions, and community organizations in order to clarify the fate of persons missing and unaccounted for as a result of the Balkan wars. Visits have also been undertaken to certain categories of detainees.

Psychological support

- In 2002 the ICRC launched a program of community-based projects that aims at encouraging the coexistence and integration of IDPs into the local community.

Respect for international humanitarian law

- The ICRC continues to run a program for the promotion of international humanitarian law, which is aimed at the authorities, schools and universities, the media, the armed and security forces, and KFOR in Kosovo.

Security

- Following hostilities in southern Serbia in late 2000, the ICRC launched a program to ensure that the local population were aware of the risk of mines and unexploded ordnance in their region. The program targeted both adults and children and was undertaken in partnership with the National Red Cross Society.

The ICRC has been able to address a broad range of needs faced by a society in transition following a decade of conflict. One reason that the organization has been in a position to do this is due to its presence in the region throughout the conflict and the knowledge that it had built up through this presence. Another important element has been its ability to form partnerships with the National Red Cross Society, with government ministries, and with local NGOs in Serbia in order to carry out its activities in the transition period, which Serbia and Montenegro have been experiencing for some five years. For the most part the ICRC's activities in this period of transition have been carried out at an individual level and with the participation of the beneficiaries, but also ensuring the inclusion and partnership of the relevant authorities. These approaches have helped to ensure the success and relevance of the programs as well as ensuring a more credible withdrawal as the authorities' participation provides a guarantee that they have a responsibility toward their own citizens once humanitarian organizations, such as the ICRC, have left.

Through its approach in Serbia and Montenegro the ICRC has applied a combination of the two models detailed earlier. The basis for the ICRC's presence, its protection-related activities, and the assistance targeting it adopted conform with the legal institutional (protection) model. The influence of the social development (assistance) model can be seen through the adoption of an income-generation program, the cash-assistance program run in conjunction with the Ministry of Social Welfare, and assistance and reconstruction of part of Serbia's primary health care system.

Operational Considerations in Transition Situations

A number of key factors need to be taken into account by humanitarian organizations that wish to be operational in transition periods. These include:

- The need to undertake transparent and thorough needs assessments.
- The devising of clear entry and exit strategies prior to conducting activities.
- The necessity for beneficiaries and authorities to be included in the planning and implementation of activities.
- An awareness and possible link of activities to peace initiatives.

Given the unpredictable nature of transition periods, all program planning needs to be long-term and flexible. Working with the national authorities forms a vital part of this long-term planning, as it will be them who continue to build on the work undertaken by humanitarian organizations in the years to come. There is need for new state institutions to feel responsible for their citizens, and humanitarian organizations can assist in this by including them in the planning, implementation, and monitoring of programs.

A vital point to note is that effective humanitarian responses demand that protection and assistance are provided on the basis of need and in a neutral and impartial manner.

Societies in transition generally suffer from a lack of global interest. During times of active conflict there is normally a high level of media interest, which generates attention from donors and humanitarian organizations alike. When the conflict is over and the country "falls off the global map," there is less interest from humanitarian organizations, partly linked to the limited resources available for low profile contexts (even though some activities carried out in such contexts can be considered as life-saving).

SUMMARY AND CONCLUSIONS

The increased number of wars and political emergencies, together with the limited success in restoring peace and stability to affected populations, has resulted in an ever increasing number of people throughout the world living in unstable conditions and lacking basic human rights. Global political institutions continue to be dominated by a small number of powerful states that are blinkered in their approach to intervening in societal disputes. Their preferred option is statehood in line with existing Western states, and any postmodern deviations are viewed with skepticism and distrust. These same organizations control the aid budget and therefore have a major say in setting the reconstruction agenda.

NGOs frequently find themselves at the coalface of the state-reconstruction process, trying to satisfy their uncommitted pay-masters and divided communities who are frequently loath to offer unconditional acceptance to a new regime given their previous experiences. These NGOs are heterogeneous, with different policies, mandates, and experiences. Their potential differences are exacerbated by the intense competition that surrounds the process of procuring funding contracts.

Approaches to state reconstruction tend to be governed by the theory of state building. Both donor-driven and internally led approaches vary in many respects including their immediate aims, the cost and direct beneficiaries, the options available to them, and the difficulties they face. However, both are similar in that they strive to establish legitimate institutions that are broadly acceptable to both the citizens of the state and the international community.

Two conceptual frameworks (models) were forwarded for steering the reconstruction process, namely the legal-institutional (protection) model and the social development (assistance) model. The former focuses on the protection function and adopts a rights-based approach while the social development model adopts an assistance approach and seeks to address the root causes of the problem. Both models have advantages as well as certain limits. The advantages of the legal-institutional model include its recognition under international law, that it is accepted almost globally, and that it has endured over time. However, on its own it is limited in scope in that it offers little by way of a durable solution. While the social development model offers both scope and durability, it is also limited in that if applied in isolation it requires a longer-term commitment and a high level of coherence among all actors, and stakeholders have to be willing to compromise on issues that can be of fundamental importance to their respective organizations.

Either model if applied alone risks addressing only a limited part of the root causes and results of conflict. The two models should in fact be considered as mutually complementary, and a combination of the two frameworks is therefore proposed as the optimal approach for humanitarian organizations operating in transition situations.

The approach taken by the ICRC in Serbia and Montenegro provides a good example of how these two frameworks complement one another. The ICRC, which is traditionally recognized for its protection mandate, has valuable assets to bring to the transition process. Its privileged position as guardian of IHL, together with the experiences and knowledge of the context, is invaluable to the reconstruction process. Sudden exit from the post-conflict situation or a role limited to protection or both could be viewed as a loss of cultural and symbolic capital, which will have a domino effect in building trust and confidence that are crucial components of social capital. The ICRC can play a leading role in bridging the protection assistance gap by utilizing its position to build social capital and manage a planned exit that is acceptable to the international community and internal actors, including the national society. However, caution is advised in ensuring that Circus mandate or relationship with the most vulnerable is not compromised.

9

Internal Displacement in West Africa: Challenges and Constraints

Claudia McGoldrick

INTERNALLY DISPLACED PEOPLE (IDPs) are among the most vulnerable victims of conflict and human rights abuses worldwide—numbering just under twenty-four million at the end of 2005.[1] Without the legal protection and assistance afforded by the 1951 refugee convention to those fleeing across an internationally recognized border, IDPs remain largely dependent on their governments who more often than not are either unwilling or unable to protect and assist them. As a result large numbers of IDPs remain exposed to further violence, malnutrition and disease, and are often forced to flee several times. Yet despite, or because of, the scale of the worldwide displacement crisis, international attention has consistently focused more on refugees—who globally are much fewer in number than IDPs but usually much more visible.

The African continent has more IDPs than the rest of the world put together, with over twelve million internally displaced by conflict in twenty countries. This is almost four times the number of refugees from Africa.[2] While the largest displacement crises currently include the Sudan, the Democratic Republic of Congo (DRC), and Uganda, the most significant regional displacement crisis is undoubtedly in West Africa. The total number of IDPs in the four countries directly involved in West Africa's regional conflict—Liberia, Sierra Leone, Guinea, and Côte d'Ivoire—may currently be well under one million, yet the potential for renewed and increased instability and massive population movements is acute.

Since the conflict started in Liberia in 1989, eventually pulling in its three neighbors, the resource-rich region has continued a downward spiral of political chaos and socioeconomic decay, creating a chronic humanitarian and human rights crisis that has been largely hidden from the outside world. Vested interests of belligerent parties and their sponsors in all four countries to maintain the revolving conflict and nonfunctioning of the various states have contributed to the failure of the faltering and often halfhearted attempts at peace building over the past seventeen years. But with limited strategic interest in the region, international interventions have mostly been based on quick-fix solutions, entailing deployment of peacekeepers, incomplete disarmament of fighters, and the accelerated return of refugees and IDPs, often ahead of premature elections. Interventions have also tended to respond to national conflicts in isolation while overlooking the intrinsic regional character of the violence. Such hollow "success stories" presaged a slide back to war in Sierra Leone in 1996 and Liberia in 1997, and left Côte d'Ivoire facing the prospect of renewed conflict following the collapse of elections in October 2005. Yet Liberia's inauguration of a democratically elected female head of state following elections in 2005 did appear to represent a tentative first step towards the restoration of the country's severely battered credibility.

Root causes of conflict in all four countries—endemic poverty, inequitable distribution of resources, corruption, and lack of governance, among them—remain largely unchanged. The continuing conflict in Côte d'Ivoire, the political fragility of Guinea, the export of mercenaries from Sierra Leone and Liberia, poorly planned disarmament and reintegration in Liberia, and the widespread availability of arms in resource-rich yet crushingly poor areas are just some of the factors that leave West Africa teetering on the brink of regional conflict. Adding to the regional instability is the violence that erupted in Togo following disputed elections in April 2005.

At the same time the overall humanitarian response has been grossly inadequate, with IDPs often at the bottom of the list despite their extreme vulnerability. National authorities in the four countries have, in differing degrees, been either unwilling or unable to provide adequate protection and assistance to IDPs—not least since in all cases they have been a principal agent of displacement—and in turn they have hampered the international response by restricting access. Humanitarian response has been further constrained by an acute lack of funding as well as muddled if not chaotic "coordination." In three of the four countries the UN "integrated missions" have to varying degrees been criticized—particularly by nongovernmental organizations (NGOs)—on the basis of humanitarian imperatives being subjugated by political ones, and, in the case of Liberia, this bitterly divided the humanitarian community.

The challenges of effective humanitarian response and peace building here are clearly intertwined: the situations of internal displacement across the region cannot be durably resolved unless both issues are addressed. One problem feeds the other in a vicious circle: without long-term commitment to tackle the root causes of conflict there will be a repeated pattern of internal displacement and humanitarian crisis, and unless displaced populations are effectively stabilized through adequate protection and assistance, there can be no hope of achieving sustainable peace.

So how can there be an effective humanitarian response to IDPs in a region with such a legacy of failure on all levels? While the "collaborative response" system developed by the international community in the absence of a single IDP agency has so far clearly failed to adequately address the needs of IDPs, an improved model of this arguably remains the most viable way forward. Unlike other response models, it has the potential to enable the international community to react both flexibly and comprehensively to such complex internal displacement situations as are found in West Africa. The new "cluster" approach borne of the 2005 Humanitarian Response Review[3]—whereby UNHCR agreed to take on sectoral responsibility for IDP protection, emergency shelter, and camp management—may prove to address at least some, but not all, of the inherent weaknesses of the current system. These weaknesses include lack of leadership and accountability, inconsistent agency commitment, and unpredictable political support from donor governments. At the time of writing (March 2006), implementation of the new approach was embryonic, and its potential impact yet to be felt. But beyond the "cluster" reform, further important measures must still be taken, particularly toward strengthening leadership and capacity and mobilizing donor support.

Failure to improve the humanitarian response system in West Africa will not only maintain the enormous problem of internal displacement as both a cause and result of perennial conflict, but also export yet greater instability from the region. This will ensure the continued suffering of millions of vulnerable civilians and cost the international community much more in the long run.

INTERNAL DISPLACEMENT: A NEGLECTED CRISIS

The international normative and institutional framework for response to situations of internal displacement remains weak largely because states are reluctant to comply with what they see as interference in a sovereign issue. This is true of the UN Guiding Principles on Internal Displacement—developed in 1998 by the then special representative of the Secretary-General on IDPs, Francis Deng—which are based upon existing international humanitarian law and human rights instruments. The Guiding Principles are intended to serve as an international standard to guide governments as well as international humanitarian and development agencies in providing assistance and protection to IDPs. Although an increasing number of governments have acknowledged the importance of the Guiding Principles and in some cases incorporated them into national legislation, for example in Angola and Colombia, there are precious few examples of this being translated into practical action in terms of finding and implementing durable solutions for IDPs.

The main focal point for the coordination of international assistance and protection to IDPs in the UN system is the Emergency Relief Coordinator (ERC). But at the operational level there is no single organization mandated to protect and assist IDPs, due partly to the magnitude of the problem, but also to inter-agency rivalry. These same issues hamper the "collaborative response" designed by the UN's Inter-Agency Standing Committee (IASC) in 1999, which requires a wide range of humanitarian actors to work together in a transparent and cooperative manner to respond to the needs of IDPs on the basis of their individual mandates and expertise. Poor coordination, competing mandates, and lack of resources have all contributed to ensure the very limited success of the collaborative response.

In 2004 the ERC took various measures aimed at improving the international response to IDPs. He strengthened the Inter-Agency Internal Displacement Division (formerly IDP Unit) within the UN Office for the Coordination of Humanitarian Affairs (OCHA) and focused its work on eight priority countries (including Liberia) with the aim of supporting UN field operations in IDP crises. And in an attempt to improve the "collaborative response," the UN's revised IDP Policy Package[4] was endorsed and disseminated to all resident/humanitarian coordinators in the field, which among other tools provides detailed guidance on developing an IDP response strategy.

Also in 2004, the UN Human Rights Commission adopted a new mandate for the UN Secretary-General's Representative on IDPs, emphasizing more the human rights aspects of his work. Walter Kälin, who was instrumental in developing the Guiding Principles together with Francis Deng, was subsequently appointed to the position.

In his 2005 report on UN reform, Secretary-General Kofi Annan stressed the need "to strengthen further the inter-agency response to the needs of internally displaced persons."[5] At the same time humanitarian reform globally resulted in various initiatives that could—potentially—impact positively on the international response to internal displacement situations. Central elements of the reform include the creation of a new UN emergency fund, launched in March 2006; the development of a standby team of protection experts; and the assignment of lead agencies for neglected humanitarian sectors or "clusters," with a priority in relation to the protection and care of IDPs. UNHCR agreed to take on sectoral responsibility for camp management, emergency shelter and protection—with Liberia identified as one of three pilot countries for 2006 (the others being Uganda and DRC).[6]

Implementation of the cluster approach was in its early stages at the time of writing, and its effectiveness yet to be assessed. Various crucial issues had yet to be resolved—not least the question of additional funding and resources to allow UNHCR to fulfill its new responsibilities.

Indeed, the overall donor response to situations of internal displacement remains woefully inadequate—particularly in protracted crises that are out of the media spotlight, and even more particularly in Africa. Even the response to the massive displacement crisis in Darfur was too little too late, not just in terms of funding but also the lack of criticism of the state's role in creating the crisis. In some underreported situations IDPs are almost completely off the agenda, as in Guinea. Again, it is still too soon to assess the impact on such situations of the $500 million UN emergency fund, meant to provide immediate funding for humanitarian aid in cases of "sudden onset emergencies, rapid deteriorations and neglected emergencies."

BACKGROUND TO THE WEST AFRICAN CONFLICT

When civil war broke out in Liberia at the end of 1989, it triggered an intractable cycle of conflict and displacement that would directly affect three other countries and indirectly affect several more. The violence that has ebbed and flowed between Liberia, Sierra Leone, Guinea, and more recently Côte d'Ivoire has created an extremely complex situation of displacement, both internally and across borders.

While accurate figures simply do not exist, virtually all of Liberia's three million citizens are estimated to have fled their homes at some time during fourteen years of intermittent conflict, most of them becoming internally displaced—some for a few weeks and some for several years, and many of them several times over. Up to one-third of Sierra Leone's population of six million was estimated to have been internally displaced at the height of the country's eleven-year civil war which ended in 2002. Up to 360,000 people became internally displaced when conflict erupted in Guinea in 2000–2001, and as many as 1 million Ivorians fled within Côte d'Ivoire when an abortive coup in September 2002 effectively split the country in half.

The end of Sierra Leone's civil war in 2002, followed in 2003 by Liberia's peace agreement and the eventual inauguration of a new democratically elected president in January 2006, gave rise to optimism that both countries are firmly on the road to recovery. Yet peace remains fragile. The UN peacekeeping operation in Sierra Leone (UNAMSIL) finally packed up and left at the end of 2005, while hundreds of thousands of refugees had returned. At the same time Liberia's highly criticized disarmament process left, by late 2005, some twenty-six thousand former combatants still waiting for places in reintegration projects, with few prospects of gainful employment. The program to return internally displaced people to their areas of origin was in many cases of questionable safety and sustainability. Root causes of the conflict in both countries—including endemic poverty and lack of economic opportunity, inequitable distribution of rich natural resources, poor governance, and cross-border flows of weapons and mercenaries—remain largely unchanged.

Côte d'Ivoire's beleaguered peace process seems particularly fragile. Ethnic tensions in the polarized country remain acute, and continue to periodically erupt into violence causing death and displacement. The conflict, in varying degrees, has so far eluded all military and diplomatic efforts to end it—including the deployment in 2004 of a six thousand–strong UN peacekeeping mission (UNOCI) on top of an existing contingent of four thousand French peacekeepers, and the Linas-Marcoussis Accord signed by all parties to the conflict in January 2003. While parties to the conflict were discussing disarmament, ex-combatants were reportedly being recruited.[7] The postponement of October 2005 elections and a troubled transition period—including the imposition of UN sanctions against three individuals in February 2006 following targeted violence against the United Nations—further exacerbated political tensions. Any further setback could result in a rapid spread of violence causing massive displacement not only in Côte d'Ivoire, but also affecting the populations of Liberia, Guinea, Burkina Faso, and Mali—countries from where about one-quarter of the country's sixteen million population originate.

The situation in Guinea is also explosive, particularly in the southeastern Forest Region that is bordered by Sierra Leone, Liberia, and Côte d'Ivoire, and that has been home to hundreds of thousands of refugees from all three countries. Thousands of former Guinean militiamen as well as Liberian fighters live in this impoverished region that has seen a steady rise in banditry and trade in small arms, and where interethnic tension is high.

The potential for regional instability was raised yet further by Togo's political upheaval following the death of former President Gnassingbe Eyadema in February 2005 and the subsequent declaration by the army of his son Faure Gnassingbe as head of state. Although Gnassingbe was forced to step down and call elections in April 2005, violent protests erupted when he was declared the winner in a disputed poll. In a fierce crackdown by Togolese security forces on opposition supporters, thousands of people fled mainly to neighboring Benin and Ghana, and there were also some reports of relatively small-scale internal displacement.

Apart from West Africa's regional conflict, separate situations of internal displacement also exist in Senegal, Guinea-Bissau, and Nigeria. In Senegal, a long-running separatist rebellion in the southern Casamance province officially ended in 2004, raising hopes for the return of several thousand IDPs—although divisions within the rebel movement itself erupted into renewed fighting in early 2006. Up to sixty-four thousand people may have been internally displaced during the conflict, thousands killed, and many others injured by landmines.

Guinea-Bissau's civil war of 1998–1999, sparked by an attempted military coup, caused up to 350,000 people to flee their homes. Most of the IDPs were believed to have returned to their homes within a couple of years. However, lingering political tensions have continued to jeopardize efforts to consolidate the peace and prevent renewed violence—not least the encroachment of periodic fighting into the border region from neighboring Senegal.

And in Nigeria, which is Africa's most populous nation, a multitude of religious, ethnic, and political fault lines that periodically erupt into communal violence has created a sizeable, albeit fluctuating, internally displaced population—particularly since the return of democracy in 1999. Government sources say that the cumulative total of people displaced within Nigeria since 1999 may be as high as three million, although there has never been systematic registration or verification of numbers. There is clear cause for concern, however, that the level of conflict—and with it the level of internal displacement—may increase as the 2007 presidential elections draw nearer.

However, these situations are quite separate from the regional conflict and as such will not be considered here.

COMMON CAUSES OF DISPLACEMENT

Although there are numerous causes at the root of West Africa's regional conflict, one of the main catalysts was undoubtedly Charles Taylor, the megalomaniac warlord who in 1989 plunged Liberia into the region's bloodiest and most destructive civil war since Biafra's attempt to secede from Nigeria.

Leading the National Patriotic Front of Liberia (NPFL), and with varying degrees of support from Côte d'Ivoire, Burkina Faso and Libya, Taylor launched an armed rebellion in the north of the country ostensibly to topple the Samuel Doe regime. Fighting quickly reached the capital, Monrovia. In 1990 the Economic Community of West African states deployed a Nigerian-led peace-keeping mission (ECOMOG) to Liberia to restore order. ECO-MOG's control did not extend beyond Monrovia, however, and the rest of the country was ruled by Taylor and other self-styled freedom fighters battling over the country's rich natural re-sources, principally timber and to a lesser extent diamonds.[8] Tay-lor effectively controlled the Liberian countryside through the instigation of ethnic massacres and gross human rights violations. An estimated 150,000 people were killed and several hundred thousand internally displaced during the first phase of the con-flict that lasted for 7 years.

Taylor was also directly responsible for starting Sierra Leone's civil war in 1991, training and sponsoring the Revolutionary United Front (RUF) rebels to effectively act as his proxy in the diamond-rich areas in the east of the country.[9] What began as a small incursion from Liberia turned into a brutal campaign of terror against civilians throughout the country that displaced mil-lions and killed tens of thousands.

In 1997 the demagogic Taylor won the legitimacy he craved through the ballot box, winning a landslide victory in the presi-dential contest. With enough ill-gotten wealth to shower voters with food and cash, Taylor was held in fear and awe by a largely illiterate population, and as such had no need to rig the elections. He held the key to Liberia's destruction and ironically, to its reconstruction. "For many, Mr. Taylor was a pragmatic choice—a choice based not on the lesser of evils but on the reasonable assumption that, if Mr. Taylor lost the elections, he would make Liberia ungovernable."[10]

But peace in Liberia was short-lived. Predictable problems quickly surfaced: factional and ethnic tensions continued across the country, exacerbated by Taylor's tendency to brutality and despotism, and only about half of the estimated sixty thousand Liberian fighters had been disarmed by the ECOMOG peace-keeping force. Less than two years after the elections, Liberian dissidents based in Guinea attacked northwestern Liberia. Fighting between government forces and the rebel Liberians United for Reconciliation and Democracy (LURD) spread throughout much of the country, worsened by the appearance of another rebel movement in 2003, the Movement for Democracy in Liberia (MODEL), which launched attacks on border areas with neighboring Côte d'Ivoire. Sporadic but intense fighting caused almost continuous displacement, eventually engulfing the Monrovia in June 2003 and causing a major humanitarian and human rights crisis that attracted, albeit briefly, unprecedented international attention.

Meanwhile the violence continued to escalate on a regional level. In 2000–2001 Guinea, which hosted hundreds of thousands of refugees from both Liberia and Sierra Leone, suffered a series of increasingly violent cross-border attacks from both countries. In many cases the perpetrators of these attacks were forces loyal to President Taylor, targeting bases of Liberian dissidents (many of them refugees) in Guinea, although RUF rebels from Sierra Leone as well as a Guinean rebel group were also responsible for the mayhem.[11] The fighting resulted in the mass displacement of civilians, particularly in the resource-rich Parrot's Beak area. It was no coincidence that Guinea also has large diamond reserves and the conflict was widely seen as having "much, if not everything to do with Taylor's quest for economic reward and advantage."[12]

Then, in September 2002, a failed coup by disaffected soldiers marked the worst postindependence crisis in Côte d'Ivoire, once a beacon of stability and economic prosperity in the region. Mass displacement was caused by fighting and human rights violations on all sides that left the Mouvement Patriotique pour la Côte d'Ivoire (MPCI) rebels in control of much of the predominantly Muslim north of the country, and government forces holding the largely Christian south. Two new rebel factions soon emerged in the west of the country—the Mouvement pour la Justice et la Paix (MJP) and the Mouvement Populaire Ivoirienne du Grand Ouest (MPIGO)—whose fighters included both Liberians and Sierra Leoneans.[13] The campaigning NGO Global Witness has reported on Charles Taylor's direct role in setting up these rebel groups, in collaboration with Liberian logging companies, with the ultimate aim of destabilizing the government of Laurent Gbagbo in Côte d'Ivoire and installing a "friendlier" one. There was also evidence that in 2003 Taylor—(correctly) fearing indictment for war crimes by the Special Court in Sierra Leone—was planning to reignite the conflict there and regain access to the diamond resources.[14] A subsequent report showed links between Taylor, the RUF in Sierra Leone, and diamond trading by al Qaeda.[15]

Taylor was thwarted however when in August 2003, under huge international pressure and surrounded by rebel forces, he went into exile in Nigeria. Clearly, however, Liberia's—and the region's—problems did not end there. In May 2005 a report by the Washington-based Coalition for International Justice confirmed that through a complex network of collaborators Taylor was continuing to finance armed groups and political parties with the aim of influencing not only Liberia's 2005 elections but ultimately the balance of regional power.[16]

Nigeria's agreement in March 2006 to allow Liberia to take Charles Taylor into custody, in response to a formal extradition request by President Ellen Johnson-Sirleaf, was widely hailed as a great day for justice across West Africa. Taylor was subsequently delivered into the custody of the Special Court in Sierra Leone where he was the first former African head of state to face prosecution for war crimes.

The four countries at the heart of West Africa's regional conflict also have common internal factors that lie behind the violence, providing fertile ground for manipulative politicians and warmongers to stoke unrest and achieve their own ends. Liberia, Sierra Leone, Guinea, and Côte d'Ivoire all suffer crushing poverty—despite their abundance of natural resources—with unremittingly bleak human development indicators.[17] The overall lack of economic opportunity, exacerbated by the inequitable distribution of resources by corrupt or inefficient governments, has in each of these countries produced a vast pool of frustrated youth who are easily incited to fight—many of them in several conflicts.

A March 2005 report by Human Rights Watch documented the testimonies of these "regional warriors" who "unanimously identified crippling poverty and hopelessness as the key factors which motivated them to risk dying in subsequent armed conflicts." Many of the fighters were forcibly recruited as children either by Liberian or Sierra Leonean rebels, and "thrust into a world of brutality, physical hardship, forced labor and drug abuse, they emerged as perpetrators, willing to rape, abduct, mutilate and even kill"—as well as to loot and pillage. Failures in disarmament and reintegration processes have also helped to ensure the continuing availability of these mercenary fighters.

Although none of the conflicts have been specifically over ethnicity, this has in varying degrees been a factor in both conflict and displacement. The existence of identical ethnic groups across the four countries has contributed to instability in border areas and has influenced the complex patterns of population displacement in the region. For example, the Mandingo and Krahn ethnic groups in Liberia have a strong ethnic affinity with identical groups in Guinea and Sierra Leone. There is also an ethnic affinity between the same groups in the southwest of Côte d'Ivoire and the eastern part of Liberia.[18] Ethnic Mandingo and Krahn people in Liberia were traditionally regarded as allies of the repressive Doe regime and as enemies of Charles Taylor, who found support among the Gio and Mano tribes.

As a result, throughout the Liberian conflict civilians on all sides have often been targeted for attack and human rights abuses on the basis of their ethnicity and perceived political allegiance.[19] The LURD rebel movement is also dominated by members of the Mandingo (or Malinké) ethnic group, which is allied with the same group in Guinea. President Lansana Conté, the current head of state, belongs to the Soussou people of western Guinea, while a third major group—the Peuls of central and northern Guinea—are seen as allied with many of the smaller tribes in the Forest Region. As internal pressures have grown against the authoritarian rule of Conté—including an assassination attempt in January 2005—fears have been raised of widespread ethnic conflict in the country.[20]

Ethnicity and nationality, as well as religion, have been used by politicians as a propaganda tool to incite conflict and cause displacement, most particularly in Côte d'Ivoire. For more than three decades after independence from France in 1960, the autocratic but tactical rule of Côte d'Ivoire's first president, Félix Houphouet-Boigny, ensured religious and ethnic harmony as well as relative economic prosperity until his death in 1993. Houphouet-Boigny's successor, Henri Konan Bédié, sowed the seeds of ethnic discord in 1995 when he introduced the concept of "*Ivoirité*" in order to restrict candidature for presidential elections, and specifically to exclude his main political rival, Alassane Ouattara, a Muslim from the north of the country whom Bédié insisted did not have two Ivorian parents as stipulated by the constitution.

This was a key cause of the September 2002 coup attempt by disaffected soldiers that presaged the civil war. Since then the current head of state, President Laurent Gbagbo, has at best failed to resolve the heightened ethnic and religious divisions in the country, and these have been used by both sides to the conflict to justify widespread killing and human rights abuses that have caused the internal displacement of up to one million people.[21] Although Gbagbo, under intense pressure from South African president Thabo Mbeki, finally agreed to allow Alassane Ouattara to stand against him in the aborted 2005 elections, Ivorian opposition parties, including rebel leaders (united into the Forces Nouvelles) have consistently accused Gbagbo of reneging on his promises and commitments under the peace accord.

PROTECTION CONCERNS

The conflicts in Liberia, Sierra Leone, Guinea, and Côte d'Ivoire have all been characterized from the outset by horrific human rights abuses against civilians. Internally displaced people have consistently been identified as one of the most vulnerable groups to abuses by government forces, militia, rebels, and armed bandits—yet adequate protection has rarely, if ever, been provided either at the national or international level. This is largely because governments and their allied militia have in many cases been a principal agent of displacement, and on the international level because of constrained and often muddled response.

In Liberia, the assisted return of some 314,000 registered IDPs was expected to be completed by April 2006 and IDP camps officially closed. The presence of fifteen thousand UNMIL peacekeepers contributed toward the restoration of peace across the country. Yet there are ongoing concerns about human rights violations against both returning IDPs and those still in camps, partly as a result of disgruntled ex-combatants who lack rehabilitation and reintegration opportunities and have on several occasions held violent protests, and the fact that Liberia and its neighbors remain awash with weapons. Throughout 2005, Human Rights Watch documented recently disarmed Liberian combatants—including children—being recruited to fight on behalf of the government in Côte d'Ivoire, perpetuating the regional cycle of conflict and displacement.

In particular, displaced or returning women and girls are one of the groups most vulnerable to ongoing human rights abuses by armed gangs and former militia members—especially to rape and other forms of sexual violence. Killings, abductions, forced labor, and destruction of property continued to be perpetrated in parts of Liberia even as preparations for the October 2005 elections—"the key to peace" in the country according to senior UN officials—were well underway. Indeed, a "badly planned disarmament and demobilization process" as well as a "poorly designed reintegration assistance package" may pose continuing protection risks for returning IDPs.[22]

Rape and other forms of sexual violence have been so pervasive throughout the Liberian conflict that it has been described as a weapon of war.[23] During the height of the fighting in Monrovia in the summer of 2003, rape and sexual violence was widely reported in the city's overcrowded IDP centers. In the Samuel Doe Stadium, where as many as fifty thousand IDPs took refuge in August 2003, Amnesty International said that within one week forty

women and twenty girls had reported being raped. Concerned
Christian Community, a local relief agency that offers psychological and social counseling to displaced civilians, said that out of
1,500 women and girls it had counseled since the beginning of
June 2003, 626 were victims of rape.[24] A 2004 Watchlist report
further highlighted the vulnerability of displaced Liberian girls in
camps to rape, sexual abuse, and prostitution.[25] According to the
Norwegian Refugee Council, young women and widows living in
IDP camps have often turned to prostitution as a survival mechanism, sometimes exchanging sexual services for food. And in
2005, the UN's Inter-Agency Internal Displacement Division reported a range of continuing protection concerns in the IDP
camps, in particular continuing and increasing reports of sexual
and gender-based violence, while the response was inadequate.[26]

In the run-up to the October 2005 elections, human rights
organizations warned that while some progress had been made
during the transitional period, Liberia's prospects for peace continued to face numerous threats, including an incomplete demobilization program, the widespread availability of small arms, a
culture of impunity, endemic corruption and mismanagement, a
weak judicial system, ethnic discrimination, and crushing poverty.
Rights organizations called on the new government to urgently
address these issues, particularly judicial reform.

Sierra Leone's eleven-year civil war was likewise characterized
by widespread and systematic sexual violence and rape, as well
as mutilation of civilians—many of them while fleeing.[27] Lack of
adequate protection of internally displaced populations was a
major cause for concern throughout the conflict. Large parts of
the country had no law enforcement system for several years, and
while civilians outside rebel-held areas received some protection
from civil defense militia and the West African ECOMOG forces,
this was clearly inadequate. The atrocities meted out on civilians
by RUF rebels during the January 1999 attack on Freetown were
just one example of this failure.

As in Liberia, rebels in Sierra Leone regularly abducted children, either to fight in combat or as domestic and sex slaves. According to Save the Children-UK, children constituted about 60
percent of IDPs in Sierra Leone and as many as 1.8 million children may at some time have been displaced since the outbreak of

the war in 1991—making them extremely vulnerable.[28] More than five thousand parents reported their children missing just in the wake of the rebel attack on Freetown in January 1999.

Since the end of Sierra Leone's civil war in 2002 and the subsequent resettlement of hundreds of thousands of IDPs, the country has started to recover from more than a decade of trauma and devastation. The RUF was officially disarmed, and a UN-mandated Special Court indicted several people for war crimes, including Charles Taylor. The UN peacekeeping force, UNAMSIL, finally withdrew at the end of 2005 after successfully contributing to the restoration of peace and security in the country.

Yet the overall situation remains fragile and challenges remain to ensure the consolidation of state authority and maintain security throughout the country, particularly in border areas. Economic recovery has been very limited, with poverty, high unemployment, and continuing corruption and mismanagement within the government all presenting urgent challenges. Frustration, especially among young demobilized fighters who lack sustainable reintegration opportunities, constitutes a major risk to continuing stability, more so in light of reports of continuing cross-border flows of diamonds, arms, and mercenaries. And while many of the egregious human rights violations that caused or resulted from the civil war are no longer taking place, there is still not a general culture of respect for basic human rights. While the Truth and Reconciliation Commission completed its mandate in 2004, the government has yet to prepare a comprehensive action plan for implementing the recommendations.

In Guinea, IDPs to a large extent integrated with resident populations. As was the case with many Sierra Leonean and Liberian refugees displaced by the fighting in Guinea, it became apparent that Guinean IDPs also suffered human rights abuses during flight. According to an Amnesty International report published in 2001, Guinean civilians were killed, beaten, raped, and abducted by armed political groups, including the RUF, in cross-border attacks from Sierra Leone.[29] Women and children, estimated by the United Nations to make up 60 percent of the IDP population, have been at particular risk.

While large numbers of Guinean IDPs are believed to have returned to their homes by late 2002, there is scant data on the scope of the country's displacement crisis. The last official IDP total was eighty-two thousand according to a government census in 2002. The continuous movement of populations in the border areas and confusion about the categorization of IDPs, refugees, and Guineans returning from neighboring countries has complicated efforts to identify the internally displaced as a group with particular needs and vulnerabilities.[30]

Protection needs remain acute amid growing concern over ethnic tensions and tensions between refugees and host communities in the Forest Region—both worsened by a steadily declining economy. Border areas remain highly volatile, with an abundance of small arms and roaming fighters from Guinea as well as Liberia and Sierra Leone ready for recruitment by the highest bidder. This has also increased the risk of forced recruitment of children, sexual and gender-based violence against women and children, rising levels of crime and armed banditry, and increased levels of HIV/AIDS. Deteriorating security in Liberia or Côte d'Ivoire or both, with the resulting population movements, would further impact on the situation in Guinea.

Throughout the crisis in Côte d'Ivoire, IDPs have been particularly vulnerable to serious and widespread human rights abuses committed by both government and rebel militia and youth groups, mostly with impunity.[31] There have been continuing reports of attacks against civilians in general by all parties to the conflict—including killings, disappearances, torture, and destruction. Extortion and racketeering are rampant throughout the country. Sexual and gender-based violence, particularly against displaced women and girls, is of major concern. Repeated displacement and lack of access to education has resulted in rising levels of prostitution and domestic slavery. Sexual exploitation of displaced girls by the "impartial forces" (covering both UNOCI and French peacekeepers) has also been reported by humanitarian agencies in Côte d'Ivoire. More than one reliable source has given detailed information about the "procurement" of displaced girls for sex by peacekeeping troops, including inside IDP centers.

Due to the ongoing inflammation of ethnic and religious tensions, displaced Ivorians have been particularly vulnerable to abuse at the hands of armed fighters as well as local communities, particularly in the cocoa-rich western region. There, UNOCI's Human Rights Division reports constant intercommunity clashes and displacements, particularly where IDPs no longer have access to their plantations. Militant youth groups continue to be particularly active between Guiglo and Blolequin, toward the Liberian border.

Important protection issues have also been raised by the premature return of IDPs to their areas of residence in the western region. Although landowners have in some cases encouraged the return of IDPs to prepare for the start of the agricultural season, local populations have reportedly been alarmed and frightened by the return of "non-native" settlers. Likewise, some IDPs are unwilling to return before disarmament takes place. In some cases where return has been encouraged, for example by the UN's pilot return project in the village of Fengolo, returnees have found their plantations occupied, resulting in dangerous intercommunity tensions and urgent calls for local peace and reconciliation work.[32]

As a result, some communities are effectively stuck in a situation of internal displacement: for example, many ethnic Baoulé, from the northern town of Bouaké, displaced in Yamoussoukro are unwilling or unable to return home because of security fears. Without access to employment, IDPs have thus become particularly vulnerable to recruitment by both government and rebel forces. In the rebel Forces Nouvelles areas, for example around the northwestern town of Man, child soldiers (including girls) are widely in evidence particularly at checkpoints.

In Abidjan, the government policy of destroying shantytowns housing largely West African immigrants who were perceived to support the rebellion—at its height in late 2002—has left an estimated 120,000 IDPs in the city, many of them in an extremely precarious state. With ethnic tensions never far from the surface, immigrants, northern Ivorians, and Muslims—including the many internally displaced—remain particularly vulnerable to attacks by pro-government militia that are active in many areas of the city.

In an unprecedented move, the UN Security Council imposed sanctions in February 2006 against three Ivorian political figures it considered guilty of a range of serious human rights abuses and who constituted "a threat to the peace and reconciliation process in Cote d'Ivoire." These included two leaders of the Young Patriots, a pro-government militia, as well as a rebel leader. The decision to impose the travel ban and freeze the assets of the three individuals finally came after several days of orchestrated violence against UN peacekeepers and humanitarian offices in January—incited largely by pro-government militia—that forced the retreat of hundreds of troops and civilian staff, and caused millions of dollars worth of damage.

CHRONIC HUMANITARIAN CRISIS

The repeated cycle of violence and displacement in West Africa over the past seventeen years has held the already impoverished region in the grip of permanent humanitarian and human rights crisis that has been largely hidden from the outside world.

Throughout Liberia's conflict humanitarian access to the interior of the country was extremely limited, and the numbers and needs of displaced people often guesswork.

As humanitarian access gradually improved with the deployment of UNMIL troops from late 2003, the scale of the crisis became apparent.

While the United Nations reported in late 2005 that around 80 percent of all IDPs who had returned may have actually stayed in their areas of return, due in part to the increasing absorption capacity of communities, there is still clearly a serious lack of basic services and infrastructure in key areas of return—such as northwestern Lofa county which was once home to many of Liberia's IDPs and which was almost entirely devastated in the war. Almost two-thirds of communities in Liberia do not have adequate shelter. The health care system throughout the country remains in emergency phase, with agencies and NGOs implementing more than 90 percent of health service delivery as of early 2006. More than 75 percent of the population has no access to referral care services such as essential and emergency obstetric care, resulting in some of the highest infant and maternal mortality rates in the world. The lack of water and sanitation facilities is a matter for serious concern: less than 10 percent of the rural population is estimated to have access to safe water, resulting in various water-borne diseases.[33]

Liberia is also one of the most food insecure countries in the world, with less than 10 percent of arable land being cultivated. This is attributable to a number of factors, including the continued disruption of agricultural systems due to the displacement of farming communities, limited access to food due to the absence of market mechanisms, high unemployment and lack of economic opportunities, socioeconomic dislocation and the breakdown of family and community coping mechanisms, especially among IDPs who have been displaced, in some cases, up to seven times since April 1999. Childhood malnutrition in particular remains high, with 39 percent of children under the age of five stunted.[34]

The humanitarian situation of IDPs remaining in camps has also continued to be grim. With the official IDP return process expected to end in April 2006, many camps have been closed, the huts demolished, and services such as health posts largely reduced. According to some NGOs, the conditions in the remaining camps—including those officially closed but still housing thousands of unregistered IDPs (i.e., those without a valid food ration card)—are deplorable. Not only have service providers been pulling out of the camps, partly due to lack of funding, but landowners have in some cases been stripping the camps of water pipes and other infrastructure. Shelters are in a state of collapse, and water and sanitation facilities are seriously lacking. The absence of a clear plan for the consolidation and integration of IDPs who for various reasons do not wish to return has exacerbated the situation. Reasons cited include inadequate return packages and lack of transport, continuing security fears, and lack of infrastructure and services in home areas.

In Sierra Leone, almost 250,000 IDPs were resettled in their areas of origin by the end of 2002, officially ending the internal displacement crisis in the country and further consolidating recovery after more than a decade of devastating civil war. But many IDPs returned to areas with no basic infrastructure or social services in place, creating acute humanitarian needs and causing some resettlers to drift back to urban areas. Resettlement assistance was only provided for registered IDPs, not for the many

thousands who were either unregistered or who did not wish to
be resettled for various reasons, including security fears. Homelessness in the capital, Freetown, has become a serious problem.

While the agriculture sector has been recovering since the end
of the conflict in 2002, with food production gradually moving
towards prewar levels, food security is still weak, particularly in
eastern and southern areas to where many IDPs returned. WFP
food aid for vulnerable populations is still required. Access to
food is restricted in many cases by high prices, rampant unemployment, and overall lack of economic opportunity, as well as
poor infrastructure. Major rehabilitation of the education and
health care sectors is also still needed.

The humanitarian situation of IDPs in Guinea remains fragile
almost six years after the height of the fighting. While some emergency assistance was provided at the time of the conflict, longer-
term needs have generally been neglected. There has been no
assessment of the current needs of IDPs in Guinea, and no assistance with return and reintegration. The situation has been further blurred by the fact that most IDPs took refuge with
overburdened host communities in urban districts.[35]

Fighting in the border areas of Guinea's Forest Region caused
major destruction in towns such as Guéckédou and Macenta,
where 90 percent of destroyed homes and public buildings still
need to be rebuilt or repaired.[36] In Guéckédou, at least 25–30
percent of returned IDPs are in need of food and shelter assistance. While some returnees have been able to resume agricultural activities, the majority lack the necessary seeds and tools.
Host communities have borne the brunt of assisting the IDPs, putting an enormous strain on already limited school and health care
facilities and resulting in food shortages and increased morbidity.
Overall living conditions and coping mechanisms have steadily
eroded as economic conditions continue to worsen.

In rural areas, access to arable land is still limited and the
United Nations has reported that some 90 percent of the population is suffering from hunger and malnutrition. One in three
households is reported to be confronted with severe malnutrition, with children under five and pregnant and lactating women
most affected. The nutritional situation has deteriorated considerably and is most worrying in the Forest Region. Lack of access

to basic health and water services, poor hygiene, as well as precarious living conditions have contributed to malnutrition as well as to the reemergence of diseases such as polio, yellow fever, and cholera. Most IDPs willing to return to their areas of origin, or to integrate into their areas of displacement, need assistance with protection, return and reintegration packages, including access to arable land, agricultural inputs, basic health, water and sanitation, and education services, according to the United Nations.

Since the onset of Côte d'Ivoire's crisis in 2002, IDPs have generally been neglected and in an extremely vulnerable situation. Less than ten thousand IDPs live in established camps or centers; approximately eight hundred thousand are estimated to be effectively hidden in desperately overburdened host communities.

The humanitarian situation of IDPs and other vulnerable groups is particularly fragile in the north and west of the country where basic social services are poor if not nonexistent. The main issues for concern include the lack of potable water, food insecurity, and lack of access to health services and to education. Malnutrition rates remain high, particularly among children under five. Waterborne diseases are rife and curable diseases have been on the increase, while the HIV/AIDS prevalence rate has reached at least 7 percent—the highest in West Africa—which may increase further in the event of renewed population displacements. At the same time access to health care is extremely poor—for IDPs and other vulnerable groups alike—with some six hundred thousand people in the western region lacking access, according to international NGOs.

In rebel-held areas, many schools have not been functioning since the outbreak of the crisis in 2002, not least because large numbers of teachers (and other civil servants) remain displaced in major towns in the south. In the northwestern town of Man— which hosts an unknown number of IDPs (although substantially less than southern towns)—the nonfunctioning of schools has been an overriding concern of both residents and humanitarian agencies. The United Nations estimates that in Côte d'Ivoire more than seven hundred thousand children, mostly girls, have been denied access to primary education since 2002 due to a lack of teachers and worsening living conditions. However, in February 2006 the interim government announced a new plan to restore schooling in the northern half of the country that could pave the way for more than ninety thousand students to sit key exams within a matter of months or even weeks.

In the economic capital Abidjan, an estimated 120,000 vulnerable IDPs are living an extremely precarious existence, many of them in shantytowns housing West African immigrants as well as Ivorians of predominantly northern ethnic groups. With the destruction of many shantytowns in Abidjan by government forces and their allied militia in 2002–2003, the arrival of new IDPs added to the burden of residents in making ends meet. Yet with the exception of some immediate, albeit ad hoc, emergency assistance by various agencies in the aftermath of shantytown destruction, the longer-term humanitarian needs of the urban displaced in these areas have been completely overlooked.

Clearly, the lack of information on the numbers, locations, and needs of the displaced has been a fundamental obstacle to an effective response. Ongoing low-level displacement together with small-scale spontaneous return has made existing estimates less and less precise. A UNFPA-funded IDP survey, carried out in five key areas in the government zone in late 2005, was expected to provide a clearer picture of IDPs' numbers, locations, and needs.

Constrained Response

Despite, or because of, the fact that the issue of internal displacement in West Africa presents a humanitarian challenge of enormous proportions, the response has on the whole been entirely inadequate. The responses in all four countries share some common constraints: weak or nonexistent national response capacities; endemic insecurity resulting in limited humanitarian access; an acute lack of funding for humanitarian programs; and weak if not chaotic "coordination," often entailing fierce turf battles between humanitarian and political imperatives. Liberia, Sierra Leone, and Côte d'Ivoire have all had peacekeeping missions that hindered at least as much as helped humanitarian response. Failures in disarmament, demobilization, and reintegration (DDR) programs, most strikingly in Liberia, have contributed to continuing instability and renewed displacement. Elections in Liberia and Sierra Leone (as well as Côte d'Ivoire) are effectively the last item in what the International Crisis Group aptly describes as an "operational checklist" of peace building, which in the absence of long-term commitment by the international community will help ensure that these countries will remain "vulnerable to new fighting and state failure."[37]

Liberia

The October 2005 elections provided the first essential step toward restoring Liberia's credibility internationally after years of pariah status. Liberia's international isolation reached its depths during the rule of Charles Taylor, who fled into exile in Nigeria in August 2003, but who in March 2006 was finally brought before the UN Special Court in Sierra Leone to face prosecution for war crimes.

A UN sanctions regime, banning the sale or supply of arms, diamonds, and timber, as well as travel, was again renewed by the Security Council at the end of 2005, on the basis that the situation in Liberia continued to constitute a threat to international peace and security. At the same time donor support to humanitarian assistance in Liberia has been extremely low—notwithstanding the departure of Charles Taylor in 2003—largely as a result of rampant corruption within the transitional government.

Donors have therefore been encouraged by the government's endorsement, in September 2005, of the Governance and Economic Management Assistance Program (GEMAP) that aims to stamp out corruption and achieve financial accountability by placing foreign experts in key administrative positions. The United Nations also welcomed the adoption of the GEMAP agreement, saying it carried "much promise" in addressing the problems that have in the past hampered donor funding.

The previous National Transitional Government of Liberia did not have the financial or technical resources to fulfill its primary responsibilities for IDP protection and assistance. While hopes may be high that the new government will usher in a new era of positive change, it is clear that at present the national agency responsible for coordinating assistance to IDPs—the Liberia Refugee Repatriation and Resettlement Commission (LRRRC)—

continues to be hampered by a serious lack of capacity and resources.

Given the previous transitional government's incapacity, as well as the overwhelming humanitarian needs in Liberia—and within that the magnitude of internal displacement—there has been a relatively huge international presence, bringing with it confusing and sometimes highly divisive coordination mechanisms.

The UN Mission in Liberia (UNMIL)—with almost fifteen thousand troops one of the largest peacekeeping missions in the world—is headed by a Special Representative of the Secretary-General (SRSG) supported by two deputies who include the Humanitarian Coordinator. A key concern, particularly among international NGOs in Liberia, has been the fact that the SRSG effectively manages not only the UN Humanitarian Coordinator but also all the UNMIL military contingents, raising fears that humanitarian mandates take second place to political and military ones.

International NGOs in Liberia have consistently voiced concerns that humanitarian coordination, particularly of the return process, has been politically driven by UNMIL. The UN's desire for a "success story" ahead of October 2005 elections in Liberia, they have claimed, has been the main reason for what they see as a rushed and poorly planned reintegration process. They have argued that the necessary safeguards of voluntariness, the availability of full and objective information, and the declaration of return areas as safe based on an objective assessment, all risked being jeopardized. A dire lack of services as well as continuing protection concerns in areas of return has reportedly resulted in IDPs returning to the camps, or creating new settlements near Monrovia, according to NGOs.

However, the year 2005 also saw some significant humanitarian reforms aimed at strengthening IDP response at the international level, including the assignment of clear responsibilities to lead organizations in various sectors, with a priority in relation to the protection and care of IDPs. UNHCR's new role as lead agency responsible for camp management, emergency shelter, and protection—in three pilot countries, including Liberia—was largely welcomed by UN agencies and NGOs, despite a number of unresolved issues including that of additional funding and resources.

A national policy framework—the Results-Focused Transitional Framework (RFTF)—was adopted by the international community and the transitional government in 2004, designed to address all aspects of Liberia's rehabilitation, including IDP and refugee return. At the end of 2004 both humanitarian and targeted transitional needs were integrated into the RFTF Humanitarian Appeal. However, donor reluctance to continue supporting reconstruction activities in view of government corruption— resulting eventually in the endorsement of GEMAP—also threatened the release of funds for urgent humanitarian activities. The United Nations therefore issued a consolidated appeal for 2006, requesting $121 million to address priority humanitarian needs, which was seen as a more effective way of ensuring sustained donor support. The term of the RFTF is due to end in March 2006, while discussions have been underway on the launch of a Common Country Assessment/UN Development Assistance Framework (CCA/UNDAF) process as well as an interim Poverty Reduction Strategy Paper during 2006.

Pending the full development of the CCA/UNDAF, and with the official return program of registered IDPs expected to be completed in April 2006, UNDP, UNHCR, UNICEF, and WFP have established a Joint Action Plan for Community Based Recovery (2006–2007). This provides a framework for a collaborative response to the reintegration of displaced populations in Liberia—targeting community-based projects aimed at the restoration of basic services, protection, productive livelihoods, shelter, and community infrastructures. The action plan also supports national institutions to progressively take the lead in directing the recovery process.

Sierra Leone

While some hailed Sierra Leone's resettlement process as a success story in which the wishes of internally displaced people themselves prevailed, others insisted it was a highly flawed and politically driven process.

President Ahmad Tejan Kabbah first took office in 1996 in wartime elections, was toppled in a military coup one year later, and was subsequently reinstated with help from West African peace-keepers and British troops. At the beginning of 2002, with a large UN mission deployed across the country and disarmament completed, Kabbah declared the war to be officially over—just four months ahead of presidential elections that won him another five-year term in office. By this time resettlement was proceeding at full speed. Displaced Sierra Leoneans were resettled in accordance with the national government's resettlement strategy, which applied to IDPs as well as refugees and ex-combatants with their dependants, and was meant to apply only when resettlement areas were "sufficiently safe to allow for the return of displaced people in safety and dignity." UNHCR was one of numerous agencies that helped to plan and implement the strategy, aiming to harmonize the resettlement of refugees and IDPs. Both groups were offered resettlement packages, which included a two-month food ration, household utensils, plastic sheeting, and, in some cases, transportation. Some 220,000 registered IDPs were resettled in several phases in 2001 and 2002. Many more returned home spontaneously. Officially, at least, this left no more IDPs in Sierra Leone.

Not surprisingly, the resettlement process raised some thorny issues—all of which may be applied to the ongoing process in Liberia. Firstly, nobody could be sure of the real number of IDPs in the country since during a decade of conflict there were always large numbers of unregistered IDPs. Only registered IDPs were eligible for assistance in the camps and for resettlement packages. With registration itself often unreliable, it was reasonable to assume that there was still an unknown number of IDPs who were not recognized and would not be assisted to return home.

Secondly, there were also many IDPs who did not wish to be resettled for various reasons. Some were traumatized, some had security fears related to their areas of origin, some had lost their coping mechanisms and had become dependent on camp life, while others were unwilling to return to areas where they knew there was a lack of infrastructure and basic services. Many had become urbanized in Freetown, adding to a growing problem of homelessness. NGO sources in Sierra Leone privately reported that about ten to twenty thousand "unofficial" IDPs remained, mostly in urban areas. Since one of the principles of the government's resettlement strategy was to discourage dependency on humanitarian aid and prolonged displacement when areas of return were declared safe, there was little if any assistance available for "residual" IDPs.

Another contentious issue was that some IDPs may have been resettled to unsafe areas. The declaration of areas as "safe for resettlement"—the main factor in effectively ending displacement—was based on a number of criteria spelled out in the government's resettlement strategy. These criteria included the complete absence of hostilities, unhindered and safe access of humanitarian workers, and sizeable spontaneous return movements. While the entire country was eventually declared safe for resettlement, concern was expressed in some cases that certain areas were prematurely classified as safe, or that established criteria were not properly applied, especially in light of the volatile situation in Liberia. The downsizing and eventual withdrawal of the UN peacekeeping force, UNAMSIL, heightened anxieties for some. Allegations were also made that insufficient or even misleading information was given to displaced people about conditions in their areas of origin.

A further cause for concern was that inadequate resettlement packages, combined with a chronic lack of shelter and basic services in areas of return, caused many IDPs to return once again to urban areas. Plans for community rehabilitation programs had in many cases not yet been developed, partly due to insufficient donor funding.

NGOs were among the harshest critics of the government-led resettlement program. MSF claimed that the government, with the United Nations, practically forced people to return—ahead of elections and ahead of the planting season in order to avoid food aid dependence for another agricultural season; that in many cases return could not be described as voluntary because IDPs were not given the information to make an informed decision; that inadequate support during both the transit and rehabilitation phases meant that IDPs were returning in neither safety nor dignity, as required by the UN Guiding Principles on Internal Displacement; and that in some cases resettlement was taking place to areas considered by the United Nations as too dangerous for its own staff.[38] While the United Nations acknowledged that numerous challenges had arisen during the resettlement process, which needed to be urgently addressed, it also said that the MSF report to some extent focused on specific issues out of context, thereby misrepresenting the full reality of the situation. However, various other NGOs were also critical of the enormous security, political, and socioeconomic pressures faced by IDPs in their "voluntary" return home.

The parallels with the current situation in Liberia are stark. Although Sierra Leone's peace has held so far, due partly to continuing UK military support to strengthen the country's armed forces, it remains very shaky—susceptible to both the internal and external pressures outlined earlier. The international community has yet to demonstrate the long-term commitment and investment required to help the government effect sustainable peace-building measures—tackling the endemic problems of corruption, poor governance, weak rule of law, and economic ruin.

Côte d'Ivoire

Côte d'Ivoire is in many respects following on the same path that Sierra Leone and Liberia embarked upon several years earlier: deployment of peacekeepers, faltering attempts at disarmament, and dogged preparation for elections despite chronic insecurity in various parts of the country. There has as yet been no official IDP return or resettlement program—arguably in part because the vast majority of IDPs are effectively hidden within host communities and there is less political mileage to be won where there are no camps to be emptied and closed, but more importantly because the country is still effectively divided in half with not even a semblance of conditions conducive to return.

The response of the Ivorian government to the IDP problem in the country has been generally weak and inconsistent, since at both the policy and operational levels there is little knowledge or experience in tackling humanitarian crises in general. There is no central government coordination mechanism for humanitarian response and no state body with overall responsibility for IDPs. While there is a Ministry of War Victims (Ministère des Victimes, des Déplacés et Exilés de Guerre) this has been preoccupied with seeking compensation for all victims of the conflict, and has had no real relevance to IDP response.

This situation has been compounded by the continuing absence of local administration and social service workers from many parts of the country, particularly the rebel-held north as well as insecure areas of government-held territory in the west. Although some efforts have been made to reestablish state administration, principally through the Comité Nationale de la Redéploiement de l'Administration, the lack of services combined with a deteriorating humanitarian situation remains of major concern. Humanitarian organizations have therefore been working directly with various government institutions aiming to complement their work, but in many cases effectively substituting for them.

At the local level, crisis committees (*comités de crises*) are responsible for registering IDPs and for coordinating and managing humanitarian aid mobilized at the national level—but this has been inconsistent and generally poorly managed, according to international agencies in the country. And in areas under the control of the rebel Forces Nouvelles, the capacity to deal with the humanitarian needs of vulnerable populations has been even more limited, and access to humanitarian agencies patchy at best.

At the international level, UN response to the humanitarian crisis in Côte d'Ivoire is headed by the Humanitarian Coordinator, who is also the Deputy Special Representative of the UN Secretary-General, and is supported by UN OCHA. The United Nations and humanitarian agencies have faced various constraints in responding to the needs of IDPs in Côte d'Ivoire—the lack of government counterparts, lack of IDP data, restricted access, and funding shortages among them. Coordination issues have also been problematic, not least the tensions between the UN Mission (UNOCI) and NGOs, with many of the latter complaining about the constraints of working alongside a mission that integrates its peacekeeping and humanitarian components. These tensions came to a head following the resumption of hostilities in Côte d'Ivoire in November 2004, when the response of French troops was widely viewed as highly partial, and by association, that of UNOCI as well. With UN peacekeepers perceived to be taking sides in the conflict, and due to the nature of the integrated mission, some NGOs argued it was very difficult to resume activities in the conflict-affected areas and still be seen as impartial and independent humanitarian agencies.[39]

Yet the 2005 UN OCHA initiative of bringing together international humanitarian actors in a Protection and IDP Network with the aim of collecting and acting on protection-related information (with internal displacement just one component of broader protection concerns) may—potentially—make the international response more effective.

Guinea

In Guinea, IDPs have effectively been an invisible problem, and the humanitarian response to them negligible at best, a situation exacerbated by a serious lack of resources. The government of ailing President Lansana Conté—reelected for another seven-year term in December 2003—has been accused of crushing opposition and failing to implement reforms related to rule of law, respect for human rights, and economic recovery. As a result, in 2004 most international donors—including the European Union, the World Bank, and the International Monetary Fund—cut their bilateral cooperation and suspended their activities in the country. This in turn has been used as an excuse by the government for failing to maintain basic social infrastructures and services, and exacerbating the subsistence needs of vulnerable groups such as IDPs, Guinean returnees, and host communities. The United Nations warned this could lead to a humanitarian crisis even in the absence of a war or a natural disaster.[40]

However, 2005 saw a measure of political progress—including the resumption of dialog with the opposition and preparations for municipal elections—that resulted in renewed cooperation by key donors.

Yet various factors continue to hamper effective IDP response in Guinea. The government body with primary responsibility for coordinating humanitarian assistance, including for IDPs, is the Service National pour l'Action Humanitaire (SENAH). Although SENAH is present in all four regions of Guinea, it is limited in both capacity and resources. Other than the immediate emergency response to the 2000–2001 attacks in Guinea's border areas, there has been scant assistance for IDPs, partly due to the lack of data on their numbers and needs. There has to date been no comprehensive vulnerability assessment of the relief and recovery needs of IDPs, returnees, and host communities.

Moreover, Guinea hosted nearly one million refugees for almost ten years, with some sixty thousand refugees from Liberia and Côte d'Ivoire remaining in camps in 2005. The lion's share of humanitarian assistance has been targeted at refugee populations. The 2005 Consolidated Inter-Agency Appeal (CAP) for Guinea requested $39 million to provide assistance to conflict-affected populations, including IDPs, in and around the Forest Region, Haute Guinea, and other areas. While 51 percent of this amount was eventually funded, the majority was for UNHCR programs.

The lack of a proper framework for tackling the protection and assistance needs of IDPs in Guinea is a fundamental issue. In most cases IDPs benefit only incidentally from relief and rehabilitation assistance provided to vulnerable groups in general. This includes improvement of access to health services, water, education, agriculture, food security, and income-generating programs in the Forest Region and Haute Guinea—often implemented by UN agencies and NGOs using funds from their bilateral country programs rather than through the CAP. Yet social indicators among communities hosting IDPs are comparatively lower than those among refugees living in camps, and are continuing to slide ever lower.

As a result of the extreme volatility of Guinea's Forest Region and its strategic importance vis-à-vis its neighbors, the UN Security Council in 2004 recommended the inclusion of Guinea in all regional strategies aimed at stabilizing the subregion. The UN Office in West Africa (UNOWA) subsequently established a task force to prepare a regional strategy that aims to synergize UN initiatives related to human rights violations, small arms trafficking, DDR issues, and the humanitarian situation of vulnerable groups in conflict-affected countries—effectively a region-wide integrated protection strategy.

WHAT NEXT?

The constrained and largely ineffective humanitarian response to internal displacement in West Africa, coupled with tenuous and shortsighted peace-building efforts over the past seventeen years, have contributed not only to a persistent and worsening humanitarian and human rights crisis, but also to the extreme volatility of the region.

So what can be done? History has clearly shown that incomplete and ineffective DDR processes have contributed to the cyclical return to war and displacement in the region. For any chance of success in securing lasting peace, UN peacekeeping missions involved in DDR programs must convince fighters that it is worthwhile to hand in their weapons and change their way of life. Crucially, solid reintegration packages must be offered, with opportunities for vocational training, access to education, and jobs. Sufficient donor funding must be made available for this. Politically driven agendas of UN missions—with their often artificial deadlines not only for DDR but also for IDP and refugee return, and in many cases for elections—must be coldly reviewed in the light of their disastrous legacy of failure. IDP return and resettlement programs cannot succeed until they can be carried out in conditions of safety, dignity, and sustainability, as required by the UN Guiding Principles on Internal Displacement. Holding elections before peace has been achieved has also been proven on more than one occasion to be a recipe for disaster. Quick-fix solutions such as these, based on accelerated "reform" programs, have achieved, at best, hollow democracies prone to collapse. In short, in order to achieve sustainable peace-building measures that tackle West Africa's endemic problems of corruption, poor governance, weak rule of law, and economic ruin, the international community must be willing to provide the necessary long-term engagement and investment.

To focus specifically on the humanitarian response to situations of internal displacement, the "collaborative response" system developed by the international community has also been strikingly inadequate, particularly in a region such as West Africa where the patterns of displacement are particularly complex and are interrelated in several countries. Inherent weaknesses in this system have included lack of leadership and accountability, the reluctance of UN agencies to divert resources from their core mandates, and the failure of donor governments to provide coherent political and sufficient financial backing vis-à-vis UN agencies and host governments.

However, the new "cluster" approach—by clearly assigning responsibility to individual agencies for ensuring a timely and comprehensive response in sectors where major gaps have been identified—aims to ensure more accountability and predictability, and could therefore address at least some of these issues. The expanded mandate assumed by UNHCR in 2006—taking a lead role for IDP camp management, emergency shelter, and protection (with UNDP becoming the "cluster lead" for early recovery)—effectively marks the first time the refugee agency has accepted global responsibility for key areas of IDP protection and assistance.

Yet while the "cluster" approach may—if properly implemented—lead to fundamental change within the current response system, it is not a panacea for all its weaknesses. Further important measures must still be taken toward improving accountability, enhancing agency commitment, strengthening leadership and capacity, mobilizing donor support, developing the role of the Inter-Agency Internal Displacement Division, and strengthening NGO involvement.

Lack of accountability has been a particular weakness of the collaborative response. Although Resident/Humanitarian Coordinators (HC) have primary responsibility under the inter-agency IDP policy to develop and implement a comprehensive response plan, this often fails to happen—and in the absence of specific reporting mechanisms, this failure is without consequence. Although HCs are required to report to the Emergency Relief Coordinator (ERC), this link is often weak and their loyalty and reporting is primarily directed to their respective agency headquarters. In integrated missions there is yet another reporting line to the Special Representative of the Secretary-General (SRSG). This has caused controversy, especially in Liberia and Côte d'Ivoire, where the respective HCs are also deputies to the SRSG, and where NGOs in particular have criticized the perceived primacy of political mandates over humanitarian ones.

The reporting line to the supervisor most relevant for IDP response, the ERC, has generally been the weakest. But much may also depend on the particular personalities and performance of individual HCs, and it is for this reason, arguably, that the same integrated mission structure has been somewhat smoother and less controversial in Sierra Leone, where the HC during the immediate post-conflict recovery phase was widely praised.

The "cluster" approach has the potential to address some—but not all—of these concerns. In order to further strengthen accountability, and achieve a better level of consistency, the ERC should be requested to report to the IASC on the progress made with regard to implementing the revised IDP policy package adopted in September 2004.[41] Similarly, Resident and Humanitarian Coordinators should be required by their terms of reference to regularly report to the ERC on their efforts to develop and implement an IDP action plan. The action plan should be developed in consultation with NGOs and should include clearly defined benchmarks against which progress can be measured. Donors should play a stronger role in monitoring the implementation of action plans. In addition, there should be procedures in place providing for the regular evaluation of the HCs by the ERC. Such checks and balances may greatly have helped the situation in Liberia, for example, where the IDP action plan formulated in November 2004 never became much more than a statement of intent.

The new "cluster" approach may also go far in bolstering agency commitment to the collaborative response, which in practice has often been undermined by competition for influence, visibility, and funding. Agencies in the field may not even be fully aware of the new policy package agreed at headquarters level. Citing budgetary constraints and other obstacles, agencies in many situations are reluctant to take on IDP-related responsibilities not strictly falling under their core mandates. This adds to the inconsistency and unpredictability of IDP response, and leads to important protection and assistance gaps. This is particularly evident in Guinea, where a multitude of excuses have been used by agencies for the lack of specific IDP response.

IASC members should formally integrate the new policy package in their agency policy and operational documents, and ensure that all relevant field personnel are familiar with the policy.

Relevant agencies should clarify their policies with regard to their involvement in addressing situations of internal displacement so as to ensure predictability in their responses.

Another crucial issue within the collaborative response that needs to be urgently addressed is that of strengthening leadership and capacity. While resident/humanitarian coordinators are assigned a key role in developing a comprehensive and systematic response to internal displacement at the country level, they often are not fully aware of their IDP-related responsibilities, do not have the necessary background and support capacity to carry out this function adequately, or are limited in their interest in IDP issues, in particular where IDP protection conflicts with their other responsibilities. In many emergencies, the UN Resident Coordinator, often the head of the UNDP country office, is designated Humanitarian Coordinator (as is currently the case in Liberia, Côte d'Ivoire, Guinea, and Sierra Leone) although he or she may have little or no humanitarian background and his or her agency agenda may not be consistent with assuming a proactive role with regard to IDP issues. In Liberia, although the HC/SRSG ultimately responsible for the IDP return program was from UNHCR, the overall lack of capacity and relevant experience particularly within the IDP Unit of UNMIL's Humanitarian Coordination Section was extremely problematic.

The ERC should therefore ensure that only candidates with a strong humanitarian background be recommended and appointed for the position of Humanitarian Coordinator in consultation with the IASC. Candidates from outside the traditional UN environment should be considered where appropriate. The positions of Resident Coordinator and Humanitarian Coordinator should normally be separated, but until such a policy is adopted by the United Nations, measures should be put in place, in particular by UNDP and other agencies, to improve selection processes and ensure that all resident coordinators are properly trained and equipped to deal with situations of internal displacement, both during an emergency and in the post-emergency phase. As a rule, HCs should be supported by a long-term senior IDP adviser in humanitarian emergency situations involving IDPs. The IDP adviser should normally report directly to the HC and should be tasked with assisting to develop and implement an IDP strategy and action plan. Although this was the case in Côte d'Ivoire, there has been a lack of continuity in the position of IDP adviser, which has contributed to limited knowledge among agencies of the IDP strategy and action plan, and even more limited implementation.

In early 2006, various reforms aimed at strengthening the Humanitarian Coordinator system were being discussed by the Inter-Agency Standing Committee, including the creation of a pool of appropriately qualified HCs. At the same time, HCs were granted access to immediate funding through the new UN Central Emergency Fund, enabling them, in theory at least, to respond quickly and more predictably to emergency situations.

Indeed, the mobilization of sufficient donor support is critical to the success of the collaborative response, and within that to the success of the "cluster" approach. Although most donor governments have committed themselves publicly to the collaborative response, several donors are reluctant to put their full weight behind it and the donor community in effect remains split on the issue. Donors rarely provide political backing for coordination mechanisms or hold agencies accountable for uncooperative behavior.

Those donor governments that have not yet done so should develop IDP policy documents highlighting the vulnerabilities and specific protection and assistance needs many IDPs have. Such policies should also include a clear commitment to supporting IDP-related coordination mechanisms. Donor governments should ensure that these commitments are actually translated into political backing for the collaborative response at the country level. The "Good Humanitarian Donorship"[42] initiative that aims to enhance donor accountability by ensuring that the responses of donor governments are effective, equitable, and consistent with humanitarian principles—and which has been piloted in the Democratic Republic of Congo and Burundi—could be adapted to the West African context.

Donors should also ensure a coordinated approach with regard to using their influence as members of agency governing boards with regard to holding agencies accountable for complying with their IDP-related responsibilities, including those under the inter-agency IDP policy.

In the chronically neglected West African region, such donor support could be mobilized through a high-level advocacy campaign led by the ERC, perhaps together with the head of UNHCR. The current ERC, Jan Egeland, whose influence yielded results in northern Uganda and Sudan among others, has yet to focus similar attention on West Africa.

In addition, the Inter-Agency Internal Displacement Division (IDD) has an important role to play in supporting country teams with regard to developing and implementing IDP strategies and action plans. The IDD should continue to develop this role, complementing and supporting field-based IDP advisers. Although Liberia is one of the IDD's chosen priority countries, any impact of this has been limited. The IDD would be the first to admit that the IDP Action Plan it helped to develop in November 2004 was never implemented for many of the aforementioned reasons, which is why overall IDP response in Liberia has been so poor. While the IDD recently developed a "watching brief" for Côte d'Ivoire, it has largely focused on Liberia in isolation. Clearly it is important to at least take into consideration the regional aspects of both the causes and consequences of internal displacement in the country, and for response plans to be adapted accordingly, particularly with regard to IDP return in volatile border areas. Furthermore, the ERC, IASC members, and donors should support the IDD in monitoring the collaborative response and promoting the policy package among all relevant actors at headquarters and in the field.

Lastly, the involvement of NGOs in UN-led coordination structures should be strengthened. Although NGOs make a significant contribution to the response to internal displacement in many countries, they are in many cases not invited to participate in the country team and thus remain outside IDP-relevant coordination structures (a particular bone of contention, again, in Liberia). It is therefore important to involve NGOs in the country teams where this is not yet the case. And NGOs themselves should play a more active role in monitoring and implementing the collaborative response.

Critics of the collaborative response may be dismissive of sticking with a model that to date has clearly failed. But so far no credible, viable alternative has been proposed either. Recent humanitarian reforms may—if properly implemented—address some of the major weaknesses of the collaborative response. Yet further efforts and sustained commitment are required to improve and strengthen the response system if it is to have any hope of success. In West Africa—where the intertwined conflicts are so complex, the needs so overwhelming, and the overall response so poor—the effort will be almost herculean. Failure, however, would be devastating: massive levels of internal displacement as both a cause and result of perennial conflict, spiraling instability, and ultimately an entire region consigned to being a forgotten emergency.

Part 4
The NGO Perspective

10

Coordination and Collaboration: An NGO View

Charles F. MacCormack

EVENTS OVER THE past fifteen years have produced dramatic changes in the environment for humanitarian response organizations. The number of manmade and natural crises has accelerated to the point where there are two or three major crises—and dozens of lesser catastrophes—every year. The proliferation of wars and civil strife is a result of the end of the Cold War, expanding poverty in some parts of the world, the breakdown of traditional norms, especially among young people, the increasing availability of weapons, increasing population pressures, and migration from the countryside to urban areas. In terms of natural disasters, more and more people are living on more and more marginal lands. Events that would have impacted relatively few people a generation or two ago now affect hundreds of thousands.

This constant and accelerating demand for action has definitely led to improved performance on the part of the international humanitarian community. The need to work together on a regular basis has led to the identification of best practices and the establishment of stronger inter-organizational relationships. There has been significant staff migration among the leading humanitarian organizations, a reflection of the often obvious, and neither surprising nor necessarily sinister, competition among humanitarian organizations. The quality and number of meetings to improve coordination has increased significantly. Having said this, the external environment confronting the humanitarian community continues to become increasingly complex.

One factor that complicated global humanitarian work throughout the 1990s was the proliferation of failed and failing states. Failed states lack effective political, economic, and social institutions. They are not just simple underachievers; instead, they demonstrate an inability to perform such classic state functions as exercising sovereignty over the national territory, providing a common defense, or maintaining law and order. They also are profoundly deficient in such modern state functions as resolving gross inequality, ensuring sound economic performance, and enhancing social welfare. States that are failing eventually become conflict-ridden and are prone to political violence and corruption; they serve as havens for a range of criminal enterprises; and they become hotbeds of instability and refugee flows that can affect societies far beyond their own borders.

Although there are many reasons for the proliferation of failed states, one major factor is that the Cold War structure suppressed many ethnic and other conflicts. With the Cold War's demise these problems reemerged. Consequently, in the 1990s, humanitarian organizations worked much more often in conflict situations. As these conflicts proliferated, so too did the need to allocate money toward post-conflict reconstruction, relief, and conflict prevention, as compared to long-term development. These trends have created a situation whereby emergencies and crises have redirected an ever larger percentage of donor funding away from long-term development efforts. The unfortunate result is that, increasingly, the global humanitarian community's efforts are now geared toward short-term issues, rather than tackling long-term solutions and conflict prevention.

HUMANITARIAN WORK AND THE LESSONS OF THE 1990s

As the 1990s unfolded, so did a series of crises—Somalia, Haiti, Bosnia, Kosovo, East Timor, Congo, and Rwanda—and for various reasons, few in the humanitarian community were good at managing these situations. To begin, we had inadequate plans for the political solutions and the military resources many of these crises required. Humanitarian workers found themselves in recurring hopeless situations. For example, in Rwanda, they pleaded for the French, the Americans, the United Nations—almost anyone—to bring military force to end the genocide. Yet no one was willing. This experience drove home several important lessons.

Lesson One: Security Is Critical

The first was that in violent situations, adequate military support was essential to deliver a humanitarian response. As a result, in the 1990s humanitarian organizations and militaries began to develop more useful rules of engagement. The net effect was greater appreciation for the complexity of contemporary humanitarian operations, for without security there could be no social development, but without social development there could be no long-term security.

Lesson Two: The Need for Coordination

A second lesson the 1990s taught the humanitarian community was the need to work together more effectively. At the beginning of the decade, responsibilities were unclear, with individual UN agencies focused primarily on their own operations, and with every humanitarian agency behaving likewise. No one was in charge. Coordination and planning were poor. Not surprisingly, this was a recipe for confusion, redundancy, and inefficiency. Too much of one thing would get done, but not enough of another. Even though lack of coordination was a major failing, the primary problem was that the sum of all resources to meet humanitarian needs was grossly inadequate.

One major challenge facing the humanitarian response community is that much of the work depends on commitments and priorities from donor nations. Government donors obviously reflect the priorities defined by national political processes. Private donors also often give based on their social, cultural, or religious identities in their home regions. For example, Catholic Relief Services, Church World Service, Lutheran World Relief, and Mennonite Central Committee are partly the mechanisms used by people of particular faiths to express their concern for those in need. Likewise, individuals interested in children, women, the environment, or other focused purposes also support specialized organizations closely aligned with their particular priorities.

On the one hand, this responsiveness to specialized groups serves to mobilize and involve much larger numbers of people in global relief and development than would be the case if these faith-based movements and communities of concern did not exist. In fact, if there were an effort to force organizational consolidation in the field during emergencies, either a great deal of identity group support would be eliminated or concerned people would find some other way to express their commitment. This reality suggests that solutions to inadequate consolidation at the field level must come through communication and coalition building, rather than by trying to force unification at the country level. Additionally, both the scale of major humanitarian initiatives and the complexity of sectoral needs—shelter, water and sanitation, health, protection, and education—create a reality where there is more than enough work to occupy an organizationally diverse humanitarian effort. It is better planning, prior policy development, and improved on-the-ground coordination that is needed, not a consolidation of organizations that, in any case, cannot be achieved.

Although competition, poor coordination, and a lack of overall planning all too often characterized international relief efforts in the 1990s, by the decade's end the humanitarian community had learned more about how to work together more effectively. For example, those who direct the world's major relief organizations now meet together to coordinate their efforts, formulate policies, and craft contingency plans in semiannual meetings. Teleconferences and issues-specific meetings take place throughout the year. As a result, the coordination between humanitarian organizations today is much better than it was a decade ago. Among the UN family of agencies, the creation of DHA (now OCHA) addressed the need for greater coordination. Additionally, InterAction, the coalition of more than 160 U.S.-based relief and development organizations, has significantly increased its efforts to rationalize humanitarian response activities among its members.

Today, roughly two hundred nongovernmental organizations (NGOs) operate in the realm of emergency and crisis response, led by about a dozen very large global families accounting for the bulk of nongovernmental humanitarian relief. Each of these large NGOs functions more like world movements. For example, Save the Children/U.S. has more than twenty-five other Save the Children national counterparts (in Norway, Sweden, Japan, Italy, the United Kingdom, New Zealand, Australia, etc.). We work as a global federation, as do most other principal actors, including the Red Cross, CRS/Caritas, CARE, Oxfam, World Vision, and Doctors Without Borders. Our operations are not insignificant. NGOs account annually for about $4 billion worth of activity, which is an important component of worldwide humanitarian response activities.

The crisis in Darfur, Sudan, illustrates the value of improved inter-agency coordination. The majority of Americans probably had no idea where Darfur was when the area exploded into the single largest humanitarian crisis in the world. Over a million people were "cleansed" and driven from their homes in Darfur in the first three months of 2004; in addition, tens of thousands more were killed, raped, and abused. The situation was critical, yet very few paid attention. For its part, the Sudanese government initially limited news media access and humanitarian assistance to Darfur, which reduced public knowledge of the crisis and any concerted effort to address it. Against this dark backdrop, Save the Children, CARE, and two or three other organizations joined forces. We arranged for journalists to visit, we wrote op-ed pieces, and we engaged the U.S. Congress, the National Security Council, and other foreign policy decision makers. In the end, by focusing attention on the crisis, enough pressure was exerted on the Sudanese government so that they agreed to allow increased humanitarian access to Darfur. Whether the situation will improve permanently or not, the prospects of improvement are better today because major humanitarian agencies worked cooperatively, rather than each agency acting alone.

Although the Darfur crisis clearly illustrates the importance of inter-agency cooperation, learning to cooperate has not been easy, even within a single organization. For example, as mentioned, there are more than twenty-five different autonomous agencies within the Save the Children Alliance alone, all working to develop common strategic plans and coordinated policies around the world. If the challenges of better coordination within a federation like Save the Children are difficult, the challenges of working across federations and with the United Nations (whose many agencies also operate with considerable autonomy) are greater still.

Different national political cultures and government priorities create different strategies among donors and humanitarian agencies. For example, European bilateral donors and nongovernmental organizations tend to be more rights-oriented, more focused on the state as the primary focus for economic and social development, and more inclined to allocate resources toward government ministries in responding to a crisis. Conversely, the U.S. government and its NGOs consider civil society organizations a primary driver of national development, and tend to allocate resources to community and other nongovernmental associations. Additionally, Japanese, Australian, Canadian, and other governmental and NGO donors also bring their own distinct national priorities to their relief and development work.

These national differences can create real difficulties for global organizations such as United Nations' specialized agencies, the International Save the Children Alliance, or the Federation of Red Cross and Red Crescent Societies. In the end, there is no way for representative, large-scale organizations to completely remove themselves from the realities of different national cultures and political views. Each must manage the inevitable tensions that arise from responding to the different priorities of different national constituencies. In spite of the difficulties, most global families have worked diligently and relatively successfully to bridge these differences. Given the polarization that often exists among governments, these efforts on the part of humanitarian nongovernmental organizations to demonstrate multinational strategies are an important contribution to more effective humanitarian response.

Lesson Three: Underlying Political Causes Must Be Addressed

A third lesson the 1990s taught the humanitarian community was that our organizations often needed to have a political, and sometimes military, commitment from governments in order to succeed, especially commitment from the leading states. Bosnia's conflict, for example, was a tragic situation that remained stalemated until there was significant military intervention to end the conflict. Other recent humanitarian efforts involving external military forces were Somalia, Kosovo, East Timor, Rwanda, Afghanistan, Darfur, Ivory Coast, Haiti, and Iraq. There is no question that the intertwining of military conflict and humanitarian action is both increasing and likely to mark emergency response for the foreseeable future.

The nongovernmental humanitarian community is divided on if, and when, military intervention is the necessary and appropriate last resort. When such interventions take place, there is also great disagreement on how the humanitarian community should individually and collectively relate to the armed forces. One of the serious challenges the humanitarian community will need to address over the coming years is developing a more coherent approach to armed forces when military and humanitarian efforts are being implemented side by side.

Lesson Four: The Need for Advocacy

Finally, over the past dozen years, we also learned that we needed to engage in advocacy and policy in a significant way—tactics that we have traditionally avoided. This lesson required many humanitarian agencies to rethink their traditional philosophy and means of operation. How can a humanitarian agency work effectively in, say, Bosnia or Darfur, where the root problems are in fact political? You can save lives year after year, yet still make no permanent difference unless you are able to get governments to change their policies. In fact, there were clearly times, such as the early years of the Balkan wars, when political leaders were using humanitarian response as a substitute for needed political and military commitment. So humanitarian organization often had to abandon their traditional doctrine of neutrality and engage in policy advocacy.

At Save the Children, we have three basic criteria by which we do this. First, we seek to leverage the knowledge and credibility gained from operational experience. Unlike think tanks, our credibility comes from the fact that we are actually on the ground, and in many cases we know things that no one else does. Second, we have contacts in the media that pay attention to us, and that we can call upon on the right occasion. We only take this step, however, if we have something to add to what is already known,

and we usually prefer to address issues quietly rather than publicly. Finally, we try to focus our advocacy where we believe we can
make a concrete difference for children and families in need.
There are situations where change is simply not going to take
place or where Save the Children's intervention will not make a
difference.

In a number of ways, then, some critical aspects of humanitarian
relief had improved before the 2001 terrorist attacks. There was
much more cooperation on a global basis, more transnational
problem solving, greater cooperation between NGOs and the
United Nations, and more effective large-scale planning across the
international relief community itself. There was greater recognition of the need to provide security. Political solutions were more
often addressed, and more and more humanitarian organizations
strengthened their advocacy efforts to achieve these goals. However, the horrific events of 9/11—and equally important, the
heightened security reactions to them—have produced even
greater changes in humanitarian work and greater challenges too.

HUMANITARIAN WORK POST-9/11

In terms of changes over the past dozen years, one of the more
significant developments for Save the Children is that we no
longer strive to be completely neutral in all emergency situations.
While not necessarily commenting on foreign policy or political
issues beyond our areas of experience and expertise, we do make
recommendations that can have political implications when the
basic rights of children are severely abused. In the current environment, there are some circumstances that compel us to assume
a more pronounced advocacy position, even if that position runs
contrary to official U.S. government policy. In most instances we
advocate not via press conferences, but rather by working with
our counterparts in Congress, the U.S. Agency for International
Development, and the Department of State. We present our views
to U.S. and other government officials suggesting why existing
policies are not working, and what might be done instead. The
challenge of the American war on terrorism has increased the

need for ongoing problem solving and dialog between humanitarian organizations and the U.S. government.

A second major change has occurred regarding institutions that have historically played minor roles in implementing humanitarian work, namely, the military and private corporations. Traditionally, the military provided security and corporations assisted relief efforts by improving war-torn infrastructure (e.g., dredging harbors and fixing oil wells). Today, however, these roles are sometimes reversed. Private corporations and civilian contractors now provide security, while the armed forces are deployed to help repair schools, immunize infants, and provide nutrition. This development represents a major change in both actors' historic missions and can create potentially large problems for all involved. Using combat troops in humanitarian efforts in Iraq, for example, is a very expensive way to conduct humanitarian relief, and limits the use of Iraqi nationals in such endeavors. Employing civilian contractors to provide security poses its own unique risks. Nevertheless, there is every reason to believe that the contracting out of protection and armed force will continue, and probably expand. The humanitarian community must try to understand and to forge a common response to this new reality.

Besides changes in the operational philosophy of NGOs, and the advent of new humanitarian and security roles for the military and private sector, the post-9/11 era also has presented new challenges to global humanitarian relief workers. Unfortunately, one challenge is simply to avoid becoming targeted as combatants. Historically, humanitarian workers could count on the acceptance of local populations for security, and they worked hard to achieve it. They put thousands of hours into meeting the leaders on all sides of a conflict, explaining what humanitarian organizations did and who they represented. For example, Save the Children stressed the fact that it was an international organization and that our only mission was to help children. In this way, skepticism often gave way to acceptance and offered greater security for our personnel. Since 9/11, however, this strategy no longer provides the security benefits it once did. In Iraq, for example, not only was the Red Cross targeted, but so was the United Nations—both of whom were among the more neutral, independent, and multilateral entities in the country. It did not matter that these agencies were not American nor received any money from the Coalition Provisional Authority; they were targeted nonetheless. The targeting of humanitarian workers represents a significant challenge that has complicated relief efforts in war-torn areas around the world.

A second challenge we face is how to work within increasingly complicated post-9/11 security measures. The Patriot Act and the Office of Foreign Assets Control (OFAC) regulates humanitarian work more today than ever before. To cite just two examples, American humanitarian grants must not be offered to any recipient that has contact with terrorist groups or individuals. NGOs have had to establish an expensive and complex worldwide compliance system in order to respond to these requirements. Nor, without explicit exemption, can they work in any regions or countries that have been prohibited by U.S. law (which includes Iran, North Korea, and nineteen other countries on the OFAC list). The consequences of this prohibition can be unfortunate.

For example, when an earthquake devastated Bam, Iran, Save the Children could not initially offer any aid despite the ample supplies of medicines and tents we had available just two hours away in Pakistan. As with every other complex issue, finding the right balance must be struck between the war on terrorism and the need to engage effectively with humanitarian crises in remote and difficult circumstances.

KEY ELEMENTS IN A SUCCESSFUL HUMANITARIAN MISSION

All humanitarian efforts should involve both the long-term need to establish sustainable political and economic development solutions, as well as emergency operational interventions to meet immediate survival requirements. However, the impact of short-term humanitarian interventions on long-term change is often limited. Such change usually requires favorable geopolitical conditions; positive national-level political, economic, and cultural trends; and sustained, adequate financial support. Needless to say, these variables are often absent in humanitarian crises. Additionally, the capacity of organizations engaged in emergency response to decisively influence these historic conditions is often secondary to larger trends.

However, in the post–World War II cases of Greece, Italy, France, and Korea, in the 1970s and 1980s the humanitarian community helped influence long-term solutions. The same might be said, in the 1970s and 1980s, for countries such as Malaysia, Thailand, Tunisia, Mexico, and Brazil. More recently, the global humanitarian community has rallied around the Millennium Development Goals as a strategic intervention to address the underlying conditions that influence individual crises. Additionally, in the United States, a number of humanitarian organizations have united around the "One" Campaign—an effort to build a more sustainable constituency for addressing basic causes of instability and armed conflict. This Campaign involves celebrities, such as U2 singer Bono, networks of churches and religious groups, and the national volunteers of leading humanitarian organizations.

InterAction, the U.S. coalition of more than 160 international nongovernmental organizations, is coordinating a Campaign Partnership for Global Effectiveness. This effort identifies and disseminates best practices in humanitarian and development assistance. Another collective effort to create long-term solutions to humanitarian crises is the SPHERE Project. This initiative sets standards to improve the long-term impact of humanitarian work.

Humanitarian organizations must, nonetheless, recognize the limited leverage they have in most crisis situations. Governments will make the final decisions. Many governments are suspicious of the efforts of international nongovernmental organizations. The attention of the media, and political leaders, tends to be short-term. The underlying causes of most conflicts run deep. Humanitarian organizations need to maintain a great deal of humility about their ability to decisively influence the larger political, cultural and historic forces that condition so much of their work.

Regarding short-term, lifesaving help during humanitarian crises, however, the work of Save the Children and other organizations is increasingly important and cost-effective. The constant crises of the past dozen years have provided an enormous amount of practical experience, lessons learned, proven staff, and networks of like-minded professionals. The following are some of the characteristics that mark a successful humanitarian action at the operational level.

1. Establish Informal Collaborative Networks

If one reflects on the Somalia crisis in the early 1990s, humanitarian efforts were marked by a lack of coherence, coordination, and cooperation, and a great deal of competition and fragmentation. In the 1990s, things did improve, and by the early part of this decade there were coalitions of NGOs working more closely with the United Nations and bilateral donors to provide assistance. After more than a decade of collective responses to situations such as the crisis in East Timor, Somalia, Bosnia, and Rwanda, humanitarian professionals learned who to work with and how to cooperate.

Additionally, the key leaders of major NGOs now meet regularly to discuss security, advocacy, and program and policy issues. Through these meetings, the level of cooperation has increased. The efforts of InterAction, the Steering Committee on Humanitarian Response, the SPHERE Working Group, and a host of other consultative arrangements between the United Nations, governments, and nongovernmental organizations all establish networks that can be called upon in a crisis situation. Given the fact that humanitarian organizations are largely the manifestation of varied citizen priorities in donor countries, establishing such networks of common understanding and personal confidence are essential to a more effective response on the ground.

2. Draw on Extensive, Worldwide Staff Capabilities

On a more concrete level, the single most important variable in the effectiveness of a humanitarian organization is the quality and experience of its staff. It's the people on the ground and their capabilities, dedication, experience, breadth of knowledge, and commitment that makes all the difference, after which everything else can fall into place. In the absence of experienced and committed staff, all the other capacities of a humanitarian organization will not suffice to bring about significant results on the ground.

Experience demonstrates that capable managerial, sectoral, and logistics staff cannot be assembled from scratch at the beginning of each new crisis. There needs to be a critical mass of staff in a large emergency response who understand the policies, procedures, and systems of the parent organization. It is also essential to have individuals who have in-depth experience with other emergency response situations. An enormous amount of effort and good will are often wasted when inexperienced individuals go through the painful process of learning anew the accepted lessons of the past. Having worked with UN agencies, bilateral donors, host governments, and other humanitarian organizations previously can produce knowledge of the organizational cultures and policies of other members of the humanitarian team on the ground. International agencies and NGOs can normally draw on experienced indigenous staff that are deeply familiar with the language, culture, and political sensitivities of their particular region.

And, while experience and integrity are critical, among the most challenging requirements related to staff excellence is to recruit the staff leadership team that is needed in order to bring about successful programs. It is demanding and difficult to work under the conditions that exist in humanitarian response situations, particularly with the deteriorating security situations in many countries. Humanitarian workers are typically not accompanied by their families, which can lead to feelings of isolation. And, of course, some of the outside activities that give life additional quality and diversity, such as films, theater, or other types of entertainment, are absent, which means that staff are working "24/7," often over extended periods. Simply maintaining one's health can also be a challenge in these situations. An astute leader must be sensitive to the inherent dangers in such stressful conditions and ensure that institutional and peer support mechanisms are in place to maintain staff well-being and effectiveness. The need of humanitarian organizations to both maintain staff continuity and carefully nurture new leaders is enormously important.

3. Build in Long-term Approaches from the Beginning

In is important that a crisis response includes activities with the expectation of a later transition to reconstruction and long-term

development commitments. It is, therefore, essential to implement crisis interventions in a way that strengthens local people,
involves host national organizations, and takes a self-help approach from the very beginning. For example, in most emergency
response situations, Save the Children promotes preventive
health services so that local workers can bring these skills back to
their villages of origin once a political settlement makes such a
return possible.

4. Leverage Modern Technology and Management Systems

There are also all the managerial and technological requirements. Using Darfur as an example: it is a very remote and unde-
veloped area, so to run a large, modern operation in a place that
lacks roads, computers, communications infrastructure, and basic
office supplies and equipment means that it is necessary to build
a complex, large-scale administrative and program operation off
a minimal base, while simultaneously managing millions of dollars of operational activity. In Bam, Iran, site of the 2003 earthquake, Save the Children/U.S. did not have a prior presence, and
most facilities that did exist had been destroyed by the earthquake, requiring the use of, literally, "offices in a box." Without
access to such modern technological resources, it can be irre-
sponsible to send people out to try to carry out humanitarian
work.

5. Actively Address Civil-Military Relations and Staff Security

The militarization of humanitarian response, and the complex
new ways the military has become involved in humanitarian response situations, will need to be tailored on a case-by-case basis.
However, the mechanisms for conducting this dialog definitely
remain underdeveloped. The idea that military support is needed
in certain crises has been long recognized, but there is a consensus in the humanitarian community that this involvement should
focus on providing security and not on the delivery of humanitarian assistance. There are a number of reasons for this assessment—one is to preserve the independence and neutrality of

NGOs, which would provide the protection that is usually afforded to those individuals who are involved in delivering aid. What the humanitarian community wants is to be allowed to do what it does best, and for the military to do what it does best—the military shouldn't be vaccinating children and we shouldn't be driving tanks.

The attacks on the UN compound in Baghdad, in the attack on the Red Cross, the killing of CARE's country director in Iraq—all organizations that were explicitly neutral and which had gone out of their way to communicate with people about their neutrality at the local level—clearly indicate that under current conditions in many areas of conflict, the humanitarian cover does not exist. Now it is possible that humanitarian workers are seen as "the enemy." These trends go far beyond the blurring of military and NGO roles, and emphasize the need to do everything possible to maintain staff security in dangerous times. This requires maintaining, as much as possible, the distinction between combatants and humanitarian workers, but humanitarian workers definitely run greater risks than ever before.

These trends have increased the need for very thorough and professional approaches to staff security on the part of humanitarian organizations. Almost all major NGOs have significantly strengthened their approach to staff safety and security. They have headquarters and field personnel assigned these new responsibilities and have developed global and country-level safety and security plans and policies. Field programs undergo regular consultations and assessments. They conduct simulations of potential safety and security crises as a means of developing and testing our management response procedures. Extensive communications channels and technologies have been made available. Needless to say, all of this is very costly in time and money. Unfortunately, however, the nature of much humanitarian response work now requires such investment if any organization is going to seriously consider itself fully supportive of its staff in the field.

6. Leverage Experience with the Media

Experience with media is another key factor. It is important that the messages going out to the public are consistent, thorough, and helpful, and having staff on hand who are familiar with how the media operates, and who can work together with media representatives on messaging, is critical. The international community now faces dozens of humanitarian crises at any given moment. Without political will and adequate funding, these crises almost always result in chronic problems for affected children and families. Geopolitical factors are a major factor, but the difference between a "forgotten crisis" and one that receives at least the basics of an adequate response is the capacity of humanitarian organizations to assure significant media attention.

Such was the case in Ethiopia in the 1980s, Somalia in the early 1990s, and the Balkans later in the decade. However, the focus of the media usually is on "new," short-term crises. To generate the long-term attention usually needed to resolve a crisis is extremely difficult to achieve. This can sometimes be done through op-ed pieces, special publications, events at the grassroots level, and interviews by returning field staff.

7. Engage in Credible Advocacy

Closely related to managing the media aspects of humanitarian response situations is an organization's credibility with respect to advocacy positions and an ability to articulate the public policy issues that are related to humanitarian crisis situations. Sometimes the crisis is long-term and multinational, such as responding to the HIV/AIDS pandemic, improving the provision of quality education in armed conflict, or directing proven solutions to the tragedy of newborn and child mortality. At other times, the crisis involves country-specific policy or political issues, such as ethnic conflict in Sudan, chronic food insecurity in Ethiopia, or civil unrest in Haiti.

In these and many other situations, both long-term and short-term solutions can only come from mobilizing political support at the local, host national, donor government, and UN levels. Once again, this is most successful when there have been years of relationship building and responsible dialog at every level. It also requires professional staff who know both the substantive issues and the best channels of communications to produce helpful policy outcomes or political solutions. The humanitarian community is not of one mind regarding the best approach to advocacy. Some organizations prefer advocating over a very wide range of issues, often in very public ways. Other organizations identify a relatively select number of policy issues, try to bring significant resources to bear on the problem, and work outside the media limelight to encourage solutions. There is undoubtedly the need for a range of responses, and most humanitarian organizations have recognized that working on long-term policy solutions is a vital component of achieving our humanitarian mission.

8. Global Reach

The ability to communicate and cooperate—in terms of staff recruitment, advocacy, media, fundraising, and networking—not only with home country entities, media, and politicians, but also with such groups on a global basis, is a key factor for success. For Save the Children member organizations, this is where international alliances can really make a difference. Whether it is an immediate crisis like Darfur, Iraq, or Afghanistan, or a longer-term crisis, such as HIV/AIDS, it is important to be able to communicate with publics, for example, in Western Europe, Japan, Canada, and Australia with similar messages, in order to get the job done.

Most of today's major humanitarian crises require a global response; concerted action from major donor nations such as the United States, European Union members, and Japan, UN agencies, relevant regional organizations such as ASEAN, the OAU, or the OAS, and host governments. Both governments and intergovernmental organizations are most likely to be active when their citizens and voters are engaged and when credible recommendations are being provided to decision makers. Therefore, contributing to long-term solutions in situations of complex emergencies requires the orchestration of public communications and advocacy on a global basis.

The diversity of national responses to many of these humanitarian crises, sometimes based on geographic or political factors, often makes the development of a coherent global response to a humanitarian crisis very challenging work indeed. It often requires a willingness to reach compromises on recommendations that might be more or less acceptable to any particular national audience. It is a challenge to pull together a common policy across the barriers of distance, culture, organizational history, and language. There is no question that it takes longer to develop a multi-country strategy and messaging than it would to do this within any single national organization. Nevertheless, forging a common strategy on a global basis is more likely to produce a successful result.

9. Adequate Resources

Most humanitarian efforts are woefully underfunded. UN consolidated appeals are usually under-subscribed. Commitments made by governments at pledging conferences are often not matched by actual disbursement of funds. What funds there are available are predominantly allocated to those crises in the media spotlight or possessing significant geopolitical relevance. Much the same can be said for private fundraising in emergencies. Most individual donors tend to follow those crises that are receiving extensive media coverage. Both governmental and private donors often restrict their contributions for those activities that match some more narrow set of priorities.

It is increasingly important to have adequate resources at least at the tactical and operational level. Given the imperative to provide as much staff security and safety as possible; given the need for reliable communications and technology support in remote and difficult circumstances; given the need to manage vehicles and facilities in situations where maintenance is a major challenge; and given the scale and severity of the problems being addressed, responding to crises in today's world without at least the basic resources needed to get the job begun can be dangerous as well as unprofessional.

Therefore, access to a broad range of both governmental and private donors is essential. It is important to be able to draw on resources from a range of donor governments, hopefully thereby being able to put together the needed range of sectoral and logistical support systems. On the private sector side, corporations, foundations, and individuals each have their particular contributions to make. Given the complexity of many of today's humanitarian crises, this breadth of resource acquisition capability is more and more important. Consequently, in the chronically un-derfunded world of humanitarian action, the need to work to-gether to expand total funding for relief and development remains urgent. In 2006 the United Nations established a Central Emergency Response Fund of $500 million to enable UN agen-cies and their implementing partners to enhance response time and strengthen humanitarian elements especially in under-funded crises.

CONCLUSIONS

The experience of the humanitarian community over the past dozen years has helped clarify what contributes to successful hu-manitarian action. At the macro level, it is crucially important to have supportive national political and economic conditions, a high-priority geopolitical context, and adequate and sustained financial resources. Since these conditions rarely apply, it is equally important to attempt to influence the global, national, and local political context. While acknowledging that humanitar-ian organizations often have only a limited impact on the larger issues affecting our work, a sustained, long-term collective effort to address underlying causes of humanitarian crises, profession-ally implemented, is likely to make a strategic difference in the long run.

In terms of meeting immediate needs, there is a menu of proven capacities to draw upon:

- Established informal collaborative networks
- Worldwide name recognition
- Extensive, worldwide staff capabilities
- Media capacity
- Credible advocacy
- Global reach
- Adequate resources

If adequate resources are allocated there will be continued prog-ress on long-term development. In spite of all the difficulties, the development community will continue to reduce significantly newborn and child mortality over the next twenty years; girls' education will increase, and consequently, more people will enjoy better lives. At the same time, though, the different development levels between regions will likely become more pronounced. Even today, we cannot speak credibly about the "South" or the "underdeveloped world" anymore. East Asia has clearly transcended these categories and other regions will too. China and India, for instance—where fully half of the world's six hundred million poor people reside—will both likely experience a real development breakthrough over the next fifteen to twenty years.

The trends of the 1990s toward better transnational cooperation within and among humanitarian organizations will also expand, and within the next fifty years these global partnerships will become much more institutionalized. These improvements, however, will not occur automatically, but only through a sustained, concerted effort. Although more work needs to be done in improving the delivery of humanitarian assistance, the real challenge is creating the political will to apply the basic lessons that have been learned through decades of hard experience.

11

Being With Them

Lluis Magrinà, S.J.

ETHICAL DILEMMAS ARISE in situations because of inappropriate relationships between Jesuit Refugee Service (JRS) humanitarian workers and the people who have suffered disaster.

APPROPRIATE RELATIONSHIPS

Jesuit Refugee Service is fortunate to have a clear mission statement that defines what is expected of our relationships: "In our work with forced migrants, The Jesuit Refugee Service accompanies many of these brothers and sisters of ours, serving them as companions, advocating their cause in an uncaring world."

Once you come to know the suffering of refugees, a pastoral approach makes sense. Many refugees are in shock. Many carry a deep sense of loss and grief. Many are humiliated, afraid, anxious, depressed, or disoriented. Many feel wronged. They have suffered atrocities—or committed them. Their tension is great. They are people on the alert, skeptical, often suspicious. Family structure is often destroyed. Fathers may still be at war or were killed. Refugee settlements are disease traps. In them there is often overdependency, corruption, injustice, and deceit. Among those suffering loneliness, abandonment, and cramped living conditions, promiscuity is common. Morale and morality are easily lost or abandoned.

Yet one still finds in such miserable settings great determination to keep families together. There is heroic courage and a remarkable readiness to forgive. One act of forgiveness can redeem and save a settlement of twenty thousand people. We have found many reasons to accompany such people—and to delight in doing so. Knowing their suffering, a pastoral approach makes sense.

Jesuit Refugee Service (JRS) Vision

Pastoral service is at the heart of the JRS mission and can be found in the reports and reflections of JRS field workers, for understanding JRS's own style of pastoral service. True, many aspects will seem obvious to those with field experience, but it is important to articulate our shared vision.

In a letter written on his birthday, November 14, 1980, Father Pedro Arrupe, S.J., the Father General of the Society of Jesus (the Jesuits), announced the foundation of JRS, explaining that "the help needed is not only material: in a special way the Society is being called to render a service that is human, pedagogical and spiritual."

In the field, our JRS pastoral role is exercised in three ways: in services that are specifically pastoral, by our presence, and by the witness that gives a pastoral dimension into all that we do. The conditions of flight (which may have been precipitous, exhausting, and either provoked by sudden violence or carefully planned) and the place of asylum (whether in camps, cities, or detention centers) influence the way we choose to witness to the Good News among the refugees. But our accompaniment and service are always pastoral. In JRS we are guided by the mission given to us: "to accompany, serve and plead the cause of the refugees and forcibly displaced people, by our accumulated experience."

ACCOMPANIMENT

Accompaniment is an essential element of our mission and our methodology. To accompany means to be a companion. To accompany others is itself a practical and effective action. Frequently now this is the way protection is provided. Accompanying refugees is a way to "internationalize" a situation. The presence of an international team has been known to prevent attacks on refugees. Moreover, our presence with them can be a sign. When a free person chooses to accompany faithfully those who are not free—who have no choice but to be there—this is itself a sign, a way of eliciting hope.

As pastoral workers we focus on our vision and are not side-tracked by political maneuverings and ethnic divisions, whether among the refugees or among agencies and governments who decide their fate.

What about the humanitarian workers?

Many of us live ordinary lives. We are used to planning what we will do during the day or during the week. This is not the case working with refugees, who constantly bring up urgent new problems. We are called to live ready for the unexpected event and the unexpected guest. Often we live simultaneously in more than one culture, that of the host country and that of the refugees for a start. We may be exposed to shocking events without warning. We are pulled in many directions, experiencing new surprises every day. This introduces a new kind of turbulence into our life. To persevere in refugee work with integrity, a JRS worker needs a strong life of the Spirit.

Hospitality is a key feature in developing a JRS team. It helps to define our way of living and working together, accompanying one another and serving. Certainly we need one another. There is a high risk of loneliness and isolation in refugee work. A centrifugal force pulls at anyone who works with marginalized people, creating a sense of being at the outer edge of the circle, marginalized ourselves. Accompanying refugees together should work to strengthen our companionship.

A DISCERNING TEAM

In the long term, even a strong but individualistic spiritual life is not enough. JRS workers rarely act alone. They need to share what is happening to the refugees and to themselves. Within our JRS structure there is a constant reference to regional, country, and project directors, who are all meant to exercise pastoral care among their team members—and in turn receive care. We aim for solidarity and frequent communication among members of project teams and within country programs. JRS work requires a cycle of discernment that leads to planning, evaluating, and reporting, in the light of our common mission. By reflecting together on our experiences, we have the chance to discern again and add fresh input to our decisions. Reflection and self-criticism helps to prevent us being overwhelmed by the great needs we face. It may also save us from favoritism or "taking sides." By serving all, we become agents of reconciliation. But living such ideals requires the cooperation and fidelity of all.

Discernment is a key element in JRS methodology. This means sifting the reality around us using all of our methods of learning and understanding—our social and political analysis, what we have heard from the people, what we realize is tugging at our hearts. All of this—shared, discussed, and reviewed—can help us know what the Spirit is asking of us. JRS workers are all invited to share the search for faith. If we value one another we will listen to each other, and valuing one another means caring for one another. This does not always happen spontaneously in teams drawn from diverse cultures, ages, and formation patterns. Yet if we want it we will work for it.

FREE FROM DEPENDENCY

How can we accompany the refugees in a way that helps them to stand on their own two feet? The challenge for the pastoral worker is to establish a relationship of mutuality with those we serve. We aim for a relationship that helps displaced people stand free of dependency, especially when an individual has urgent needs. Certainly we can feel effective if we are "loved" by the people. But let us not be deceived. We must not be loved only for the money or goods we bring.

FINDING HOPE OR BRINGING HOPE

Do we bring hope, or do we find it there? The richness of human spirit that we discover among refugees, including a vibrant hope, is always a surprise. Obviously there is sadness in the exile's song. While there may be no rational grounds for believing that what a refugee longs for will actually come about, we may also find hope in his hope. For hope is not optimism. Optimism expects that things will get better. Hope is a virtue grounded in suffering. It is a grace that gives strength. Hope is a promise that takes root in the heart and is a guide to an unknown future. The challenge for the pastoral worker is to search for and find the seeds of hope, to allow them to grow, to fan the feeble spark into a flame. Hope is what enables us to live fully in the present moment. Our role is to help change a refugee camp from something to survive in to a time and place for growth.

Refugees have a message that our world needs to hear. JRS has a mission to help the world learn from the experience of forcibly displaced people. We members of a worldwide community are privileged to make that first step of conversion, through listening to the stories and hopes of the survivors of human conflict.

LISTEN TO THE REFUGEES

Surely the only way to learn about the real needs of refugees is to listen to them. Our biggest temptation on seeing the distress of the refugees in a camp or in a city is to begin projects, to give material things, to decide en masse what the refugees need. They often arrive in exile without shoes, with only one torn shirt, hungry, without a clear plan. But they did not undergo this experience in order to get a shirt or shoes. Their human experience calls for respect. They are traumatized by violence, lonely, rejected, exhausted in body certainly, but also exhausted by losing their place in a stable society—and sometimes feeling guilty about what they did in order to survive. They want to be understood, to be heard. Their frequent question is, Why is God doing this to me? They have a right to ask this question. But it cannot be asked unless someone listens. This is our primary role, to listen to the questions, to the longing, and to the fundamental human need of the refugees.

INFORMATION AND COMMUNICATION

Often we and other voluntary workers are the first and only people whom a refugee can trust after the trauma of flight. They left in fear and live in shock. We have a responsibility not only to listen but also to speak, and to facilitate communication. Refugees need to be informed and to learn the truth. Refugees are so often excluded from decisions concerning their lives. Wherever possible, JRS includes the refugees in our own planning and decision making. Our communication must be transparent.

One of the greatest sufferings of displaced people is losing contact with their dear ones. Great ingenuity is employed in passing messages and in finding out what is happening at home and among loved ones. We do everything possible to open lines of communication and enable refugees to be well informed. Many times this service is reciprocated. They, in return, keep us much better informed.

ACROSS BORDERS

JRS is one of the few agencies that will place itself on both sides of a refugee border. This was the case in Vietnam, Cambodia, El Salvador, Ethiopia, and Rwanda—and now Burundi, Liberia, Sudan, and Angola. When a conflict continues, it is immensely difficult even for us in JRS to maintain open communication across borders. Imagine how difficult it is for the refugees. The border in question may be mined or patrolled. And there may be political obstacles. But there are also sure to be obstacles of the mind: ideological differences, racist prejudices or sheer misinformation. Cross-border communication is one of the most important services we can offer, but it requires a high level of self-awareness, self-criticism, and capacity for analysis. We are often too little aware of our own ideological interpretations and prejudices. It is natural for us, after listening all day to the refugees' stories, to take on their interpretation of events.

FORGIVENESS AND HEALING

Today many people talk about reconciliation—which is not a developed art or ministry but a pioneer field. Possibly the most effective reconciling actions are the unselfconscious ones. Formation for peace can be integrated into our normal services. An agent of reconciliation must be close to the people, but may not take sides. With a Christian group, we can offer opportunities and conditions for a change of heart within a liturgical context. But even outside occasions of worship, depending on the culture, the community may be helped through theater and dance, songs and choirs, counseling, and formation of the teachers and other leaders. Reconciliation with one's own past involves remembering what happened, healing the memory and preparing for the future.

ACCOMPANYING OUR COLLEAGUES

Generally JRS teams include people who are more senior and more experienced than typical members of voluntary agencies. Care for our fellow refugee workers, a valued service, is mostly offered through simple friendship, and also by joining as equals in the forums for exchange and solidarity. But at times we also offer counseling. Many workers, through their privileged encounters with the refugees, or faced with extreme situations of suffering, are touched and start to question their own lives. They, too, deserve to be accompanied.

Shaping JRS Priorities

The pastoral dimension of JRS helps shape our criteria for selecting where, among whom, and how we shall work. Pastoral reasons, for example, cause us to go beyond the Geneva Convention definition of a refugee, which might otherwise limit the range of persons JRS serves. When we speak of "great human need," we are speaking pastorally—pointing to the needs of the whole person, spiritual and material.

ADVOCACY AND ACCOMPANIMENT

If we listen to the refugees and discern what they say to us, their message can be better heard. "Accompaniment" is itself an aspect of the kind of advocacy that JRS undertakes. We are not so much a "voice for the voiceless," but assist those without voice to express themselves. They have a primary right to speak on their own behalf. Finding ways to facilitate their communication is a challenge to our creativity. Meanwhile, simply by being with them we give witness to their situation. We call attention to what is happening.

SOME DILEMMAS OR FACTORS WORKING AGAINST APPROPRIATE RELATIONSHIPS

Ethical dilemmas spring up as factors that work against our best practices in appropriate relationships. The intention of accompanying people in the aftermath of crisis and loss and the JRS ideal of serving people as companions reminds us of what can happen instead.

Grassroots Consultation and Participation

Programs drawn up with no grassroots consultation and participation (the same with the operation of programs), such as doing for people rather than with them, are doomed to fail. It is now perceived wisdom to consult from the very beginning. In refugee communities, for instance, there are many qualified people, teachers, technicians, and midwives. Parents of children too have much to decide. Women have an essential input often neglected. Forming good refugee committees is important. It is easy to neglect, however, involving the communities to the maximum extent, especially in emergency situations. Here the dilemma is really the one of spending the time and effort to make the connections—rather than rushing to get a set model of operation up and running quickly.

Security and the Violence

JRS, as part of its accompaniment, has always valued the individual stories of each refugee. This privileged information needs respect and safeguarding. It is the fruit of getting to know the people well. Nowadays in many places, the lack of adequate security and the violence in refugee locations means that evacuation of staff is not uncommon. "Accompaniment" is compromised by having to evacuate staff at certain crisis times. This dilemma cannot be solved but only mitigated by clear security guidelines and understanding with the people involved. Particular issues of whether or not an organization will benefit itself with the use of armed guards are common nowadays (see, by way of comparison, MSF's recent withdrawal from Afghanistan).

Behavior of Humanitarian Workers

Maverick, nontransparent behavior of humanitarian workers, enforcing power systems of control, and badly informed or badly trained workers—all unfortunately can continue or worsen bad stereotyping and political, ethnic, religious, and social divisions within the communities they are meant to be serving. The institutionalization of this is most damaging, but the individual forms of exploitation are the ones that reach the headlines (corruption or sexual exploitation and abuse, for instance). Codes of conduct are drawn up to attend to this. The dilemma for organizations comes in how to manage complex operations with limited personnel resources and limited time to train and improve their knowledge and skills. We are called to respond with limited human means. Many of those who do respond are extremely generous people. Do we spend enough time on equipping staff with the ability to respond wisely?

Institutional Ethos

The mission and institution of a nongovernmental organization (NGO) could lead to abuse if put into action in a way that is inappropriate. JRS as a Catholic Church institution works with people of all religions (or those with no religion at all), and it does not seek to evangelize among the refugees. Some church institutions might see forms of evangelization among vulnerable people as legitimate. This sort of institutional ethos to work in humanitarian operations needs assessment. It could lead to ethical dilemmas at least for the local authorities, in whom they allow to operate in their territory. There is always the need for more people to assist, but each organization, for good and for bad, brings its own culture too.

Politicization of Aid

The transparency of who controls an organization and therefore its work, at least in part, is sometimes compromised. Iraq, since the American-led invasion, has seen the further politicization of aid. Funders, especially funding governments, have a very direct effect on if and how an NGO can operate. This leads to dilemmas of working in a place—at what cost? Or with whose funds?

Means to Raise the Funds Needed

Again other dilemmas for humanitarian agencies are the means to raise the funds needed. Now it is recognized how the dramatic and often demeaning images of suffering people at their most vulnerable are not ethically tolerable. They debase the dignity of those who have already been humiliated. (However, even the title of this input, ". . . dilemmas facing NGOs immersed in misery and human pain . . . ," panders a bit to portraying humanitarian crises as only situations of misery and pain. Certainly, we would not want to glamorize them! But the experience of JRS is that among the pain, there are stories of heroism, generosity, survival, cooperation, and relief. These are aspects often neglected. Reports of the projects that work and the hopes of the people tend to raise the interest (and the funds) of partners just as well as the stories of misery. Misery and numbers of deaths can be estimated at their maximum for the sake of drawing media and hence world attention. But is this ethically justified?

Another dilemma, in this section on means, is at what price do we make alliances and contracts? Some governing bodies require a compliance with policies that are not acceptable. Examples would be working with the Ethiopian relocation policies of the Mengistu era. A more recent controversial issue (now largely superseded, but which could resurface) was the signing of "Memoranda of Understandings" with the Sudan Peoples Liberation Army (SPLA) in Southern Sudan. Some agencies left the country for at time rather than sign.

To Be Professional

The need to be professional, to work efficiently in services, is sometimes played off against appropriate relationships: in what has just been mentioned, the means justified to raise money, but also perhaps in the competition for contracts, the enticement of competent workers from other organizations with inflationary salaries, et cetera. "Professional" in this case means "being efficient," but efficient in the competitive business sense. This is sometimes at odds with humanitarian ideals.

Dependency

A commonly mentioned syndrome in humanitarian situations is dependency. It is talked of in terms of how refugees or other vulnerable people become dependent on aid or other means of support. It is perhaps more important to note how organizations and their workers in the humanitarian field can incur and even encourage dependency. This stresses the importance of well-defined "exit strategies" for projects; something simpler in development work than in protracted refugee situations. These situations can lead some governments to complain about the strain on the host country's resources. There are, however, also host countries that have benefited considerably from the aid to refugees within their borders. The dilemma arises of who actually wants to find a solution to the crisis and who, by design or by default, is acting to prolong it?

Working across Borders

A particular syndrome in more protracted crises is that workers who have become one with the views and ideological leanings of a group of refugees, for instance, no longer have a perspective that will help to promote peace and integration back in the home country. An important help to avoiding this impasse for JRS is to have staff working across borders wherever possible. The past and the present and the future have to be reconciled. Reconciliation is a long process of social change that needs each faction to integrate a new vision (e.g., for Rwanda and Burundi where the taking of sides, Hutu and Tutsi, affects those within the countries, refugees, the displaced, and the humanitarian workers).

Advocacy Dilemmas

To avoid putting field workers more at risk, JRS has worked in partnership with human rights organizations. Information and suggestions are relayed for direct lobbying, but our identity is not used. Sometimes there will be the need to assess whether this is adequate.

Public criticism of bodies like UNHCR has to be weighed with how much they affect the working relationship. However, sometimes criticism is unavoidable if serious protection issues are not addressed.

The use of NGOs for advocacy of others, such as governments, can raise reverse advocacy dilemmas. For JRS running a radio station in Tanzania, there has to be a strong editorial policy to avoid local authorities or even UN bodies controlling it for dispersing views not acceptable to JRS, for instance on some repatriation issues. The ultimate dilemma comes at what point to close rather than to be "used" in the worse sense.

APPENDIX: CRITERIA FOR PLANNING AND EVALUATING JRS PROJECTS

Background

Over its twenty-five-year history, JRS has responded in many ways to the needs of forced displaced people. These have ranged from assistance given to an individual refugee to large-scale education programs involving several thousand students. JRS has worked with asylum seekers, refugees, internally displaced people, and people in detention. It has started and closed many projects; it has reduced some and expanded others. A process of discernment is required in making these choices on whether and how to respond to the different needs of forcibly displaced people and in order to monitor and evaluate our work. We are guided in this by our mission and by a set of the criteria that have been developed over the years. The most comprehensive set of guidelines have been developed in the area of education, pastoral work, and work with people in detention (Berlin, February 1999).

Our Roots and Sources: The Ignatian Tradition

When selecting projects, JRS uses criteria found in Part VII of the Jesuit Constitutions, for choosing ministries that match the overall Jesuit mission. JRS opts to work in situations of great need, in places where a more universal good may be served, where others are not meeting people's needs, and where it has a special contribution to make. JRS works where it is likely to be effective by reason of previous experience, or because JRS or the wider Society of Jesus or a partner agency has already established a base, or because a JRS initiative could help mobilize others.

Our Charism

The vast majority of our projects fall in a few areas, which can be considered our areas of specialization:

education and training
social services, psycho-social support and counseling
pastoral care
emergency and material assistance
legal assistance
health
research, public education, and advocacy

Criteria for JRS Projects

The following criteria are based and adapted from the Charter and Guidelines of JRS and arise from our experience.

WHO WE WORK WITH

1. The mission given to JRS embraces all persons who are driven from their homes by conflict, humanitarian disaster, or violation of human rights. We follow Catholic social teaching, which applies the expression "de facto refugee" to many related categories of people (The JRS Charter, No. 8).
2. In the selection and design of projects, particular priority is given to women, putting specific emphasis on their needs and contributions.

WHERE WE WORK

1. JRS works where there is the greatest need, with refugees who might otherwise be forgotten, where others are not providing the same service, or where JRS has a special contribution to make. It gives priority to activities that benefit the greatest number of people
2. JRS starts projects where its particular expertise is useful and only when it is assured of having the necessary personnel and financial resources for the implementation of the project.

COOPERATION AND PARTNERSHIP

1. JRS works in coordination with local Jesuit Provinces and with Jesuit institutions and personnel. (Guidelines)

2. Before setting up projects, JRS seeks to coordinate its activities and resources with those of existing groups, including local parishes and dioceses, religious communities, and research institutes.

3. Where possible, JRS facilitates the involvement of individuals, institutions, and communities in serving refugees according to their capacities and talents.

4. JRS seeks to work in collaboration with the local Church, always respecting the relationship of the Society with local Church officials.

5. JRS starts programs where it has the capacity to operate thanks to the local presence of a Jesuit community, Church, or other contacts which can give support to the team

6. JRS supports, where possible, initiatives of the refugees themselves, or it responds to invitations and requests from the local Church. It supports existing programs or starts new ones after a thorough consultation with the refugees, local partners, and all those affected by the program. Ideally, it does not support the initiatives of single individuals.

7. Strenthening the local Church in its service to refugees. JRS seeks to implement the Church's preferential option for the poor. JRS works in partnership with the local diocese, with the local Caritas, and with religious congregations and the local Jesuit province to help them better serve the refugees. It may, however, maintain its autonomy in its work and ways of proceeding. We advocate for the rights of refugees even with the local Church.

8. JRS "joins efforts with other international institutions and organizations to combat the injustices which uproot peoples from their land and families," cooperating with UNHCR and international agencies and NGOs working in the interests of refugees.

9. The collaboration is not maintained if it compromises the mission of JRS or the interests of the refugees.

10. Promoting and sustaining networks. Where possible, JRS will help refugees rebuild their own social networks and organizations that are often broken down during exile. JRS will work together with these networks and communities.

STYLE AND TYPE OF WORK

1. JRS gives priority to accompaniment and pastoral presence among refugees and forcibly displaced persons. Services are

tailored to meet local needs according to the resources available. No mode of assistance is excluded, but JRS normally offers services that are direct and personal. These include programs of pastoral care, various kinds of education for children and adults, social services and counseling, and health care.

2. JRS opts for a personal style of presence, and deliberately keeps its administrative structure as light as possible. JRS is not normally equipped to undertake large-scale emergency or infrastructure projects.

3. Emergency assistance must have clear timelines and should not be provided indefinitely. Material assistance should be reduced to a minimum and should be made available only for specific time periods.

4. JRS seeks to support refugees to be independent in the long term and supports projects which have potential for sustainability and continuity, for generation of income, or for giving the tools for the refugees to rebuild their lives. This is particularly challenging given the structural constraints of refugee life, which is unstable, ever changing, and where there is little encouragement to live a life of dignity.

5. JRS seeks to let the refugees speak with their own voices, to share equal power in a context where refugees are powerless, and are dependent on us to provide services. No JRS project ought see the refugees as passive victims. We believe that God is among the refugees. For this, JRS seeks the full participation of refugees at all levels of the planning and implementation of the work, taking care that they are involved in decision making. In hiring, priority is given to refugees.

6. JRS shows respect for the refugees, by promoting programs that affirm their dignity, their cultural and religious traditions, and defending their human rights.

7. JRS projects do not create dependency among refugees or create a beggar mentality. JRS projects encourage refugees to contribute with their own resources to the implementation of the project. JRS programs emphasize training of refugees and capacity building. JRS encourages refugees to be self-reliant, the artisans of their own lives.

8. At every level of our work, including our structures and internal organization, we must recreate experiences of justice, democracy, and participation.

9. JRS projects are a collaborative effort of Jesuits, other religious communities, and lay people.

10. Social justice has to be at the basis of all JRS work. It must determine the way we work with refugees, the way we structure our teams and our organization, and the type of work which we do.

11. JRS uses many channels to advocate refugee causes. Preferred methods of pursuing advocacy are partnerships with Jesuit social institutes and centers of research, and also with human rights organizations. Advocacy is a vital element of the JRS mission.

12. JRS follows the Universal Declaration of Human Rights, the 1951 Convention Relating to the Status of Refugees, and other international instruments in its work with refugees. When these are not respected, JRS assumes the role of advocacy on behalf of refugees and their rights.

13. We must be politically neutral, but not apolitical. We must analyze the causes and politics of displacement. We need to work toward changing structures of injustice that are at the root of forced displacement.

14. We support initiatives coming from refugees which are proposing alternatives for the future that are based on justice

15. Each project must be based on a thorough assessment and have clear, measurable objectives, methods, and timelines.

12

Transformation from Relief to a Justice and Solidarity Focus

Joan Neal

FOR OVER SIXTY YEARS, Catholic Relief Services (CRS) has been working overseas, providing emergency relief and development to economically and socially disadvantaged communities in poor countries. This chapter will present some of the organizational experiences, challenges, and successes that have transformed CRS as an agency, as well as the approaches used, the focus of its work, and the way in which impact is measured.

As the official overseas relief and development agency of the Catholic Church in the United States, and one of the largest private voluntary agencies in the world today, CRS is currently working in ninety-six very poor countries. On behalf of the U.S. Catholic community, and in partnership with local Catholic and non-Catholic agencies, CRS's staff of nearly four thousand employees support local programs of emergency assistance, educational outreach, agricultural development, micro enterprise for small-scale traders, farmers and producers, peace building in conflict-ridden societies, prevention, care, support and treatment for persons living with HIV/AIDS, and health care for vulnerable women and children. In 2004, CRS served over seventy million beneficiaries through these programs, implemented primarily by local partner agencies, many of which are faith-based.

However, CRS began as a more modest operation, focused on emergency relief and refugee assistance at its founding. The bishops of the United States created CRS in 1943, during the Second World War, to help respond to the needs of refugees in Europe and the poor worldwide. In the beginning years, CRS (then known as War Relief Services), out of its first three offices in Paris,

Rome, and Berlin, relocated Polish refugees freed from slave labor in Siberia, and assisted war orphans, refugees, and other suffering populations. Funding for these first programs came both from U.S. Catholics and the National War Fund Appeal established by President Franklin D. Roosevelt. A strong commitment to the alleviation of human suffering due to catastrophic events has continued and the agency has responded to numerous emergency situations around the world.

Over the past sixty years, major world events and trends have fundamentally transformed the organization: the Cold War, decolonization, Vatican II, globalization, war, and genocide in Africa, Asia, and Europe, as well as the war on terror. These events have influenced how CRS understands its mandate, how it carries out its programs, and how it measures impact nationally and internationally.

In the 1960s, CRS broadened its mission from one of charity and emergency response to one of sustainable socioeconomic development of local communities. For several decades, the agency viewed its work through a relief *and* development "lens." High value was placed not only on addressing the manifestations of poverty through relief activities but also on eliminating the immediate causes of poverty through development programs. CRS used this relief and development model until the early 1990s.

It is important to note two characteristics of early programs—a close relationship with local Catholic partners and significant funding from the U.S. government, particularly P.L. 480 food assistance. In subsequent decades, these two factors dramatically influenced both the quality and content of CRS's programs.

Initially, programs of assistance around the world were merely free distributions of food aid, clothing, and medicine. Over time, however, an increase in professionalism occurred both as a result of a growing awareness of the root causes of poverty and disease, and because newer agencies were also competing for government resources. Program design and evaluation standards were set and professional employees were recruited to ensure that programs dealt with causes, and not only the symptoms, of poverty, malnutrition, and disease. By the late 1980s, programs of health care, nutrition education, micro-enterprise, and agriculture achieved levels of excellence never before reached. In Africa, CRS was sponsoring over 90 percent of all U.S. government food aid, and received millions of dollars of U.S. government grant funding for emergency and developmental assistance programs, largely as a result of improved managerial capacity and its professional standards.

By 1990 CRS's self-identity was that of a highly professional socioeconomic development agency with a strong, well-respected, logistical capacity to deliver food aid and other supplies in times of emergency. The agency accessed hundreds of millions of dollars in public resources annually and the scale of operations was so large that increasingly CRS worked with local governments and international agencies in programs of national significance. As a result of the great availability of both public and private resources, CRS became one of the largest charitable organizations in the world, assisting millions of needy people without regard to race, religion, or political affiliation.

Just as the Cold War contributed to public motivation and policy to support *increases* in foreign aid in the 1950s and 1960s, so the *end* of the Cold War resulted in dramatic *decreases* in foreign aid, especially in poor African countries that had little security or economic importance to the United States. At the same time, corrupt and dictatorial regimes supported by either the Soviet Union or the United States during Cold War competition were allowed to collapse, as they were no longer useful in the new world order. Economies suffered and wars broke out or were intensified in Angola, the Balkans, Congo, Sudan, Sierra Leone, Liberia, Rwanda, and Ethiopia . . . all countries where CRS had large programs.

Consequently, the early 1990s brought international crises in quick succession, with failed and fractured states creating complex emergencies. Warlords carved up Somalia into clan-based fiefdoms ruled by the gun as hundreds of thousands went hungry. Meanwhile in Bosnia, conflict erupted on a scale unseen in Europe for almost fifty years, and the term "ethnic cleansing" entered the lexicon.

But it was the genocide in Rwanda that caused CRS to focus its efforts with a clarity it had previously lacked. It was a watershed event whose impact was felt far beyond the borders of that small

country. CRS had worked in Rwanda for over thirty years supporting relief and development when, in 1994, nearly one million
people were ruthlessly killed in just three months of organized
and cruelly methodical identity-based conflict. Thirty years of
CRS investments in development programs were wiped out in just
ninety days because, in its singular focus on relief and development efforts, the agency had ignored the fact that there was a
deep-seated pathology permeating the fabric of that society. As a
Catholic agency, CRS asked itself how it had failed to understand
that addressing this problem of hatred and distrust needed to be
at the core of its mission.

What CRS learned from the horror of Rwanda was that its work
in relief and development, though carried out effectively and efficiently, was not enough. In Rwanda, a majority Catholic country,
neither the local Church nor CRS had attended to the divisive
societal relationships that had evolved. From the time of independence, the Church had maintained a vast network of schools,
mission hospitals, and institutions. Some of the bishops had enormous influence on the policies of the government. CRS supported many of the programs of the Church at the parish,
diocesan, and national levels. But in spite of their best intentions,
these programs never resulted in substantive, sustainable change
in the underlying, unjust structures and societal beliefs.

After the genocide, CRS realized that it had unwittingly contributed to structures that perpetuated societal imbalances in
Rwanda. It had failed to support programs that fostered right relationships among peoples, among institutions, and even relationships inside the Church. CRS had essentially forgotten its Catholic
identity and taken a very narrow view of its purpose.

Clearly, CRS couldn't continue in that vein and fulfill its mission of service to the poorest of the poor. It was time to begin a
serious self-reflection, agency-wide. Staff and partners embarked
on a series of "justice reflections" that explored deeply the question of how to modify and measure the impact of humanitarian
action based on the agency's core values. These reflections concluded that the impact of CRS programs on the ability of project
beneficiaries to live in dignity and realize their full human potential is, in fact, *the* critical question.

The word "impact" implies a one-dimensional situation—similar to using a hammer and a nail. You pound the nail with the hammer until it's in place—job finished. CRS's experience as a Catholic organization working overseas has made it clear that humanitarian action is far more complex than that—that it has effects far beyond the immediate situation. Simply delivering humanitarian aid is not enough to fundamentally change the lives of the people we serve.

In the case of Rwanda, while CRS delivered goods and services that could be measured by hard indicators such as how many people were fed, or how many blankets were distributed, or how many wells were dug, those interventions only addressed the *symptoms* of the problems. The root causes of conflict and poverty remained untouched. CRS had to find another way of operating—a way to address the *systems and structures* that perpetuate violence, inequality, and marginalization while also meeting immediate needs for such things as food and housing.

After considerable reflection and prayer, CRS resolved to change the way it approached its program work around the world. The agency began to incorporate a justice-centered focus in all of its programming. Catholic social teaching, that jewel of the Catholic faith, was used to begin a transformation of the organization from top to bottom, across the world. Catholic social teaching offered a clear path to help address the questions about CRS's mission. Its vision of a just and peaceful world gives a rationale for everything the agency does.

In retrospect, limiting the terms of human development to economic growth and public health considerations, and concern for being competitive in the marketplace of U.S. government resources, may have caused CRS to fail to recognize the richness of its own Catholic tradition and all it has to offer in the promotion of integral human development and just and peaceful societies. As positive as CRS's contributions of food, clothing, shelter, and development assistance have been to millions of poor and suffering individuals around the world for over sixty years, failure to see its programs in a broader context of human sacredness, rights, and responsibilities in society, the preferential option for the poor and the common good, limited its potential as a Catholic

CRS Guiding Principles

DIGNITY AND EQUALITY OF THE HUMAN PERSON   All of humanity has been created in the image of God and possesses a basic dignity and equality that come directly from our creation and not from any action on our own part.

RIGHTS AND RESPONSIBILITIES   Every person has basic rights and responsibilities that flow from our human dignity and that belong to us as humans, regardless of any social or political structures. The rights are numerous and include those things that make life truly human. Corresponding to our rights are duties and responsibilities to respect the rights of others and to work for the common good of all.

SOCIAL NATURE OF HUMANITY   All of us are social by nature and are called to live in community with others—our full human potential isn't realized in solitude, but in community with others. How we organize our families, societies, and communities directly affects human dignity and our ability to achieve our full human potential.

THE COMMON GOOD   In order for all of us to have an opportunity to grow and develop fully, a certain social fabric must exist

agency and its ability to truly transform the lives of the poor and marginalized overseas.

Consequently, since 1997 CRS has worked to address issues of justice in all of its programs. Country programs overseas analyze their operating environments through a "justice lens," meaning they examine the policies, practices, and structures that create or perpetuate poverty and marginalization. Then they design programs that empower local communities to address these underlying causes while meeting people's immediate needs. A set of "Guiding Principles," based on Catholic social teaching, serves as a guide to all CRS programs.

CRS also had to revisit its entire approach as to how it worked with the local church in countries where the agency had decades of experience. The principle of subsidiarity—that the people themselves at the local level often know best the solutions to their within society. This is the common good. Numerous social conditions—economic, political, material, and cultural—impact our ability to realize our human dignity and reach our full potential.

SUBSIDIARITY A higher level of government—or organization—should not perform any function or duty that can be handled more effectively at a lower level by people who are closer to the problem and have a better understanding of the issue.

SOLIDARITY We are all part of one human family—whatever our national, racial, religious, economic, or ideological differences—and in an increasingly interconnected world, loving our neighbor has global dimensions.

OPTION FOR THE POOR In every economic, political, and social decision, a weighted concern must be given to the needs of the poorest and most vulnerable. When we do this we strengthen the entire community, because the powerlessness of any member wounds the rest of society.

STEWARDSHIP There is an inherent integrity to all of creation and it requires careful stewardship of all our resources, ensuring that we use and distribute them justly and equitably—as well as planning for future generations.

own problems—now guides CRS staff in relationships with partner agencies, learning to listen better and do so with the greatest possible respect. A set of "Partnership Principles" was developed to guide relationships with partners. Some country programs invest in a more thorough analysis of gender issues to ensure that they promote equity and women's empowerment.

In other cases, CRS finds that *traditional* socioeconomic development programs are inadequate to address the injustices that exist. Entire new programming areas, such as peace building, education, and capacity building have been developed to deal with these situations, either as stand-alone projects or cross-cutting themes that are found in all projects.

The addition of these new cross-cutting program sectors led CRS to adopt a holistic conceptual framework based on its core values of Catholic social teaching: the "Integral Human Development

CRS Partnership Principles

1. CRS bases partnerships upon a shared vision for addressing people's immediate needs and the underlying causes of suffering and injustice.
2. All of CRS's partnerships assign responsibility for decision making and implementation to a level as close as possible to the people whom decisions will affect.
3. CRS achieves *complementarity and mutuality in its partnerships,* recognizing and valuing that each brings a set of skills, resources, knowledge, and capacities to the partnership in a spirit of mutual autonomy.
4. CRS fosters *equitable partnerships* by engaging in a process of mutually defining rights and responsibilities, in relation to each partner's capacity, required to achieve the goal of the partnership.
5. In its relationships with partners CRS promotes *openness and sharing of perspectives* and approaches. These relationships are founded upon a spirit of respect of differences, a commitment to listen and learn from each other, and a mutual willingness to change behavior and attitudes.

framework." This framework links household and community assets to the systems and structures that can empower or marginalize households and communities, as well as the vulnerability context within which they live. The framework helps staff and partners to analyze how households build, protect, transfer, and combine their assets into strategies and the outcomes they achieve. This analysis identifies the best possible ways for CRS to strengthen the household and community asset base and support the realization of full human potential by empowering local communities to advocate for change of unjust structures.

This focus on justice also transformed the work of CRS in the United States. Previously, CRS's relationship with U.S. Catholics was one of donor and recipient. The agency simply provided information and education on its programs overseas, and U.S. Catholics provided financial support for these programs. Now, CRS engages this constituency in actions and advocacy for international justice, changing the relationship from one largely based on the transfer of wealth to one that sees sharing within a larger

6. To foster healthy partnership, CRS promotes *mutual transparency* regarding capacities, constraints, and resources.
7. By building partnerships, CRS seeks to make a *contribution to the strengthening of civil society.* CRS also encourages its partners to engage in dialog and action with other members of civil society, in order to contribute to the transformation of unjust structures and systems.
8. The engagement of CRS and the local partner in local capacity development involves a long-term commitment to complete a mutually agreed-upon process of organizational development. This commitment is characterized by a spirit of accompaniment: a close relationship that is flexible and responsive in both its institutional and personal forms.
9. CRS recognizes that all communities have capacities and coping mechanisms that should be identified, understood, and strengthened as the primary source of solving local problems. CRS and its partners *maximize community participation* in all aspects of programming to ensure community ownership of, and decision making within, the development process.
10. CRS facilitates and promotes the strengthening of partners' abilities to identify, build on, and address their vulnerabilities, strengths, and specific capacity building needs through a process that leads to sustainability.

relationship of solidarity and a growing awareness of how our consumption, investment, and trade affect the lives of our brothers and sisters in poor countries. The U.S. Operations Division reaches out to U.S. Catholics to raise awareness about injustices overseas, to increase understanding of key issues, such as international debt, trade, foreign aid, and migration, and to influence government polices and practices.

The transformation of Catholic Relief Services is ongoing, but already its impact has been profound. Today, CRS views its mission through a lens of justice and solidarity.

Not only does CRS ask if its rural development programs are sustainable and of high technical and professional quality, but also how assistance to one population group will affect relations with another: men and women, Hutus and Tutsis, Muslims and Christians, the rich and the poor, people in the North and those

Peace Building through Education in India

CRS/India works in areas where there are multiple problems, where there is a lack of food, where people are alienated from political power and processes, where there are ethnic and religious tensions that are layered within these other conflict issues. In communities experiencing political and social tension, schools can be flashpoints for violence. In India, there are numerous examples of Catholic schools becoming the focus of small-scale community violence over issues that go far beyond the institution, students, or curriculum. The underlying causes of conflict in these cases are multiple, but the lack of food security and impaired ability to meet other basic human needs are part of the problem. Schools are also places where bridges are built between people within divided communities. These relationships can be fostered among the student body, among the school and its surrounding community, or among multiple communities.

CRS and four partners who operate residential schools in tribal regions of India examined the operations of their schools to identify ways to achieve peace building outcomes alongside social development and livelihood security outcomes. From these four cases it is evident there are several practical ways that schools help build relationships and address community needs. Within the residential schools, peer conflict resolution mechanisms constructively address problematic issues within the campus. Residential schools convene regular meetings and host or support tribal festivals and dances to help strengthen relationships between and among community members. Schools and students reach out to support community literacy and development in remote areas, and work to encourage the government to increase its capabilities in servicing remote areas. Together, these activities support an integrated approach to human development that builds up the assets of people and communities and change the structures and systems within which they are currently marginalized.

in the South, emphasizing our interconnected web of relationships and the resulting obligations to one another.

Ultimately, CRS has come to learn that human development is more a question of working within society to *transform* unjust relationships (whether they are economic, religious, cultural, racial, or political) than it is a simple transferring or generating of

CRS Vision Statement

Solidarity will transform the world to:

- Cherish and uphold the sacredness and dignity of every person;
- Commit to and practice peace, justice, and reconciliation; and
- Celebrate and protect the integrity of all creation.

wealth. CRS now understands as never before that we are all part of the one human family—whatever our national, racial, religious, economic, or ideological differences—and in an ever increasingly interconnected world, loving our neighbors has global dimensions and responsibilities.

When CRS supported relief efforts in Bosnia during the war, it had to consider a priori what the impact of its distributions would be on straining already tense ethnic and religious differences. Staff ensured that Catholic Croatians and Muslim Bosnians had equal access to food. Likewise for the Serbian Orthodox communities. In this way, food relief could be used to foster right relationships and promote the common good rather than further divide suffering communities. In Indonesia, CRS was able to bring together women of different faiths through small micro-finance loans to find opportunities to build peace, no small feat in a post-9/11 world. Inter-faith dialog programs in Pakistan had started already, even before those tragic events, and have since then proven to be all the more necessary.

Inter-faith Dialog in Pakistan

CRS has worked in Pakistan since 1954. During this time, the agency's approach has shifted from a focus on socioeconomic development to one of fostering right relationships and promoting inter-faith dialog between the Muslim majority and the small Christian minority. Activities such as establishing local peace communities, educational programs in schools, training of youth leaders, musical radio programs, and publishing positive stories about tolerance, forgiveness, and respect have helped to increase understanding and reduce incidents of social, religious, and sectarian violence.

CRS also realized that its work is not just about relationships on the ground in the ninety-six countries where it works, but also about how U.S. citizens, live, consume, donate, invest, and vote. These decisions impact, for better or worse, the lives of poor and marginalized people around the world.

Catholic Relief Services has not lost any of its commitment to professionalism and management efficiency. Nor has it lessened its relationship with our government, although the nature of that relationship is changing. What has changed is that CRS now views these important aspects of the agency's work within a broader understanding of its identity as a Catholic agency and its mission of promoting more just and peaceful societies.

When CRS implements a micro-finance project, staff and partners not only ask the business questions (is the interest rate right? do villagers understand the business processes? do they have the training they need to keep the books?), but we also ask how this micro-finance project will affect interpersonal relationships— within families, with other ethnic groups, with the government, with the official banking system. Human relationships matter just as much if not more than the technical aspects of delivering relief and development.

Clearly humanitarian action can answer myriad pressing needs: basic healthcare, food, medical care, education, even dignity in work. Food for Work programs, for example, have built hundreds of thousands of miles of roads, countless schools, latrines and wells, and helped reforest and reseed untold acres. But, experience has taught CRS that it cannot simply deliver relief and development programs in a vacuum. As a Catholic agency, as part of the mission of the Church, CRS must seek to transform relationships through its work. Until the structures of injustice in the world are changed, we will never have a lasting impact on the lives of real people. Only in this way can we truly carry out Pope Paul VI's exhortation that "General development is integral; it has moral and spiritual dimensions as well as political, cultural and economic."

Consequently, CRS also uses programs like Food for Peace to build and strengthen democracy. For instance, in 2003, more than 1,800 rural women who participated in CRS food-for-work programs in India were elected to political office in their village councils. They are now serving as a voice for their communities at the local government level. This example demonstrates how empowering local communities can transform relationships and have a profound effect on society.

It is clear that CRS now sees the delivery of goods and services to the poor as a subset of a larger context. This larger context—the necessity of structural change and transforming unjust relationships—represents a long-term view, a more eschatological perspective. CRS believes that solidarity will truly transform the world. In this light, the success of CRS must be measured, today and for the foreseeable future, by the degree to which the agency contributes to making that happen.

NOTES

CHAPTER 1
PATIENTS WITHOUT BORDERS
Bernard Kouchner, M.D.

1. International Committee of the Red Cross is an independent and neutral organization ensuring humanitarian protection and assistance for victims of war and armed violence.
2. Doctors Without Borders, financial report, 2004. http://www.msf.fr.
3. "Shaping the Future," World Health Report, 2003, overview, 5.
4. World Bank statistics, 2000.
5. Rapport du Haut Conseil de la Coopération Internationale sur la coopération dans le secteur de la santé avec les pays en développement, 8. http://www.hcci.gouv.fr/travail/rapports_avis/rapportsante.html, 2002.
6. Ensemble pour une Solidarité Thérapeutique Hospitaliere En Réseau, http://www.esther.fr.
7. Georges Canguilhem.

CHAPTER 2
PROTECTION OF CIVILIANS IN ARMED CONFLICT:
A DECADE OF PROMISES
Sheri Fink, M.D.

1. K. Annan, "The Secretary-General Address to the Stockholm International Forum," Stockholm, Sweden, January 24, 2004.
2. This case is drawn from S. Fink, *War Hospital: A True Story of Surgery and Survival* (New York: Public Affairs, 2003).
3. United Nations, "Report of the Secretary-General Pursuant to General Assembly Resolution 53/35 (1998): U.N. Srebrenica Report," 1999.
4. United Nations, "Report of the Independent Inquiry into the Actions of the United Nations during the 1994 Genocide in Rwanda," S/1999/1257, December 15, 1999.
5. P. Gaillard, "Rwanda 1994: 'Kill As Many People As You Want, You Cannot Kill Their Memory,'" talk given at the Genocide Prevention

Conference organized by the Aegis Trust and the UK Foreign Office, London, January 2002.

6. P. Gaillard, "Rwanda 1994: 'La vraie vie est absente,'" talk given at the International Museum of the Red Cross and Red Crescent, Geneva, October 18, 1994.

7. Steering Committee for Humanitarian Response, "The International Response to Conflict and Genocide: Lessons from the Rwanda Experience," March, 1996.

8. United Nations, "Report of the Independent Inquiry."

9. United Nations, "Report of the Secretary-General."

10. Steering Committee, "The International Response to Conflict and Genocide."

11. United Nations Security Council, "Report of the Secretary-General to the Security Council on the Protection of Civilians in Armed Conflict," S/2004/431, May 28, 2004.

12. International Crisis Group, "Darfur: The Failure to Protect," Africa Report 89, March 8, 2005.

13. J. Egeland, "Statement by Undersecretary General Jan Egeland to the Security Council on the Protection of Civilians in Armed Conflict," June 21, 2005.

14. International Commission on Intervention and State Sovereignty, "The Responsibility to Protect: Report of the International Commission on Intervention and State Sovereignty," December, 2001.

15. K. Annan, "The Secretary-General Address."

16. The SPHERE Project, "Sphere Handbook 2004: Humanitarian Charter and Minimum Standards in Disaster Response," Oxfam Publishing, December 2003.

17. H. Slim and L. E. Egurin, "Humanitarian Protection, A Guidance Booklet: Pilot Version," ALNAP, 2003.

18. H. Slim and A. Bonwick, "Protection: An ALNAP Guide for Humanitarian Agencies," Overseas Development Institute, London, August 2005.

19. J. Fawcett and V. Tanner, "The Security of National Staff: Toward Good Practices," InterAction, 2001.

CHAPTER 3
NO JUSTICE WITHOUT POWER: THE CASE FOR
HUMANITARIAN INTERVENTION
Alexander Van Tulleken, M.D.

1. J. L. Holzgrefe, *Humanitarian Intervention: Ethical, Legal and Political Dilemmas,* ed. J. L. Holzgrefe (Cambridge: Cambridge University Press, 2003), 18.

2. Kofi Annan, "Millenium Report to the United Nations General Assembly," 2000.

3. *Le Monde*, April 18, 1994.

4. Hugo Slim, "Humanitarianism with Borders," paper for the ICVA Conference on NGOs in a Changing World Order: Dilemmas and Challenges, 2003. http://www.jha.ac/articles/a118.htm.

5. Bill Clinton, 2003, visiting the cemetery in Srebrenica.

6. Samantha Power, *A Problem from Hell, America in an Age of Genocide* (New York: Basic Books, 2002), xxi.

7. Elegantly put by Tom J. Farer in *Humanitarian Intervention*, ed. J. L. Holzgrefe, 55.

8. UN Secretary-General Kofi Annan has emphasized on several occasions the idea that "human rights, and the evolving nature of humanitarian law, will be unacceptably limited if the principle of state sovereignty is always allowed to trump the protection of citizens within those states." The quotation is from a speech made at Tilburg University, Holland, on November 21, 2002.

9. Congressional Record, 90th Congress, 1st Session, 1967, 113, pt. 1:876. Taken from Powers, *A Problem from Hell*, 85.

10. Translation from Hugo Grotius, *De Jure Belli ac Pacis Libri Tres*, trans. F. W. Kelsey, ed. J. B. Scott, *The Classics of International Law* (Oxford: Oxford University Press, 1925), book 2, chapter 5, section 8, volume 2, 584.

11. Marcus Tullius Cicero, "De Re Publica," in Marcus Tullius Cicero, *De Re Publica and De Legibus* (Cambridge: Harvard University Press, 1928), 3:xxii, 3, 211. This quotation nicely illustrates the basis of natural law in J. L. Holzgrefe's "The Humanitarian Intervention Debate," in *Humanitarian Intervention*, ed. J. L. Holzgrefe, Cambridge: Cambridge University Press, 2003.

12. John Rawls, *A Theory of Justice*, rev. ed. (Cambridge: Harvard University Press, 1999).

13. "The Report of the International Commission on Intervention and State Sovereignty," synopsis, xii. The full text of the document can be found at http://www.iciss.ca/pdf/Commission-Report.pdf.

14. Hedley Bull, conclusion, in *Intervention in World Politics*, ed. Hedley Bull (Oxford: Oxford University Press, 1984), 195.

15. The "Downing Street Memo" refers to minutes transcribed during the British prime minister's meeting on July 23, 2002, published by the *Sunday Times* on May 1, 2005.

16. The Charter of the United Nations, Article 1(1).

17. Unilateral action and the transformations of the world constitutive process: the special problem of humanitarian intervention, Michael Reisman, *EJIL* 11, no. 1. (2000): 3–18.

296   NOTES TO PAGES 57–76

18. Statute of the International Court of Justice, Article 38. The full text of the Statue can be found at: http://www.icj-cij.org/icjwww/ibasic documents/ibasictext/ibasicstatute.htm.

19. Jane Stromseth, *Humanitarian Intervention*, ed. J. L. Holzgrefe, 241.

20. Hugo Slim, "Military Intervention to Protect Human Rights: The Humanitarian Agency Perspective," http://www.jha.ac/articles/a084 .htm, March 11, 2002.

21. United Nations Department of Peacekeeping Web site, www.un.org/Depts/dpko/dpko/index.asp.

22. Report of the Secretary-General, Boutros Boutros Ghali, "An Agenda for Peace," 1992. www.un.org/Docs/SG.agpeace.html.

23. Samantha Power, "Bystanders to Genocide: Why the United States Let the Rwandan Tragedy Happen," *Atlantic Monthly*, September 2001, 104.

24. Memorandum from Deputy Assistant Secretary of Defense for Middle East/Africa, through Assistant Secretary of Defense for International Security Affairs, to Under Secretary of Defense for Policy, "Talking Points On Rwanda/Burundi," April 11,1994. http://www.gwu.edu/ ~nsarchiv/NSAEBB/NSAEBB53/.

25. "Interview With the French Media in Paris, June 7, 1994," *Public Papers of the Presidents of the United States, William J. Clinton III, 1994*, book 1, *January 1 to July 31, 1994* (Washington, D.C.: United States Government Printing Office, 1995), 1056–1057.

26. Memorandum from Under Secretary of Defense for Policy to Deputy Assistant to the President for National Security, National Security Council, "Rwanda: Jamming Civilian Radio Broadcasts," May 5, 1994.

27. See http://www.un.org/Pubs/chronicle/1994/issue4/0494p4.asp.

28. Security Council Resolution 929.

29. Julie Godoy, "France Fails to Accept Responsibility over Rwanda," IPS News Agency, 2004, www.ipsnews.net/interna.asp?idnews=23212.

30. Peter Singer, "Peacekeepers, Inc.," *Policy Review*, no. 119l, June 2003.

31. Kofi Annan, "Action Plan to Prevent Genocide, 2004, http:// www.preventgenocide.org/prevent/UNdocs/KofiAnnansActionPlanto PreventGenocide7Apr2004.htm.

32. An excellent analysis of the relationship between the conflicts in Darfur and in South Sudan can be found in Samantha Power's "Dying in Darfur: Can the Ethnic Cleansing in Sudan Be Stopped?" *New Yorker*, August 30, 2004, 56–64.

CHAPTER 4
THE HUMANITARIAN COMMUNITY AND THE PRIVATE SECTOR
Major General Tim Cross

The opinions expressed in this chapter are those of the author and do not represent official United Kingdom Ministry of Defense (UKMOD) policy.

1. The headline—and eye-catching—value of the contracts often disguises a myriad of costs which have to be borne by the companies concerned, including equipment procurement.

2. See *Emergency Relief Operations* and *Traditions, Values and Humanitarian Action*.

3. The use of contracted medical personnel was nonetheless still widespread even following the formation of a military medical service, and not always with negative consequences. Hospital Apprentice Fitzgibbon, employed under "local arrangement" by his peacetime surgeon, won a Victoria Cross (VC)—the highest award for bravery in the UK Armed Forces—during the operation to capture North Taku Fort in the second China War in August 1860; at fifteen years three months old, he is the youngest-ever VC winner. He married, had two children, and died of a stroke in Delhi, India, aged thirty-seven.

4. The British Forces—particularly the army—are unique within Europe. Conscription (National Service) is not part of our national "psyche" and is therefore historically very unusual.

5. My definition of materiel includes every commodity and piece of equipment needed to support military operations, such as fuel, food, shelter, medical supplies, spares, ammunition, and so forth.

6. The consequences of a "hot" war would have probably been catastrophic, but the risk or likelihood was pretty remote.

7. The strategic level of war is the application of military resources to help achieve grand strategic objectives—the political "end-state." The operational level is how resources are used within a particular theater of operations to enable tactical level operations to succeed.

8. Fighting power is a combination of manpower and equipment, training and sustainability, doctrine, and leadership and motivation; all work together to produce an overall "ability to fight."

9. Even on a major training exercise overseas it is not unusual to experience DNBI figures of over one thousand personnel.

10. In terms of campaign medals—not awards for particular acts of bravery.

11. This varies from nation to nation and contract to contract. At one end of the spectrum some CONDO nurses have not, in theory, been

entitled to care in the establishment in which they are working! At the other, U.S. contractors are now often issued with a "common access card" that entitles them to life support (food and accommodation), vehicle maintenance, medical support, and the use of PX facilities—all monitored under federal acquisition regulations.

12. A deployed UK medical group recently included six CONDO nurses—two from accident and emergency, two from intensive care units, and two general nurses; they proved invaluable.

13. As the operation matured in Iraq, the early use of CONDO specialists in the relatively secure Shaibah Logistic Base allowed the British Army to continue to support allied offensive operations elsewhere, without an increase in uniformed troops.

14. The term Private Military Company (PMC) has been largely dropped—it sounded too aggressive. It has been replaced by Private Security Company (PSC), which sounds more defensive—and is therefore deemed to be more acceptable.

15. The numbers vary depending on who one asks—some say ten thousand, others thirty-five thousand; my sense is of twenty to twenty-five thousand, certainly if one includes the unlicensed companies.

16. Between April 2003 and December 2005 the UK Foreign Office spent £110 million on protection for diplomatic staff, ministers, and construction workers.

17. Originally called the Office of Post-War Planning (OPWP), established under a U.S. presidential directive in January 2003 in the Pentagon under retired three-star General Jay Garner. I joined them in Washington in February 2003, deploying with them to Kuwait and then Baghdad; ORHA soon became the Coalition Provision Authority (CPA), which continues to operate in the "Green Zone" in Baghdad.

18. Tim Spicer, the boss of both Sandline and Aegis, and I were commanding officers together in Germany. The attempt to turn him into an outcast rightly failed. The British parliamentary inquiry found that Foreign Office officials had known about the arms shipments in advance, and Spicer was rightly vindicated. Under his leadership Aegis has even established a charitable foundation, under which they (and he) help schools and orphanages—people and events are seldom what they seem to be at first glance!

19. I recognize that nothing can perhaps be more irritating than being killed or wounded!

20. "Even in war, moral power is to physical as 3 parts of 4." Attributed to Napoleon in *Treasury of Thought* by Maturin M. Ballou (Boston: Houghton, Mifflin, 1899).

21. Events in various businesses around the world (like Enron) also highlight the reality that these moral pressures do apply equally elsewhere, far away from the rigors of operations in places like Iraq.

22. The 1977 Organization of African Unity Convention for the Elimination of Mercenaries in Africa, and the 1989 UN Convention against the Recruitment, Use, Financing, and Training of Mercenaries—the United Kingdom, in common with most other Western governments, has not signed up to the latter, mainly because it does not believe that it could mount a successful prosecution under the convention.

23. This recommendation came from the widespread concern over issues like the 1998 "Arms to Africa" or "Sandline Affair" referred to above, and other events throughout Africa (Ethiopia, Angola, Sierra Leone, etc.) and elsewhere like the Balkans and Afghanistan.

24. Andy Bearpark joined ORHA/CPA in the summer of 2003 shortly before I left, but we had met earlier when he came out with British Prime Minister Tony Blair to Basra; we discussed the situation together, as he considered whether or not to move out to Iraq from the Balkans where he was working for the European Commission and the United Nations. We have met and spoken since, back in the United Kingdom, on a couple of occasions.

25. See an earlier chapter of mine in this book series—*Emergency Relief Operations.*

26. Initiated largely by the churches within the United Kingdom but taken up by the G8 group of nations.

27. Like business in the round, the major NGOs are concerned with "market share" and "profitability." They often have to produce coherent business plans to secure funding from the various IOs and government aid departments—both in their home countries and when deployed in a complex emergency. Some are good at it—others not so good!

28. In addition, and building on the success of, for example, the International Diploma course on Humanitarian Affairs run by the Center for International Humanitarian Cooperation (CIHC), further diplomas on running effective humanitarian supply chains and working alongside the private sector now need to be developed—work has begun in the United Kingdom but it will take some time to reach maturity.

29. Overall around $10 billion is now spent annually on the delivery of aid around the world.

CHAPTER 5
LOOKING BEYOND THE "LATEST AND GREATEST"
Christopher Holshek

1. From an informal paper provided at the start of "Humanitarian Roles in Insecure Environments: A Strategic Workshop," U.S. Institute

of Peace, Washington, D.C., January 13–14, 2005. Notes on the workshop are available at http://www.usip.org.

2. The Challenges Project, *Challenges of Peace Operations: Into the 21st Century—Concluding Report 1997–2002* (Stockholm: Elanders Gotab, 2002), 143, http://www.peacechallenges.net.

3. Karen Guttieri, "Civil-Military Relations in Peacebuilding," *Sicherheitspolitik und Friedensforschung* (University of Hamburg) 2 (2004): 84.

4. Challenges Project, 143–44. Following bullet points are paraphrased from the report.

5. Challenges Project, 144.

6. "Humanitarian Roles in Insecure Environments." The USIP paper derives its observation on fatal attacks on humanitarians in 2003 from World vision data collected from various reports (Dennis Klug, UN security coordinator).

7. An excellent discussion of this issue can be found in the section called "Civilian Attitudes Toward Military Humanitarian Assistance and the Issue of Uniforms" (chapter 6) of Olga Oliker et al., *Aid During Conflict* (Santa Monica, Calif.: RAND National Defense Research Institute, 2004), 88–96, http://www.rand.org.

8. From an informal copy of the ACBAR bulletin obtained December 27, 2002. For further information, go to http://www.acbar.org.

9. Ibid.

10. Ibid.

11. "Humanitarian Leaders Ask White House to Review Policy Allowing American Soldiers to Conduct Humanitarian Relief Programs in Civilian Clothes," InterAction news release, April 2, 2002, available at http://www.interaction.org/newswire/detail.php?id=411.

12. In addition to the RAND publication, *Aid During Conflict*, a good discussion of PRTs can be found in a paper on PRTs (currently in draft and untitled) by Michael Dziedzic, U.S. Institute of Peace, http://www.usip.org.

13. John S. Burnett, "In the Line of Fire," *The New York Times*, August 4, 2004, http://www.nytimes.com.

14. Challenges Project, 145–48. Text is extracted from various parts of the original.

15. Christopher J. Holshek, "The Operational Art of Civil-Military Operations: Promoting Unity of Effort," in *Lessons from Kosovo: The KFOR Experience*, Larry Wentz (ed.), Command and Control Research Program, Department of Defense, Washington, D.C., July 2002, 270–71, http://www.dodccrp.org

16. Robert M. Schoenhaus, "Training for Peace and Humanitarian Relief Operations," United States Institute for Peace, Peaceworks 43, April 2002, 5–6.

17. Maj. Gen. Timothy Cross, "Military/NGO Interaction," in *Emergency Relief Operations,* ed. Kevin M. Cahill, M.D. (New York: Fordham University Press and the Center for International Health and Cooperation, 2003), 204.

18. Cross, 205.

19. Christopher J. Holshek, "Interdisciplinary Peace Operations Professional Development: Investing in Long-Term Peace Operations Success," in *Cornwallis Group VII: Analysis for Compliance and Peace Building,* ed. Alexander Edward Richard Woodcock and David F. Davis (Cornwallis Park, Nova Scotia: Pearson Peacekeeping Center, 2003), 53.

20. Cross, 205–6.

21. Department of Peacekeeping Best Practices Unit, "Handbook on United Nations Multidimensional Peacekeeping Operations," New York, United Nations, December 2003, 159.

22. Schoenhaus, "Training for Peace," 7.

23. Cheryl Bernard, "Afghanistan without Doctors," *The Wall Street Journal,* August 12, 2004, p. A10.

24. "Handbook on United Nations Multidimensional Peacekeeping Operations," 64.

25. Dziedzic paper, USIP.

26. Oliker, *Aid During Conflict,* 40–43.

27. Guttieri, 85.

28. See Christopher J. Holshek, "Concept Proposal—Interagency Training and Development Center," Potomac Strategies International, LLC, December 4, 2002, 4–5. For a copy, go to http://www.potomacstra tegies.com.

29. Chris Seiple, *The U.S. Military/NGO Relationship in Humanitarian Interventions* (Carlisle, PA: U.S. Army Peacekeeping Institute, 1996), 187.

30. Challenges Project, 150.

31. For more information, go to the PKSOI website at http://www.carlisle.army.mil/usacs/divisions/pksoi/.

32. Jon M. Ebersole, "The Mohonk Criteria for Humanitarian Assistance in Complex Emergencies: Task Force on Ethical and Legal Issues in Humanitarian Assistance," *Human Rights Quarterly* (Johns Hopkins University Press) 17, no. 1 (February 1995): 192–208.

33. Seiple, 11. Note this was published in 1996.

34. Schoenhaus, 23–24.

CHAPTER 6
NOT IF . . . BUT WHEN AND HOW?
Larry Hollingworth

1. Jane Barry and Anna Jefferys, "A Bridge Too Far," Humanitarian Practice Network 37, January 2002.

2. Sadako Ogata, United Nations High Commissioner for Refugees Press Conference, April 20, 1999.

3. General A. Joulwan and Christopher C. Shoemaker, "Lessons from Rwanda—Civil-Military Cooperation in the Prevention of Deadly Conflict: Implementing Agreements in Bosnia and Beyond," December 1998, The Carnegie Commission on Preventing Deadly Conflict, http://www.carnegie.org/sub/research/index.html#conflict.

4. Humanitarian Practice Network 37.

5. Alex de Waal, *Who Fights? Who Cares?* (Trenton: Africa World Press, 2000).

6. Ibid.

7. Martha Finnemore, *The Purpose of Intervention: Challenging Beliefs About the Use of Force* (Ithaca, N.Y.: Cornell University Press), 3.

8. Ibid., 10.

9. Ibid., 78.

10. Ibid., 56.

11. David Rieff, *A Bed for the Night* (New York: Simon and Schuster, 2002), 328.

12. Ibid., 331.

13. Dr. Rod Lyon, "Civil Military Relations in an Age of Terror," paper prepared for the Albright Symposium, University of Queensland, Brisbane, July 5–7, 2004.

14. Arthur C. Helton, "International Bureaucracy and the Debasement of Mercy," in *The Price of Indifference: Refugees and Humanitarian Action in the New Century* (New York: Oxford University Press, 2003).

15. Hugo Grotius, *De Jure Belli ac Pacis*, book 2, chapter 25, section 8, trans. Francis W. Kelsey (Oxford: Clarendon Press, 1925).

16. J. L Holzgrefe and Robert O Keohane, eds., *Humanitarian Intervention* (Cambridge: Cambridge University Press, 2000).

17. "Intervention, Protection, and Humanitarian Assistance at a Crossroads," World Affairs Council, San Francisco, March 2000.

18. Fiona Terry, *Condemned to Repeat: The Paradox of Humanitarian Action* (Ithaca, NY: Cornell University Press, 2002), 24.

19. Jacques Forster, *Human Security for All: A Tribute to Sergio Vieira de Mello* (New York: CIHC, Fordham University Press, 2004), 178.

20. Ibid

21. David Rieff, *A Bed for the Night* (New York: Simon and Schuster, 2002), 33.

22. UNHCR Handbook, http://www.hrea.org/learn/tutorials/refugees/Handbook/hbtoc.htm.

23. Jan Egeland, "Human Security For All," *Challenges* (New York: CIHC, Fordham University Press, 2004), 134.

24. Ibid., 132.

25. De Waal, *Who Fights? Who Cares?*

26. Jan Egeland, "The Challenges of Humanitarian Diplomacy," *Human Security for All: A Tribute to Sergio Vieira de Mello* (New York: CIHC, Fordham University Press, 2004), 133.

27. "The ICRC and Civil Military Co-Operation in Situations of Armed Conflict," 45th Rose-Roth Seminar at Montrose, March 2, 2000.

28. Ibid.

29. Neill Wright, speech delivered in Florence, Italy, to a NATO seminar, May 15, 2000.

30. Arthur C. Helton, "International Bureaucracy and the Debasement of Mercy," in *The Price of Indifference: Refugees and Humanitarian Action in the New Century* (New York: Oxford University Press, 2003).

31. Nicholas Morris, "No Past Mission Can Provide a Precise Blueprint for Any Future One," UNHCR occasional paper, 1997.

32. Larry Minear, *The Humanitarian Enterprise—Dilemmas and Discoveries* (Bloomfield, Conn.: Kumarian Press, 2002), 4.

33. General A. Joulwan and Christopher C. Shoemaker, "Civil-Military Cooperation in the Prevention of Deadly Conflict: Implementing Agreements in Bosnia and Beyond," December 1998, The Carnegie Commission on Preventing Deadly Conflict, http://www.carnegie.org/sub/research/index.html#conflict.

34. "The Future of Humanitarian Action," International Mapping Exercise prepared by Antonio Donini in consultation with Peter Walker and Larry Minear, the Alan Shawn Feinstein International Famine Centre. Friedman School of Nutrition Science and Policy, Tufts University, January 2004.

35. Ben Hemingway, "Civil-Military Co-operation in Post Conflict Rebuilding," InterAction, Monday Developments, March 22, 2004, http://www.interaction.org/library/detail.php?id=2860.

36. Sean Pollick. Conference of Defense Associations Institute Symposium, November 3–4, 2000.

37. Ibid.

38. Forster, "Human Security for All," 174.

39. Ibid., 177.

40. Rieff, *A Bed for the Night*, 328.

41. Jan Egeland, Tsunami News bulletin 6/2, http://www.tsunami news.com.

CHAPTER 8
PROTECTING SOCIETIES IN TRANSITION
Geoff Loane, Lois Austin, and Pat Gibbons

1. H. Slim, "International Humanitarianism's Engagement with Civil War in the 1990s: A Glance at the Evolving Practice and Theory," a briefing paper for Action Aid UK, 1997. J. Macrae and M. Duffield, "Politics and Humanitarian Aid," *The Journal of Disaster Studies, Policy and Management* 25, no. 4 (2001): 269–74.

2. The current paper defines "transition" as the passage from war to peace and not any continuum from relief to development. Societies in transition are considered as those societies experiencing this period of time following active conflict and in the buildup to relative peace.

3. Such as the International Committee of the Red Cross and certain elements of the UN system.

4. State failure, viewed in this paper as a state's failure to fulfill its envisaged roles, namely: to provide security, to represent its citizenry, and to provide a minimum level of welfare.

5. State collapse, viewed in this paper as the collapse of the state's institutions.

6. W. Weiner, *The Global Migration Crisis: Challenge to States and to Human Rights* (Glenview, Ill.: Addison Wesley Longman, 1995).

7. Ibid.

8. Slim, "International Humanitarianism's Engagement with Civil War in the 1990s."

9. F. Fox, "New Humanitarianism: Does It Provide a Moral Banner for the 21st Century?" *The Journal of Disaster Studies, Policy and Management* 25, no. 4 (2001): 275–89.

10. K. Menkhaus, "The Security Paradox of Failed States," National Strategy Forum, 2003.

11. Mialls, 2001.

12. J. Milliken and K. Krause, "State Failure, State Collapse, and State Reconstruction: Concepts, Lessons and Strategies," *Development and Change* 33, no. 5 (2002): 753–74.

13. Weberian state refers to the concept of a state administered through highly rationalized and legitimate social institutions.

14. M. Pugh, "Post-Conflict Rehabilitation: Social and Civil Dimensions," http://www.jha.ac/articles/a034.htm, 2000, document posted June 3, 2000.

15. Macrae et al., 2004.

16. M. Ottaway, "Rebuilding State Institutions in Collapsed States," *Development and Change* 33, no. 5 (2002): 1001–23.

17. Ibid.

18. Pugh, "Post-Conflict Rehabilitation."

19. Fox, "New Humanitarianism."

20. Pugh, "Post-Conflict Rehabilitation."

21. S. Burkey, *People First: A Guide to Self-Reliant, Participatory Rural Development* (London: Zed Books, 1996).

22. J.Cusworth and T. Franks, *Managing Projects in Developing Countries* (London: Longman, 1993).

23. D. Cox, "The Social Development Conceptualization of Forced Migration," International Summer School in Forced Migration, Participants Handbook, University of Oxford, 2001.

24. A goal in this context is defined as something to contribute to as opposed to a specific objective, which is regarded as aims that are specific, measurable, and fully achievable.

25. This may take many forms, such as cash-based responses (vouchers, cash transfers, micro-financing, loans), income generation, grants, and agricultural and livestock support.

CHAPTER 9
INTERNAL DISPLACEMENT IN WEST AFRICA:
CHALLENGES AND CONSTRAINTS
Claudia McGoldrick

Internal Displacement Monitoring Centre (IDMC, formerly Global IDP Project) of the Norwegian Refugee Council is mandated by the United Nations to monitor internal displacement worldwide and to make relevant information and analysis available to decision makers, humanitarian practitioners, and the general public. http://www.internal-displacement.org.

1. IDMC, "Internal Displacement: Global Overview of Trends and Developments in 2005," March 2006.

2. UNHCR, "2004 Global Refugee Trends," 2004, 90.

3. The Humanitarian Response Review, initiated by the UN emergency relief coordinator and published in August 2005, included key recommendations aimed at reforming the collaborative response, namely strengthening the role and functions of HCs and improving the selection process, and the assignment of clear responsibilities to lead organizations at sector level, with a priority in relation to the protection and care of IDPs. http://www.reliefweb.int/library/documents/2005/ocha-gen-02sep.pdf.

4. Inter-Agency Standing Committee, "Implementing the Collaborative Response to Situations of Internal Displacement, Guidance for UN Humanitarian and/or Resident Coordinators and Country Teams," Geneva, September 2004.

5. Report of the Secretary-General, "In Larger Freedom: Towards Development, Security and Human Rights for All," March 2005.

6. For more information on humanitarian "clusters" and general humanitarian reforms, see ICVA's Web site, http://www.icva.ch/cgi-bin/browse.pl?doc=doc00001560.

7. Human Rights Watch, "Youth, Poverty and Blood: The Lethal Legacy of West Africa's Regional Warriors," March 2005.

8. Lansana Gberie, *West Africa: Rocks in a Hard Place,* Partnership Africa Canada, May 2003, http://www.oecd.org/dataoecd/17/57/33905950.pdf.

9. Ian Smillie, Lansana Gberie, and Ralph Hazleton, *The Heart of the Matter: Sierra Leone, Diamonds and Human Security,* Partnership Africa Canada, January 2000.

10. Claudia McElroy, "Liberia's Hollow Democracy," *Guardian,* July 26, 1997.

11. Elizabeth Blunt, "The Guinea Conflict Explained," *BBC News,* February 13, 2001.

12. Lansana Gberie, *Destabilizing Guinea,* Partnership Africa Canada, October 2001, http://www.pacweb.org/e/pdf/destabilizing_e.pdf.

13. Paul Walsh, "Ivory Coast: Who Are the Rebels?" *BBC News,* November 30, 2002.

14. Global Witness, "The Usual Suspects: Liberia's Weapons and Mercenaries in Côte d'Ivoire and Sierra Leone," March 2003.

15. Global Witness, "For a Few Dollars More," April 2003.

16. Coalition for International Justice, "Following Taylor's Money: A Path of War and Destruction," May 2005.

17. UNDP, "Human Development Report," 2004, http://hdr.undp.org/reports/global/2004/.

18. UN OCHA, "Consolidated Inter-Agency Appeal for West Africa," March 2001.

19. Human Rights Watch, "World Report 2000: Liberia," 2001.

20. IRIN web special, "Guinea: Living on the Edge," January 2005.

21. Human Rights Watch, "Côte d'Ivoire: Accountability for Serious Human Rights Crimes Key to Resolving Crisis," October 2004.

22. Maria Clara Martin, *Review of Protection Issues in West Africa Coastal Countries,* October 2004, http://www.internal-displacement.org/8025708F004CE90B/(httpDocuments)/0180177C1D066103802570B700599DAB/$file/WFP+consultant+WAFrica+report.pdf.

23. Report of the United Nations High Commissioner for Human Rights and follow-up to the World Conference on Human Rights, Situation of human rights and fundamental freedoms in Liberia, UN Doc. E/CN.4/2004/5, August 12, 2003.

24. IRIN, "Liberia: Boy Gunmen Go on Raping Spree Among the Displaced," August 27, 2003.

25. Watchlist on Children and Armed Conflict, "Nothing Left to Lose: The Legacy of Armed Conflict and Liberia's Children," June 28, 2004.

26. Inter-Agency Internal Displacement Division, "Report of Follow-up Mission to Liberia," May 8–22, 2005.

27. Human Rights Watch, "Sierra Leone: Getting Away with Murder, Mutilation, Rape," July 1999.

28. Save the Children-UK, "War Brought Us Here: Protecting Children Displaced within Their Own Countries by Conflict," May 2000.

29. Amnesty International, "Guinea, Liberia and Sierra Leone: A Human Rights Crisis for Refugees and the Internally Displaced," June 2001.

30. IDMC, "Guinea's Forgotten Internal Displacement Crisis," February 2005.

31. Human Rights Watch, "Côte d'Ivoire: Militias Commit Abuses with Impunity," November 2003.

32. UN Security Council, "Fourth Progress Report of the Secretary-General on the United Nations Operation in Côte d'Ivoire," March 2005.

33. UN OCHA, "Consolidated Appeals Process (CAP): Appeal 2006 for Liberia," November 30, 2005.

34. Ibid.

35. UN OCHA, "Consolidated Appeals Process (CAP): Humanitarian Appeal 2005 for Guinea," November 2004.

36. IDMC, February 2005, http://www.internal-displacement.org/.

37. International Crisis Group, "Liberia and Sierra Leone: Rebuilding Failed States," December 2004.

38. Medecins Sans Frontieres, "Populations Affected by War in the Mano River Region of West Africa: Issues of Protection," May 2002.

39. Anna Jefferys and Toby Porter (Save the Children-UK), "Ivory Coast Is a Case of Too Much UN Coordination," AlertNet, November 2004.

40. UN OCHA, November 2004, http://ochaonline.un.org/web page.asp?Nav=_humanissues_en&Site=_human issues.

41. Inter-Agency Standing Committee, September 2004, http://ocha online.un.org/webpage.asp?Nav=_humanissues_en&Site=_humanissues.

42. See also http://www.reliefweb.int/ghd/index.html.

CHAPTER 11
BEING WITH THEM
Lluis Magriñà, S.J.

Reference: "Everybody's Challenge: Essential Documents of JRS 1980–2000," Jesuit Refugee Service, 2000.

CONTRIBUTORS

Lieutenant General Nadeem Ahmed, Vice Chief of the General Staff of the Pakistan Army, was the Chief Military Coordinator for the Military Wing of the Federal Relief Commission following the devastating earthquake of October 8, 2005. He is the Deputy Chair of Pakistan's Earthquake Reconstruction and Rehabilitation Authority.

Kevin M. Cahill, M.D., is University Professor and Director of The Institute of International Humanitarian Affairs (IIHA) at Fordham University, President and Director of the Center for International Humanitarian Cooperation (CIHC), Director of the Tropical Disease Center at Lenox Hill Hospital, Clinical Professor of Tropical Medicine and Molecular Parasitology at New York University School of Medicine, Chief Medical Advisor for Counterterrorism (NYPD), Professor of International Humanitarian Affairs at the Royal College of Surgeons in Ireland, and Senior Consultant to the United Nations Health Service.

Major General Tim Cross, British Army, retired, is a Director of the CIHC. He has been deeply involved in fostering military/civilian cooperation throughout his career, which had included duty in Bosnia, Kosovo, Iraq and Macedonia. General Cross is a contributor to previous books in this series, *Traditions, Values and Humanitarian Actions* and *Emergency Relief Operations*.

Sheri Fink, M.D., is a fellow of the Harvard Humanitarian Initiative and a visiting scientist at the Francois-Xavier Bagnoud Center for Health and Human Rights. Dr. Fink has worked with humanitarian agencies throughout the world, responding to complex emergencies and disasters during the Iraq war, Hurricane Katrina and the 2004 Asian earthquake and tsunami. She is the author of

War Hospital: A True Story of Surgery and Survival, a personal memoir about Srebrenica, Bosnia.

Larry Hollingworth is the Humanitarian Programs Director for both the CIHC and the IIHA. Retiring after thirty years as an officer in the British Army, he joined the United Nations High Commission for Refugees and served in Cyprus, Sudan, Ethiopia, Eritrea, and the Balkans. He has also worked on behalf of the CIHC as a humanitarian expert on UN assignments in Iraq, Palestine, Lebanon, and Pakistan. He is a frequent lecturer on relief and refugee topics in universities and is a commentator on humanitarian issues for the BBC.

Christopher Holshek is a Colonel in the U.S. Army. He has had extensive field experience in the planning and deployment of U.S. Army forces to the Balkans and served with the UN in a civilian capacity as a Logistics Officer. He is an adjunct faculty member at both George Mason and New York universities.

Bernard Kouchner, M.D., is a Member of the European Parliament. He is an internationally known activist, writer and lecturer. He was a cofounder of *Doctors Without Borders* and *Doctors Around the World*. He has served as Minister of Health and Minister of Humanitarian Affairs of France.

Geoff Loane heads the regional delegation of the International Committee of the Red Cross to the United States and Canada. He previously headed the Red Cross delegations in Serbia and Montenegro, and directed relief operations in Sudan and Somalia. He is the author of a number of articles and books on humanitarian concerns.

Charles F. MacCormack is President and CEO of *Save the Children*, a member of the Council on Foreign Relations and serves on the executive committee of InterAction. Prior to joining Save the Children, he was president of World Learning.

Andrew MacLeod was with the UN Disaster Assessment and Coordination Team following the Pakistan earthquake and served as

Chief of Operations for the UN Emergency Coordination Centre there. He now works with the Earthquake Reconstruction and Rehabilitation Authority. Mr. MacLeod has worked for UNHCR, ICRC, and as a senior political adviser, international attorney and an officer in the Australian Army.

Lluís Magriñà, S.J., is International Director of Jesuit Refugee Service in Rome. He is the author of many articles on North-South relations, development and forced migration.

Claudia McGoldrick has been a human rights advocate, primary school teacher and journalist in West Africa, Central Asia, the UK and the US. Ms. McGoldrick currently works for the Norwegian Refugee Council's Internal Displacement Monitoring Centre in Geneva, responsible for West Africa.

Joan F. Neal, Vice President for Operations of Catholic Relief Services, directs the agency's domestic programs and advocacy initiatives in faith-based actions, promoting international social justice and solidarity with poor and marginalized people.

Alexander Van Tulleken, M.D., is a resident physician at King's College Hospital, London. He has practiced medicine in refugee areas in South America, the Far East and Africa, working in Darfur, Sudan with Medecins du Monde.

THE CENTER FOR INTERNATIONAL HUMANITARIAN COOPERATION AND THE INSTITUTE FOR INTERNATIONAL HUMANITARIAN AFFAIRS

THE CENTER FOR International Humanitarian Cooperation (CIHC) is a public charity founded by a small group of international diplomats and physicians who believed that health and other humanitarian endeavors sometimes provide the only common ground for initiating dialog, understanding, and cooperation among people and nations shattered by war, civil conflicts, and ethnic violence. The Center has sponsored symposia and published books, including *Silent Witnesses; A Framework for Survival: Health, Human Rights, and Humanitarian Assistance in Conflicts and Disasters; A Directory of Somali Professionals; Clearing the Fields: Solutions to the Land Mine Crisis, Preventive Diplomacy;* the new International Humanitarian Books Series of Fordham University Press—*Basics of Humanitarian Missions; Emergency Relief Operations; Traditions, Values and Humanitarian Action; Human Security for All: A Tribute to Sergio Vieira de Mello; Technology for Humanitarian Action; Tropical Medicine: A Clinical Text;* and *To Bear Witness: A Journey of Solidarity and Healing,* that reflects this philosophy. Four volumes have been published in French by Robert Lafont.

The Center and its directors have been deeply involved in trying to alleviate the wounds of war in Somalia and the former Yugoslavia. A CIHC amputee center in northern Somalia was developed as a model for a simple, rapid, inexpensive program that could be replicated in other war zones. In the former Yugoslavia the CIHC was active in prisoner and hostage release and in legal assistance for human and political rights violations, and facilitated discussions between combatants.

The Center directs the International Diploma in Humanitarian Assistance (IDHA) in partnership with Fordham University in New York, the United Nations Staff College, and the Royal College of Surgeons in Ireland and has offered IDHA programs in Egypt and Kenya. It has graduated more than seven hundred and fifty leaders in the humanitarian world from one hundred six nations, representing all agencies of the United Nations and most nongovernmental organizations (NGOs) around the world. The CIHC also cooperates with other organizations in offering specialized training courses for humanitarian negotiators and international human rights lawyers. The Center has provided staff support in recent years in crisis management in Iraq, East Timor, Aceh, Kosovo, Palestine, Albania, and other trouble spots.

The Center has been afforded full consultative status at the United Nations. In the United States, it is a fully approved 501-C3 charity.

The CIHC is closely linked with Fordham University's Institute of International Humanitarian Affairs (IIHA). The Directors of the CIHC serve as the Advisory Board of the Institute. The President of the CIHC is the University Professor and Director of the Institute. CIHC officer Larry Hollingworth is Humanitarian Programs Director for the Institute. Peter Hansen, a Director of the CIHC, is Diplomat in Residence at the IIHA.

DIRECTORS

Kevin M. Cahill, M.D., President
Peter Hansen
David Owen
Francis Deng
Boutros Boutros Ghali
Joseph A. O'Hare, S.J.

Helen Hamlyn
Abdulrahim Abby Farah
Peter Tarnoff
Eoin O'Brien, M.D.
Jan Eliasson
Tim Cross